Text World Theory and Keats' Poetry

Advances in Stylistics

Series Editor: Dan McIntyre, University of Huddersfield, UK

Text World Theory and Keats' Poetry

The Cognitive Poetics of Desire, Dreams and Nightmares

Marcello Giovanelli

Bloomsbury Academic
An imprint of Bloomsbury Publishing Plc

B L O O M S B U R Y
LONDON • NEW DELHI • NEW YORK • SYDNEY

Bloomsbury Academic

An imprint of Bloomsbury Publishing Plc

50 Bedford Square
London
WC1B 3DP
UK

1385 Broadway
New York
NY 10018
USA

www.bloomsbury.com

BLOOMSBURY and the Diana logo are trademarks of Bloomsbury Publishing Plc

First published 2013
Paperback edition first published 2015

British Library Cataloguing-in-Publication Data
A catalogue record for this book is available from the British Library.

ISBN: HB: 978-1-6235-6112-3
PB: 978-1-4742-2289-1
ePDF: 978-1-6235-6067-6
ePub: 978-1-6235-6633-3

Library of Congress Cataloging-in-Publication Data
Giovanelli, Marcello.
Text world theory and Keats' poetry: the cognitive poetics of desire,
dreams and nightmares/Marcello Giovanelli.
pages cm. – (Advances in Stylistics)
Includes bibliographical references and index.
ISBN 978-1-62356-112-3 (hardcover) – ISBN 978-1-62356-067-6 (pdf) –
ISBN 978-1-62356-633-3 (epub) 1. Keats, John, 1795-1821–Criticism
and interpretation. 2. Poetics–Psychological aspects. 3. Style, Literary. I. Title.
PR4838.S8G56 2013
821'.7–dc23
2013009013

Series: Advances in Stylistics

Typeset by Deanta Global Publishing Services, Chennai, India

For Jennie, Anna, and Zara

Contents

Contents

Acknowledgements

I would like to thank Peter Stockwell and Kevin Harvey for their initial help and guidance when this work formed the basis of a doctoral thesis, and then for their advice on preparing the material for publication. I am also grateful to Ron Carter, who was very generous in giving his time and advice at different stages of this project, and whose helpful suggestions were very much appreciated.

I would also like to thank the editing team at Bloomsbury for their help in seeing this book through the stages of publication.

As always, my wife Jennie deserves my biggest thanks for allowing me to take advantage of her proofreading skills, and for her unswerving support in far too many ways to mention here.

List of Figures and Tables

Key to Text World Notation used in Diagrams

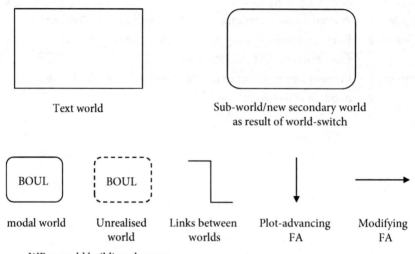

Text world

Sub-world/new secondary world
as result of world-switch

BOUL

modal world

BOUL

Unrealised
world

Links between
worlds

Plot-advancing
FA

Modifying
FA

WB = world building elements
FA = function-advancing propositions

t = time
l = location
e = enactors
o = objects

References to Keats' Poetry and Letters

All references to Keats' poems are from Barnard, J. (ed.) (1988) *John Keats: The Complete Poems* (3rd edition), London: Penguin.

All references to Keats' letters are from Rollins, H. E (ed.) (1958) *The Letters of John Keats: Two Volumes*, Cambridge: Cambridge University Press (abbreviated as *Letters*).

Introduction

1.1 Aims of this book

This book represents the first full length study of a canonical English poet using text world theory (Werth 1995a, 1995b, 1999; Gavins 2001, 2005a, 2007a). It aims to account for the use of dreams, desires and nightmares in a selection of Keats' poetry by explaining how these are conceptualized, understood and tracked by a reader in the act of the reading experience. As I explain in Chapter 2, text world theory ought to be ideally placed to undertake a study of this kind, since Werth initially presents the model as a cognitive discourse grammar capable of providing an account for the production and reception of all types of discourse (Werth 1999: 85). However, as I argue in this book, the current text world theory model has yet to be developed to satisfactorily account for dream states, or explain and deal with the distinction between types of desiring and dreaming. In addition and consequently, there has not as yet been any work within text world theory to explain more extreme types of dream experience such as the nightmare to explore their role in literary discourse. My aim here is to provide a coherent and sustainable model for dealing with dream and desire states. In doing so, I maintain the multidisciplinary approach of text world theory and consequently, this study draws widely from stylistics, cognitive psychology, cognitive linguistics, dream theory, sleep medicine, literary theory and textual and biographical studies. Above all, as I argue throughout, this book stands as a work of literary criticism.

1.2 Dreams, desires and nightmares

In this book, I treat the notion of the dream and the term *dream* itself in line with both those works in dream theory and sleep medicine (e.g. Hartmann

1998; Domhoff 2010) and within literary criticism (e.g. O'Connell 2006) as one of several associated *mentation states* running along a continuum and guided by a principle of continuity in cognitive processing. Consequently, I use the term *dream* to refer to any one of a number of different types of consciousness such as reverie, fantasy and sleep dreaming. These represent movement along a cline from prototypical awareness to what Tsur would term *altered states of consciousness*, which have functional significance and impact.[1]

> Altered states of consciousness are mental states in which adult persons relinquish to some extent the already acquired control of "ordinary consciousness". Such states help them achieve some relatively immediate exposure to reality, an immediateness which somewhat alleviates the rigid defences built up by ordinary consciousness.
>
> (Tsur 2008: 451)

Since this is a study of literary fiction, I am mindful of the need to see the inclusion of a fictional dream event as an important authorial decision that has an impact on the ways in which the literary text is read and understood. As Holland reminds us:

> the dream in literature always reaches towards a substratum of meaningfulness. A literary text, because it is authored, always has a principle of coherence. . . .the dream like everything else in the literary text, has to fit that principle.
>
> (Holland 1993: xvii)

Accounts of dreams in literature, for example in the collections by Lazar (1983), Rupprecht (1993) and Bulkeley (2001), have tended to concentrate on explaining this meaningfulness often by providing analyses of dream content only, or else interpreting dreams within a theoretical (often psychoanalytical) framework. Similar approaches are taken by those working both in dream theory and sleep medicine, where assigning an interpretation to the events of a dream has been the priority of analysis. That is not to say that this kind of approach is invalid; indeed much of my own analyses are concerned with exploring and explaining degrees of meaningfulness that can and have been assigned to various mentation states in Keats' work. However, an operational consequence of a sustained focus on meaning has been the neglect of an exploration as to how readers are led to conceptualisations through textual constraints, and how they are asked to manoeuvre their ways through and around texts that attempt to emulate the distinctive states of consciousness that make up dream, desire and nightmare states. This study therefore sets out to explore readerly projection into states of consciousness and consequent movement around these states through the act of reading a literary text. In other words, it aims to account for the experiential nature of reading and the way in which a text 'feels': what Stockwell (2009:15) terms *texture*.

In setting up a framework for accounting for these states, I am conscious of the need to treat literary dream events as representations and in doing so, to differentiate between that which is constructed for a literary purpose and that which occurs naturally in sleeping humans. For as Porter (1993: 36–7) notes, the literary dream is always foregrounded as a radically different, processed structure, and is labelled, framed and understood as a significant event in comparison to normal everyday dreams. Furthermore, the special shaping of the literary dream means that it is often radically different to accounts of dream experiences that form the body of analytical work in sleep medicine and psychological studies. Despite this, I treat the literary dream and its associated states as part of a deliberate decision on the part of the author to reproduce and emulate a certain kind of cognitive experience and consequently place unique demands on the reader in terms of textual management.

1.3 Keats

The literary focus of this study is on how the poems of Keats selected for analysis are read as experiences that involve distinct conceptualisations and movement both discretely and comparatively across different mentation states. Although the model I use to explain these processes is a relatively new one, the idea in itself is not. Much work in what is known as *New Criticism*, the dominant critical paradigm in Keats studies in the mid-twentieth century (e.g. Burke 1943; Brooks 1947; Wasserman 1953), draws attention to these types of imaginative shifts and escapist movements that have been seen as a marker of Keats' style, primarily to explore what Wilson (1993: 1) terms the 'Romantic vision of the dream as a buffer against the ordinary world'. These have resulted in accounts of the poems that stress the role of the imagination and its associated modes in Keats' poetry as critical thematic concerns either providing a revelatory power, facilitating sympathetic identification, or acting in a manner of self deception (Waldoff 1985, and see also Chapter 3). Although the changing climate of literary criticism, particularly in the latter part of the twentieth century, has placed historical and political readings and theoretical imprints over these prior concerns, they have largely remained the same. So, as Sandy (2006: 1324) states, new critical-theoretical approaches have simply 'shifted the terms of reference for accounts of Keats' style away from private emotions to the political'.[2]

Although Sandy (2006: 1327) suggests that 'in recent times there has been an increased confluence of philosophical, contextual and formal approaches in critical studies of Keats, there has to my knowledge been no significant full-length study that attempts to pull these concerns together within the field of stylistics. Where short studies exist, they tend to offer micro-level analyses of individual poems with their own particular focuses (e.g. Stockwell 2002; Bruhn 2005; Tsur 2008). Bex (1995) surveys a wider range of poems in exploring Keats' odes but only comments briefly on each one. Equally, although work in text world theory itself has begun to move outwards from the emphasis on short prose extracts that typified most early work (see Section 1.4), there has as yet been no comprehensive study of a recognised major nineteenth-century English poet within the field of cognitive poetics. This book therefore offers a sustained discussion of the work of John Keats as part of a contribution to Keats studies in general as well as to cognitive poetics.

I should also add something about my choice of poems. I have selected those that both exemplify and can be illuminated by the modifications I am suggesting to the text world theory model. As a result of limited space, it has not been possible to include poems which obviously make use of dream events and about which much has been written, for example *The Fall of Hyperion: A Dream* and 'Ode to a Nightingale'. However, the poems I do focus on provide interesting and innovative examples of text world theory in practice and range from the well documented (*The Eve of St Agnes*), to those moderately attended to in critical studies (*Isabella; or, The Pot of Basil* and 'La belle dame sans merci'), to a relative rarity ('This living hand, now warm and capable'). My analyses of these poems aim to either add to existing critical debate or, in the case of the final one, offer a uniquely detailed and radical reassessment of the poem.

1.4 Rationale for using text world theory

As an analytical framework in the field of cognitive poetics, text world theory appears to be well suited to a study of mentation states since it is a model that aims to account both for how knowledge is organised in conceptual structures and for how readers and listeners keep track of discourse events, particularly through the construction of and movements towards and from remote conceptual spaces set up through temporal and spatial shifts, modalised constructions, direct speech and other relocations such as those as a consequence of metaphor or hypotheticality. It exists therefore as a model that is concerned with the types of constraints that arise as a result of macro- and micro-textual patterns and structures, which position the reader towards adopting a particular stance. Furthermore, although text world theory stresses the importance of extra-textual knowledge in the creation of meaning through its emphasis on the negotiation of text worlds, its *principle of text-drivenness* (Werth 1999: 149), which accounts for the specific kinds of knowledge activated during the reading process, means that it remains a model deeply rooted in textual analysis.

As I mention earlier, the vast majority of early work in text world theory is based on prose extracts, and in his early papers and 1999 monograph, Werth himself tends to focus on short extracts rather than attempt to explore the conceptualisation of worlds across larger stretches of discourse. However, the landscape is changing. Although there has remained a great deal of work using literary prose fiction (e.g. Gavins 2000, 2003, 2005b, 2010; Hidalgo Downing 2000a, 2000b, 2003; Al-Mansoob 2005), the model is now being used more widely. So for example, within non-fiction, Gavins (2007a) analyses a range of different text types from parenting guides to 'lonely heart' columns, and Hidalgo Downing (2000c) uses text world theory to explore the advertising genre. Moving even further outwards across literary mode and discipline, some limited work has been undertaken using drama texts, for example, Horder (2007) and Cruickshank and Lahey (2010) and within pedagogical stylistics, for example, Giovanelli (2010). This study aims to build on the work that has been undertaken by researchers working on poetry using text world theory (Hidalgo Downing 2002; Lahey 2003, 2004, 2005, 2006; Stockwell 2005, 2009; Gavins 2007b, 2012; Nahajec 2009) by proposing a radically new way of accounting for an as yet underdeveloped area of the text world theory model. In this way, this study aims to draw on existing text world methods but at the same time propose a sustainable reconfiguration of the current model that can be tested in future analyses.

1.5 Structure of the book

This book consists of 10 chapters. Following this introduction, Chapter 2 presents an overview of text world theory. Here, I trace the model's origins in Paul Werth's dissatisfaction with generative linguistics and its connection to more general operational methods in cognitive linguistics. I provide summaries of work in theories of structured representation and tracking processing as a way of both introducing important theoretical models that have influenced, or are significantly similar to Werth's model, and fully contextualising text world theory within the disciplines of cognitive linguistics and cognitive poetics. The final part of this chapter then provides details of Werth's original model, exemplified where necessary with my own analyses from Keats' *Lamia*. I end the chapter by outlining significant modifications to text world theory that have been suggested by Joanna Gavins. These modifications are the starting point for my own additions to the text world theory model.

In Chapter 3, I draw on work from a range of connected disciplines to examine the nature of the dream phenomenon. I draw extensively and widely from work in psychology and sleep medicine to explore how the notion of dreaming can be best understood for the text world theorist. Here I suggest, following Hartmann (1998), that the term *dream* should be considered as one of a number of different states of consciousness along a continuum, arguing that text world theory as it currently stands has yet to sufficiently deal with the complexities associated with its various conceptualisations. As a way of fully contextualising my study in the light of Keats and Romantic poetry, I also present an overview of nineteenth-century attitudes to, and ideas on, dreaming, suggesting how for Romantic poets, the idea of the dream was bound to a more complex set of ideas about the role of the imagination and its associated forms.

Chapter 4 is the first of my chapters where I aim to develop the current text world theory model. In this chapter, I build on Gavins' (2005a) reconfiguration of modality within text world theory. In the opening part of the chapter, I focus on providing an overview of modality, since my own revisions to the model make use of historical and recent work in this area, particularly in the viewing of modalised constructions as representing both attitudes to, and as yet unrealised projections of, states of affairs. This is supported by reference to work in cognitive grammar (Langacker 1987, 1991, 2008) on clausal grounding and the conception of reality, and modal force (Johnson 1987; Sweetser 1990; Talmy 1988), before finally I present a model for identifying *desire* and *dream worlds*. Chapter 4 is therefore the central chapter in this book since it proposes the model from which analyses of Keats' poems extend, and its identification of the dream world forms the basis for my further suggestions for text world theory in later chapters.

In Chapter 5, I use this model to provide a detailed cognitive poetic analysis of Keats' *The Eve of St Agnes*, arguing that much of the poem's texture and meaning arise as a result of the interplay of dream and desire worlds related to the central characters of Madeline and Porphyro. Here, I also adopt a structure that I follow for the remaining analytical Chapters 7, 8 and 9, by beginning with an overview of the context of the poem's composition and of critical opinion on the poem relevant to my subsequent discussion.[3]

In Chapter 6, I build on my initial distinction between a desire and dream world to propose a distinct and extreme type of text world, *the nightmare world*. This chapter takes as its starting point the idea that the representation of a nightmare in literary discourse aims to emulate an unpleasant experience so much so that as White-Lewis suggests:

> when we encounter nightmares in literary form, we, as readers, are engaged imaginatively and physiologically by the compelling intensity of the images. We identify with the terror, we feel the anxiety.
>
> (White-Lewis 1993: 48)

The ideas of feeling, of implication, of transportation into a literary experience and of emulation are central concerns in a cognitive poetics of texture. To this end, I explore key work on the nightmare phenomenon as a way of explaining how its literary representations necessarily aim to simulate real-life experiences. I particularly draw extensively on work in sleep medicine to sketch out the defining features of a nightmare world: its inherent world switching properties as a result of waking triggers; reliance on sharply defined and intense dominant images and emotions; and its resulting ripple effect, experienced when the dreamer awakens. Here, as in Chapter 3, I contextualise my study of a Romantic poet by drawing further on nineteenth-century views on the nightmare and in particular, explore Coleridge's interest in the phenomenon. In addition, since nightmare recounts make extensive use of negation, I provide an overview of work relevant to my discussion in a cognitive context, as a way of exemplifying how nightmares rely on clusters of negative lexical items as integral world-building and enriching components. Finally, I propose a model for a nightmare world that anticipates further discussion in my final three analytical chapters.

Chapters 7, 8 and 9 are the final analytical sections of this study and use my notion of the nightmare world in different ways to each analyse a Keats poem. First, in Chapter 7, I exemplify Keats' use of a prototypical nightmare world in *Isabella; or, The Pot of Basil* as a central and defining moment of the poem. My emphasis here is on the functional design of the nightmare experience and world. I suggest that existing critical readings of the poem, focusing on the symbolic nature of characterisation and the regenerative nature of Isabella's experience with her dead lover Lorenzo, can be explained through considering the consequences and impact of the prominent nightmare world in the poem. I also suggest that this account of conceptualisation can be used to explain the educative experience that has been ascribed to the nightmare, and that the movement into and across the nightmare world can be read in the context of Keats' own philosophy on trauma as an essential part of human existence.

In Chapter 8, my focus turns to the text world notions of *accessibility, maintenance* and *tracking* in an analysis of 'La belle dame sans merci' as I focus on the texture created by the setting up of distinctive text worlds and the movement across their edges. In this chapter, I suggest that Keats sets up a series of restrictions in text world accessibility for his readers that impact on our ability to verify the accuracy of the events represented in the poem. In addition, I explore the use of two explicit negative worlds: the establishing world of the poem, which explicitly seeks to defeat any readerly expectations of the romance genre; and the climactic nightmare world of the poem, which I argue is used at the heart of a wider series of world switches that eventually cause a keenly felt sense of dislocation on the part of the reader.

I retain my focus on movement in Chapter 9, by exploring Keats' fragment 'This living hand, now warm and capable'. Drawing attention to the poem's insistence on the proximity of the reading experience and its inherently negative world detail, I suggest that the poem's invitation to be read as a cycle of haunting means undertaking a radical re-evaluation of its global structure as a series of embedded worlds within what I term a *composite nightmare world*. I argue that the experience of reading the poem is necessarily the felt experience of moving across world edges within the framing nightmare space. Furthermore, I engage with critical debate about the nature of the poem's second person address and suggest a model for differentiating between three potential types of reader involvement: *detachment, involvement* and *empathy*.

In my concluding chapter, I summarise the main findings and arguments of this book and draw attention to further implications and directions arising from my study for the text world theorist.

1.6 A note on *the reader*

Throughout this book, I use the term *the reader* or *a reader* when referring to choices, movements or the possible consequences involved in the act of reading a poem. I am aware that these terms as well as those such as *informed reader* (Fish 1980) or *idealised reader* (Stockwell 2002) are problematic since as Tsur (2008: 27) makes it clear 'In most cases, these phrases mean "a reader who complies with my theoretical analysis"'. However, there are two important points relevant to my decision to use this term. First, my discussion aims to conform to Simpson's (2004: 3) 'three "Rs"' of stylistics: being *rigorous* rather than impressionistic, and *retrievable* and *replicable* in following a sufficiently transparent framework that lends itself to comparability. Consequently, this study is concerned with keeping to a disciplined stylistics and is necessarily introspective in nature. Although there is a recent growing call for and trend in studies in stylistics to be more sociolinguistically oriented in discussion of the decisions made by *real, actual* or *ordinary readers* (Hall 2009) in given reading contexts, it is beyond both the aims and the scope of this book to offer an empirical study of the responses of readers other than myself and those critical responses to the poems with which I engage. However, as I suggest in my concluding chapter, both text world theory and my suggested additions to the model appear well equipped to undertake more empirical research within the field of stylistics/cognitive poetics.

Secondly, it should be noted that in my analyses of Keats' poems, I am aiming to map out the defining features of the structures, conceptualisations and movements within the poems that impose specific cognitive constraints on all readers. Where I do make claims for broad thematic concerns, these are based on historical critical response and the premise that more often than not readers are in relatively general agreement in their interpretations of literary texts.[4] Moreover, since clearly in a work of literary criticism, there needs to be some term by which we reference the human entity engaged in the act of reading and since there is no space in this book to engage in debate about readers, while acknowledging that such debate exists, I settle on *the/a reader* for both convenience and economy.

Text World Theory

2.1 Introduction

Text world theory is a cognitive discourse grammar, originating in the work of Paul Werth, whose early papers (1981, 1994, 1995a, 1995b, 1997) culminated in a monograph (1999), posthumously published and edited by Mick Short. Werth considered text world theory to be a model applicable to all types of discourse and one which was genuinely able to deal directly and upfront with context, which according to him, had been beyond the scope and ambition of generative linguistics. This chapter, which provides an overview of text world theory, begins by summarising the underpinning principles of a 'cognitive enterprise' in linguistics, drawing attention to Werth's emphases on discourse and context as part of his *human viewpoint* theoretical position. In this section, I also provide an overview of key work in other cognitively oriented models of knowledge structuring and discourse processing that account, in similar ways to text world theory, for how writers, readers, speakers and listeners negotiate and build rich conceptual structures in the process of communication.

In Section 2.3, I present the key components of Werth's text-world model, focusing primarily on his three architectural levels of the discourse world, text world and sub-world. Here, I summarise important phenomena within these three levels that sit at the heart of a worlds-approach: discourse types and participants; knowledge partition and retrieval; world building; sub-worlds and accessibility; incrementation; negation; and focus. Finally, in Section 2.4, I look at some of the important work on and developments in text world theory following Werth's 1999 monograph made by Gavins (2005a, 2007).[1]

2.2 Text world theory and cognitive linguistics

2.2.1 The *cognitive enterprise*

In attempting to define the discipline in the first decade of the twenty-first century, Evans (2009: 46) argues that cognitive linguistics has now come to be an 'enterprise' with a set of shared goals rather than a set of strictly uniform approaches to language and cognition. This definition reflects the wide range of work now being undertaken under the cognitive linguistics umbrella.[2]

Croft and Cruse (2004: 1–4) argue that cognitive linguistics is guided by three major principles: that language is not an autonomous faculty but rather develops in line with other cognitive abilities; that grammatical structures represent ways of presenting experiences that in themselves are meaningful; and, that knowledge about language is built up through both experience and use. These principles place the discipline as a reaction to the dominant model of generative linguistics of the mid- to late twentieth century. In addition, a fourth principle of *embodied cognition*, a cornerstone of cognitive science that emphasises the relationship between the human body moving through space, conceptualisation and linguistic form, underpins much work within the cognitive linguistic enterprise. Criticising generative linguistics, Lakoff (1987) highlights its 'abstract and disembodied' (1987: xi) nature, and contrasts this with his own theory of 'experiential realism' (1987: xv), which stresses the influence of experience and embodiment on the growth of human reason. For Lakoff, our perspective on reality is defined by the embodied nature of our being, and our use of language reflects this 'viewpoint'. Lakoff characterises his experiential realism in the following way:

> the mind works not independently but as part of our existence as embodied beings: conceptualisation is as a result of bodily experience and our interaction with the outside world;
>
>   the 'imaginative' use of metaphor and metonymy allow abstract ideas and entities not grounded in experience to be conceptualised;
>
>   thought and concepts have gestalt properties with an overall structure that is more than just the result of simple building blocks following logical rules.
>
> (Lakoff 1987: xiv–xv)

Lakoff's beliefs and views later become part of his 'generalisation commitment' (1990: 40). This stresses that there are fundamental organisational similarities between those areas of language such as syntax, phonology and semantics that generative grammars would treat as modular and distinct. Lakoff also proposes a 'cognitive commitment' (1990: 40) to keep linguistics as a discipline reflecting more widely accepted cognitive principles, informed by approaches in cognitive science, psychology and anthropology on the mind and brain.[3]

This experientialist or cognitive approach has tended to focus around the following research areas and paradigms: psychological models of categorisation (e.g. Rosch 1975, 1978, 1988; Lakoff 1987; Wierzbicka 1985); the organisation of conceptual structures into frames, schema, scripts and scenes (e.g. Fillmore 1968, 1977, 1982a, 1982b, 1985; Schank and Abelson 1977; Schank 1982; Rumelhart 1975, 1980, 1984; Cook 1994) and the projection and tracking of these conceptual structures or spaces (e.g. Fauconnier 1994, 1997; Emmott 1994, 1997; Galbraith 1995, Zubin and Hewitt 1995); prominence of figure-ground and image-schematic configurations (e.g. Lakoff 1987; Johnson 1987); conceptual metaphor theory (e.g. Lakoff and Johnson 1980; Lakoff 1987; Lakoff and Turner 1989, Fauconnier and Turner 2002); cognitive grammar and a usage-based approach to language acquisition (e.g. Tomasello 1992, 2003, 2006).[4]

Of all of the above, I would like to briefly summarise two areas that are particularly relevant to text world theory. First, the organisation of knowledge into conceptual structures has its roots in *frame semantics* (Fillmore 1977, 1982b, 1985), in which a lexical item is understood as part of a wider set of semantic relationships, which are acquired and sustained through use. This has given rise to a theory of 'encyclopaedic semantics' in opposition to the generative dictionary-based view with its straightforward dichotomy of linguistic and non-linguistic knowledge, a distinction between semantics and pragmatic meaning and ideas on context-free and context-bound meaning. With its emphasis on context, frame semantics proposes that to understand a word is to understand the world in which it is used.[5] Similarly, *schema theory* (Schank and Abelson 1977; Schank 1982) highlights how prior knowledge and experiences exist in the form of memory structures called *scripts*, which represent knowledge about the sequence of a particular event, such as going to a restaurant or buying a train ticket. These are given further structure by various types of motivational *goals* and themes, which provide contextual reasons for particular goals and offer ways of predicting likely future goals. Scripts can be progressively developed to help account for understanding new utterances and situations; essentially then, schema theory proposes a dynamic model of knowledge structure based on experience and active organisation and re-organisation of cognitive and conceptual detail.

Secondly, there are theories that define and describe the kinds of tracking processes that readers and listeners undertake in the course of discourse and text engagement. In *mental spaces theory* (Fauconnier 1994, 1997), cognitive domains are set up by means of space builders (Fauconnier 1994: xxiii) that originate from a parent space, fleshed out further by names and descriptions, references to tense and mood, presuppositional constructions and trans-spatial operators (Fauconnier 1997: 40–1), which act as linguistic guides for the reader/listener in the construction of rich cognitive structures (1997: 40). Similarly, Emmott's *contextual frame theory* (1994, 1997, 2003) is a discourse account of both conceptualisation and text processing, focusing on the *contextual frame*. This is 'a mental store of information about the current context, built up from the text itself and from inference made about the text' (1997: 121), which guides the reading process and which is used to make sense of new textual information. In this model, characters become *bound* to frames containing narrative information, remaining so until they explicitly leave and become *unbound*. When bound to a frame, characters can be either *textually overt* (explicitly mentioned) or *covert* (not mentioned but assumed to remain in the frame because they have not been unbound) (1997: 124). As discourse information is tracked, a frame becomes *primed* (1997: 123), to become the main focus of attention; a shift away from this attention is a result of *unpriming* with a new frame primed for attention, a process which mirrors the reader's perspective and which Emmott calls a *frame switch* (1997: 148). *Repriming* of a frame occurs as a result of *frame recall* (1997: 152). In Emmott's model, contexts are modified in line with contextual requirements, drawing attention to changes to 'the contextual configuration' (1997: 142) of a conceptual structure, including different versions of characters or as Emmott describes them *enactors*, which are 'past and present realisations of the same referent' (1997: 188), as well as plot and locations.

Deictic shift theory (Galbraith 1995, Segal 1995a, 1995b, Zubin and Hewitt 1995) is also a model that accounts for how readers experience narrative discourse by adopting 'a cognitive stance within the world of the narrative' and interpreting the text 'from that perspective' (Segal 1995a: 15). Deictic shift theory makes use of Bühler's *origo* of the deictic field of human language (1982: 13), at the centre of which are the *sender, place* and *moment markers* (1982: 14) 'I', 'here' and 'now', and in relation to which other constructions such as temporal adverbs and tense configurations are marked and understood (Segal 1995a: 15). The deictic centre then becomes a vantage point from which we conceptualise events.[6] Shifts between deictic centres are tracked and understood by a reader through a series of *PUSHes* into and *POPs* out of and across deictic levels or *planes* (Galbraith 1995: 47), as deictic operations that a reader performs on one or more of these deictic centre components during the process of constructing an interpretation for a stretch of narrative text. These operations involve either introducing new entities into the deictic centre, maintaining the deictic centre through anti-shifting devices or alternatively, shifting the deictic centre perceptually, spatially or temporally (Zubin and Hewitt 1995: 141) (see also Zubin and Hewitt 1995: 146–52 and Stockwell 2002: 53–5 for systematic accounts of the types of shifting and anti-shifting devices and their correspondence to each deictic centre component). In addition, a fourth kind of shift, what Zubin and Hewitt call *voiding* (1995: 141), occurs when one deictic centre component is temporarily irrelevant and ceases to be maintained in narrative tracking; a more permanent kind of voiding is suggested by Stockwell's *decomposition* (2000: 150). Segal (1995b) defines this active monitoring and processing of the boundaries between deictic centres as *edgework* (1995b: 74–6).[7]

2.2.2 A cognitive discourse grammar

Text world theory aims to be a *cognitive discourse grammar*. By this, we can say that it both draws on the principles of cognitive linguistics, and has similar properties to other cognitively oriented theories of structured representation and discourse tracking. In aligning himself to cognitive rather than generative principles, Werth sees the language event as a phenomenon that 'is intimately bound up with human experience' (1999: 19), and proposes his own *human viewpoint* that relies on 'the importance of knowledge, the central role of human experience, the inescapable effects of the situation, the discourse-driven nature of these processes' (1999: 22). Subsequently, the relationship between Werth's model and other cognitive approaches to structured representation and discourse tracking is clear. First, Werth explicitly links the cognitive linguistic concept of the *frame* or *schema* to his notion of text world, which represents the individual 'representation of a specific context' (1999: 112), both built by and in turn building areas of knowledge.[8] The frame is therefore important in Werth's concept of the role of *knowledge* in the discourse world (see Section 2.3.2).

Secondly, and with regard to discourse tracking, Fauconnier's concept of the mental space can be seen to share many similarities with text world theory in its modelling of the ways in which linguistic forms work to project alternative conceptual spaces or worlds. Equal similarities can be seen in deictic shift theory's emphases on movement between deictic centres, and the ways in which this is processed and tracked during the act of reading The influence of Werth's model on contextual frame theory is evident in the latter's notion of how degrees of knowledge in the frame is contextually reconfigured through a process that Werth would term *incrementation* (see Section 2.3.6). Furthermore, later developments in text world theory have borrowed Emmott's term *enactor* as a preferential term to character when speaking both of text world entities and the worlds they create (see Section 2.4). All in all then, text world theory is a model that has a strong commitment to cognitive principles, and is fundamentally concerned with comprehensively accounting for the types of knowledge structures, linguistic properties and discourse processing and tracking that make up the experience of reading.

2.3 Werth's text world theory model

2.3.1 Discourse world

In text world theory, the *discourse world* is 'the situational context surrounding the speech event itself' (Werth 1999: 83), a physical immediate situation in which a discourse event takes place. Discourse worlds are populated by human participants who jointly negotiate meaning construction, based on textual detail, their own knowledge and other perceptual detail. In prototypical cases, such as face-to-face conversation, producer and receiver(s) share the same temporal and spatial space, whereas a *split discourse world* exists when producer and recipient are separated.[9] Werth emphasises the cognitive and experiential dimension of the model by stressing that the discourse world cannot simply be 'a matter of sense input' (1999: 83) but relies on participants drawing upon stored knowledge frames to create rich inferences or 'states-of-affairs conceived of by participants' (1995a: 50). In this way, a 'feeding system' of individual and culturally dependent ideologies, memories, desires, memories, beliefs, dreams, intentions and imaginative acts are used by participants in, and to make sense of, the language event.

2.3.2 Common ground and knowledge

In co-constructing meaning, discourse participants follow 'discourse meta-principles' (Werth 1999: 49–50) of *communicativeness, coherence* and *co-operativeness* to build up a *common ground* (1995a: 51), which Werth defines as 'the totality of information which the speaker(s) and hearer(s) have agreed to accept as relevant for their discourse' (1999: 119). Once a common ground is established, knowledge between participants is shared in a process known as *incrementation*, where new information is processed into the common ground shared space (1999: 95).

Even where a split discourse world exists, there has to be some degree of shared knowledge for a text to be understood. Werth suggests that participants here rely on *shared knowledge* as a way of establishing and building common ground, proposing that this knowledge is *mutual* (or private) and *general* (or public) knowledge. General knowledge represents the larger body of potential knowledge available to discourse participants through their personal, social and cultural group membership. It follows therefore that general knowledge may also be thought of in more specific and defined terms or 'degrees of generality' (Werth 1999: 96). In addition, Werth further divides general knowledge into two types: *cultural* and *linguistic* knowledge.

General cultural knowledge is the 'non-linguistic information available to individuals or groups living in a particular society' (Werth 1999: 97). As I have previously mentioned, Werth accounts for its structure using the cognitive linguistic notion of the *frame*. Clearly, the degree of knowledge held by an individual will depend on that individual's position as a member of a particular cultural group. So, a senior and more qualified medical surgeon will have a more richly defined SURGERY knowledge frame than a junior doctor. In addition, the degree to which successful interaction can take place will depend on participants' frame knowledge: clearly, if one participant has far richer frame knowledge than another, this may impact on the success of the discourse. Linguistic knowledge is defined by Werth as 'the general knowledge underlying the use of language' (Werth 1999: 98) and represents the kinds of knowledge that participants have about how they might use language in given contexts.

On the other hand, mutual (or private) knowledge occurs as the consequence or the result of incrementation and as part of the on-going discourse event, where participants build a shared knowledge space centred on the construction of a text. Like general knowledge, mutual knowledge can be divided into one of two types: *perceptual* and *experiential* knowledge.

Perceptual knowledge is shared knowledge, deriving from 'mutual perceptions of the immediate situation' (Werth 1999: 99). These represent initial short-term memory experiences relating to the human perceptual system such as the distinguishing of a face or the hearing of a noise that are mutually shared by discourse participants in the immediate situation. These may later become processed into permanent memory and represent experiential knowledge a more broadly based mutual knowledge that consists of a shared experience of situations in which participants have either directly or indirectly participated.

In acknowledging that the human knowledge system is vast, Werth stresses the need for a principle to account for the following questions:

> How do we apply what we already know to a particular discourse?
> How do we access the knowledge store for the appropriate knowledge?
> How do we sort through the whole mass of knowledge to find just those propositions which are relevant?
>
> (Werth 1999: 103)

Werth addresses this through his principle of text-drivenness, which dictates that it is the text itself that both determines the degree of background knowledge required and is responsible for evoking what is necessary for a reader/listener to understand it. This can be illustrated by using a short extract from Part I of Keats' *Lamia*.

> . . . they had arrived before
> A pillared porch, with lofty portal door,
> Where hung a silver lamp, whose phosphor glow
> Reflected in the slabbed steps below,
> Mild as a star in water. (378–82)

In the context of the poem, two lovers, Lycius and Lamia (who unknown to Lycius has previously metamorphosised from a serpent to a woman) have arrived at Lycius's home in the city of Corinth. In the reading of these lines, the principle of text-drivenness acts as a controlling mechanism to evoke only the following background knowledge needed by a reader acting as discourse participant to understand the situation:

- architectural knowledge about pillars, porches, doors and steps
- the nature and function of a lamp
- the use of phosphor as an element exhibiting luminescence
- the principle of reflection
- the reflection of stars in water

It is possible of course that not all discourse participants will have the same degrees of background knowledge, and it is clearly the case that some of the above may be incomplete or partial, for example, in the case of understanding the use of phosphor in lamps. Here, Werth proposes a 'double function' (1999: 152) of text-drivenness through the process of *accommodation*, in which the text provides sufficient detail for inferencing to take place to compensate for deficient background knowledge. So for example, a reader unaware of the nature and function of phosphor in lamps is able to infer the missing detail through the reference in subsequent lines to reflection and the analogy offered of the stars reflecting in water, as a way of understanding the quality of luminescence that phosphor must hold.[10]

2.3.3 The text world: World-building elements and function-advancing propositions

The second level of Werth's text world theory model is the text world, defined as 'the situation depicted by the discourse' (Werth 1995a: 53), deictically structured, dependent on knowledge and further enriched by

> . . . some manifest portion of the discourse world, perceived by the participants; or by the experiences remembered by the participants, i.e. the contents of memory; or else by speculations created by the participants, i.e. produced by the imagination.
>
> (Werth 1995a: 53)

A text world is a conceptual space negotiated as part of the *process of discourse* by participants. In prototypical face-to-face discourse, there may be more emphasis on those parts of the discourse world that are mutually perceived or experienced by participants; for written texts, operating in a split discourse world, conceptualisation is more likely to result from memory and imagination, particularly in those instances where

> the writer might intend to 'evoke' some particular kind of situation which for the reader might be entirely unfamiliar, and thus instead of recapturing an existing memory, will be totally new information.
>
> (Werth 1995a: 55)

In conjunction with participants' knowledge, *world-building elements* are responsible for providing spatio-temporal parameters and nominated entities which set up and build these conceptual structures. Although for prototypical face-to-face discourse, these may be elements that are mutually manifest to the participants, the 'here-and-now' (Werth 1995a: 76), for less prototypical examples (and certainly for the majority of examples of written discourse), these will need to be made explicit in the text itself. Werth identifies the following as a 'classified list of examples of text world builders':

> **Time** (t): time-zone of verbs; adverbs of time; temporal adverbial clauses, e.g. *it was a dark and stormy night, in 1979, at two minutes past midnight on April 7th, 10⁻⁹ seconds after the Big Bang, as soon as John realised*
>
> **Place** (l): locative adverbs; NP with locative meaning, locative adverbial clauses, e.g. *on the table, at Lewes in the county of Sussex, there was an old barn. . . . ., where the sea meets the sky.*
>
> **Entities** (c and o): noun phrases, concrete or abstract, of all structures and in any position, e.g. *my friend Susan, these are the voyages of the Starship Enterprise, a policeman who had lost his way, the square root of − 1, your attitude to market forces.*

> (Werth 1995a: 76)

It is possible to exemplify Werth's classified list of world-builders by returning to the extract from Part I of Keats' *Lamia*, which was initially used to explain the principle of text-drivenness in the previous section.

> . . . they had arrived before
> A pillared porch, with lofty portal door,
> Where hung a silver lamp, whose phosphor glow
> Reflected in the slabbed steps below,
> Mild as a star in water. (378–82)

Although the discourse world participants, here Keats and the reader, are removed both spatially and temporally and consequently share a split discourse world, the world-building process allows for a successful negotiation of a rich text world. The location of the city of Corinth, understood from the extract's co-text, is further specified by the locative adverbial 'before a pillared porch'. Entities in the text world are the characters of Lycius and Lamia (again gleaned from the co-text), the porch itself and the parts and properties detailed: 'pillared,' 'lofty portal door' (379), 'silver lamp', 'phosphor glow' (380) and 'slabbed steps' (381). These world-building elements are shown in Figure 2.1.

In addition, explicitly mentioned entities will have 'associations with frame knowledge already present in the minds of participants' (Werth 1995a: 58). In this case, a fully enriched conceptualisation of the two lovers sheltering in the porch away from the hustle of the city will depend to some extent on the reader utilising whatever general knowledge they might have about 'runaway lovers', love in the context of what has occurred up to this point in the poem, and biographical and historical knowledge of Keats and his poetry such as the

Text World
WB t: past l: Corinth c: Lycius and Lamia o: pillared porch PROPERTY: pillared PARTS: lofty portal door, silver lamp (with phosphor glow), slabbed steps

Figure 2.1 World-building elements in lines 378–82 of *Lamia*

commonly held allegorical readings of the poem. In the process of reading this extract and beyond, a developing sense of location and character is formed as part of the process of incrementation of shared knowledge between Keats and his reader.

In contrast to world-building elements, function-advancing propositions are non-deictic constructions that 'advance the discourse in order to fulfil whatever purpose it is meant to have' (Werth 1995a: 59). The difference can be seen by looking at these examples:

1. While the news was on, John finished his dinner
2. While John was eating his dinner, the phone rang

(examples from Werth 1999: 190)

Here, the subordinate *while* clauses situate the temporal parameters and introduce the world-building entities 'the news' (o) and 'John' (c). In contrast, the main clauses act to modify the situation conceptualised and develop the plot through of temporally structured clauses built around the function-advancing propositions 'finished' and 'rang'.

Werth proposes that function-advancing propositions are one of two types: those representing *changes in state* and those relating to *steady-states*. Predications relating to changes in state, both physical and conceptual, are seen as *path statements* (Langacker 1987) that map changes in the form of movement from a source to a goal situation (Werth 1999: 198). In essence, these match *material processes* in systemic functional linguistics (Halliday and Matthiessen 2004: 179). In contrast, steady-state predications are processes that modify existing world-building elements descriptively, which Werth subdivides into *state*, *circumstance* and *metonymy modifications* (1999: 197–8). Although Werth's treatment of these and his subdivisions are not always

Text World
WB t: past l: Corinth c: Lycius and Lamia o: porch
FA Lycius and Lamia ↓   had arrived porch → pillared porch → portal door silver lamp → on door lamp → has phosphor glow light → reflects in steps steps → are below the porch

Figure 2.2 World-building elements and function-advancing propositions in lines 378–82 of *Lamia*

clear, broadly speaking his ideas correspond to systemic functional linguistic notions of *intensive, possessive* and *circumstantial relational processes* (Halliday and Matthiessen 2004: 216). In line with what has now become standard text world theory notation, Werth proposes that path statements are represented by vertical arrows, while states, circumstances and metonymies are represented by horizontal arrows (1995a: 60).

Returning to the extract from *Lamia*, it is possible to show how function-advancing propositions in the text help to modify the deictic and referential world builders. First, our knowledge of Lycius and Lamia as wilful agents of a material action intention process 'they had arrived' fulfils a plot-advancing function. Elsewhere, a series of steady-state predications map out the parts and properties of the porch in a process that both modifies and enriches the conceptual space represented in the text world. So, the property of the porch as 'pillared' (379) is an intensive process, which defines 'pillared' as an attribute of the porch and in systemic functional linguistic terms can be seen as fulfilling an attributive function. Other metonymic elements fulfil a descriptive-advancing function in the form of the 'portal door' (379), the 'lamp' (380) and the 'steps' (381), each of which are possessive attributive processes in so far as they provide details of what the porch contains (or possesses). The richness of this world is seen through further modification: the door is 'lofty' (379), the 'hung' lamp is 'silver' and possesses a 'phosphor glow' (380) which is 'reflected' in the 'steps' that are 'slabbed' and 'below' (381) the deictic space in which the lovers find themselves. In fact, the intensity and minutiae of detail in this scene are representative of the intense world the lovers momentarily find themselves in, cut off from the external dangers present in the 'busy world' (I, 397) which eventually destroys them in Part II of the poem. That these lines are heavily descriptive rather than plot advancing is in keeping with the setting up of a richly conceptualised enclosed space that accommodates the lovers at this point in the poem. Using the conventions of diagrammatic text world theory notation, lines 378–82 can be presented as shown in Figure 2.2.

2.3.4 Sub-worlds and accessibility

Werth defines a simple text world as one where the 'deictic properties and function advancing propositions are entirely in correspondence with each other' (1999: 204) and which can loosely correspond to adhering to the 'classical Greek Unities of Person, Place, Time and Action' (1999: 204). In contrast, *sub-worlds* are more complex structures formed from modalised constructions (attitudes, belief systems, wishes and desires or the forcing of obligation and necessity), shifts in time and space, thought and speech processes and hypothetical and imaginary situations.

Whereas all text worlds are created by participants in the discourse world, sub-worlds may be created both by discourse world participants and by text world characters. Sub-worlds created by discourse participants who share the same ontological status are, in line with general principles of communicative co-operation, constructed through negotiation by using textual detail and participant cognitive resources. In this way, these sub-worlds remain *accessible* to both parties. In text world theory, Werth defines *accessibility* as the degree of truth and reliability that can be attached to worlds created by participants and characters.[11] Since the worlds created by discourse world participants are open to verification by co-participants who can accept them as reliable, such worlds are termed *participant-accessible* (Werth 1999: 214). On the other hand, characters that exist as text world entities and have no presence in or access to the discourse world can only build out from a text world level to create *character-accessible sub-worlds*. In the context of literary reading, since a reader acting as a discourse participant has no way of assessing the reliability or truth value of an entity who exists at a different ontological level (fictional characters are clearly not bound by the same co-operative principles as participants), these worlds are inaccessible to a reader.[12] I return to the notion of accessibility in my discussion of Keats' 'La belle dame sans merci' in Chapter 8, where I explore how a cumulative sense of dislocation is enforced through the absence of access afforded to the reader.

2.3.5 Defining features of the sub-world

Werth categorises sub-worlds in the following way:

> deictic: departures from the basic deictic 'signature' of the conceptual world, e.g. 'flashbacks', 'direct speech', 'windows' on to other scenes

> attitudinal: notions entertained by the protagonists, as opposed to actions undertaken by the protagonists in the discourse

> epistemic: modalised propositions expressed either by participants or by characters

(Werth 1999: 216)

In Werth's model, deictic sub-worlds are the most typical kind of alternative structure and are the result of shifts in the basic deictic parameters of time and place, as for example in the case of flashback and flashforward. Character flashbacks, which are by nature character-accessible, are often prefaced by mental predicates such as 'remember' and 'recall' (Werth 1999: 218). In addition, direct speech, which alters the time-signature of the text world by transporting a reader into a character's discourse world, can also be considered sub-world forming as can both direct and reported thought. Werth's second kind of deictic sub-world is the 'Meanwhile back at the ranch' departure from the current text world space to an alternative location (1999: 224). In these cases, the formation of a sub-world may be seen as a 'window on an alternative scene' (1999: 224), which despite activating a spatial deictic shift maintains the temporal aspects of the text world. In this way, it can be understood as an extended comment on the matrix text world, varying in relative importance to its parent space. This can be seen, for example, in the split screen cinematic technique, allowing a reader/listener/ viewer to 'toggle' between alternative spatial spaces (Werth 1999: 224–5). The final kind of deictic movement is based not on a temporal or spatial shift but on some aspect of 'entity displacement' (Werth 1999: 226). In this instance, new characters or objects are set up and attention is focused on them, displacing previous text world entities.

Attitudinal sub-worlds are represented by desire (want worlds), belief (believe worlds) and purpose (intend worlds) (Werth 1999: 227). Desire worlds, initiated by predicates such as 'wish', 'hope' and 'dream', are stipulative (1999: 230) in that they build a remote conceptual space, expressing desired outcomes in the matrix text world. I explore Werth's treatment of desire within his text world theory model in more detail in Chapter 4 using Gavins' modifications (2001, 2005a, 2007a) as a springboard to suggest a distinction between *boulomaic dream* and *boulomaic desire* worlds.

Werth discusses belief worlds using the following example (where *Pear* and *Banana* represent competing computer manufacturers' models):

John believes that a *Pear* is better than a *Banana*.

(Werth 1999: 234)

This proposition is contextualised by placing it within a series of events whereby John, having previously thought his *Banana* was the superior machine, tested a *Pear* on the basis of several computer magazine reviews which concluded that a *Pear* was better than a *Banana* on all accounts. Having used a *Pear*, he now accepts that it is the better machine. As a belief context, the proposition 'a *Pear* is better than a *Banana*' is taken as given and accepted in the common ground and it is John's attitude towards this, or 'the fact of his belief' (1999: 235) rather than the content of the belief itself that initiates a sub-world. The conceptual space formed by the sub-world serves to present John's attitude to the proposition rather than the truth value of the proposition itself. Werth's final kind of attitudinal sub-world is the purpose world, which presents intentions deictically placed within some future time zone (Werth 1999: 238–9).

Of all the parts of Werth's initial model, the classification of sub-worlds has come under closest scrutiny and criticism. Further discussion and revision of Werth's ideas on sub-worlds are provided in Section 2.4, and in Chapter 4.

2.3.6 Incrementation

A key principle of text world theory is that text worlds are not static but rather dynamic spaces in a discourse event, and are continually open to modification and revision based on participant knowledge held in the common ground which defines them. It is therefore possible to explain how they are updated to represent these alterations through the process of *incrementation* (Werth 1999: 289).

Werth (1999: 310) views incrementation as an integrated process of reference, deixis and predication updating, arising from a sense of *discontinuity*. In terms of referencing, Werth explains how the 'anaphora rule' (1999: 292) works to ensure that any anaphor explicit in the text world is understood by its relation to an entity in the common ground through the monitoring of an elaborate system of frame relationships (1999: 292). Werth uses the following example to show how this monitoring can solve any possible ambiguity:

> 1. (b) We raised a subscription at the Cricket Club to send him home, but the blighter wouldn't go. The fellow said he liked *the place*, if you please.
>
> (Werth 1999: 293, original emphasis)

In this example, Werth explains how the anaphor 'the place' is more likely to refer to one location than another based on our frame knowledge built up from the preceding discourse and more general knowledge of the kinds of situations being explained. Reference updating is therefore concerned with how we keep track of and amend our conceptualisation of entities in any given text world.

In contrast to reference-updating, deixis-updating occurs as result of time shifts across sub-worlds, while predication-updating is a radical updating of the conceptualisation of a text world through transformational predications: Werth provides an example of how a series of predications describe how an ecological disaster permanently alters the landscape in Pierre Ouellette's (1994) science-fiction novel *The Deus Machine*.[13] At its most extreme, the incrementation process can account for severe discontinuities that cause a discourse participant/reader to radically alter his or her conceptualisation of a particular text world through either *world-repair* or in the most extreme cases *world-replacement* (Gavins 2007a: 141–2).

2.3.7 Negation

In Chapter 6, I explore the role of negation in the creation and conceptualisation of a particular type of dream world, which I term the *nightmare world*. Here, I provide an initial overview of Werth's treatment of negation.

Werth asserts that negation must be viewed as a more complex phenomenon than the mere assigning of a negative value to an affirmative proposition and sees negative constructions as holding a foregrounding discourse function as a result of a figure-ground conceptual reversal.[14] Negation is therefore primarily based on the denial of a degree of expectation held in the common ground and is concerned more with micro and macro contextual matters than with pure syntax or semantics.

> You cannot . . . negate something unless there is good reason to expect the opposite to be the case. The explanation for this is perfectly common-sensical: to deny the existence or presence of an entity, you have to mention it. The very act of denying brings it into focus. It also has the effect of restricting possible interpretations of the sentence in isolation to just those which are compatible with, and cohere with, the given context.
>
> (Werth 1999: 251)

Werth differentiates between two types of negation. In the first type, which Werth views as the 'prototype of negation' (1999: 253), an expectation is explicit in the common ground and subsequently identified in the text world. A permanent change in text world parameters occurs through the introduction of a negative construction denying the expectation, which generates the conceptualisation of a negative sub-world. Since this is a sub-world and sub-worlds are world-building movements away from a matrix text world, the negative sub-world presents an alternative deictic structure that defeats the expectations held in the common ground and made explicit in the matrix text world. This change has to be viewed as a permanent one, unlike say temporal or spatial shifts since some of the original world's parameters are deleted. Negation can therefore be seen to alter text world parameters as a type of incrementation.

Although Werth views the denying and defeating of common ground expectations as the most usual function of negation, he also draws attention to a less prototypical type, *negative accommodation*, where an entity is both introduced into the common ground and yet deleted at the same time with striking effects (1999: 254). Werth uses the following example from E. M. Forster's *A Passage to India* to illustrate this:

> There are no bathing steps on the river front, as the Ganges happens not to be holy here; indeed there is no river front, and bazaars shut out the wide and shifting panorama of the stream.
>
> (Werth 1999: 255)

Werth argues that here a reader does not need to rely on the encyclopaedic knowledge of whether the Ganges is a holy river and whether cities on the

Ganges have bathing steps, since the phrases 'no bathing-steps' happens not to be holy' and 'no river front' suggest these expectations anyway through the act of negating them. Indeed, the text suggests that these ought to be there, and the use of negation functions to both draw attention to this and confirm their absence. Despite the focus on the processing function of negative accommodation in the absence of background knowledge, Werth does acknowledge that some frame knowledge will determine the probability of examples being treated as genuinely possible. Werth argues that the dynamic and coherent nature of discourse processing will ensure that a sentence such as the following would not be considered genuine or coherent in comprehending the novel as a whole since it would not evoke a plausible frame, consistent with the image of Chandrapore built up in the text so far.

> There are no ice-cream stands on the river-front, as the Ganges happens not to be holy here; indeed there is no river front, and restaurants shut out the wide and shifting panorama of the stream.
>
> (Werth 1999: 255)

In acknowledging that negative accommodation evokes frames in order to deny the expectations in them, Werth calls into question the suitability of the sub-world machinery to account for negation as a phenomenon. In Section 2.3.5, I explained that Werth characterises the sub-world as either a temporary departure from the parameters of a matrix world or the projection of attitudinal or epistemic notions and propositions often accessible only to text world enactors. With this in mind, since prototypical negation alters deictic parameters permanently rather than on a temporary basis, while negative accommodation, in its mentioning only to deny, can be seen as the most extreme kind of inaccessibility, Werth appears to suggest that negation is best seen as part of the process of incrementation. I return to negation in Chapter 6 where I review Werth's model and incorporate negation into my model of the *nightmare world*.

2.3.8 Focus

In this section, I refer to Werth's (1995b) to introduce his ideas of *focus*, which I use in my analysis of *The Eve of St Agnes* in Chapter 5.

In an analysis of the opening section of Thackeray's *Vanity Fair*, Werth likens the positioning of narrative point of view afforded by the originating participant-accessible text world as similar to 'the camera-position in a movie'

(Werth 1995b: 187). Later, in the same chapter, he states that the development of the text world due to the introduction of function-advancing propositions should be understood in the following way:

> our representation must be thought of not as a picture or a photograph, but rather as a movie-film, made up of a large number of 'frames', succeeding each other in time.
>
> (Werth 1995b: 192)

Werth uses this important analogy to introduce his idea of *focus* (1995b: 194), which like a sub-world is a departure outside the text world to another set of deictic parameters. Although both the focus and the sub-world can be thought of as types of cinematic projection, the difference remains that a sub-world extends outwards from its originating space, while a focus is a 'concentrating of attention inwards' to an 'earlier viewpoint at a later stage' (1995b: 194).

This difference can be highlighted by using the same extract from *Lamia* with which I exemplified Werth's notions of text-drivenness, world-building elements and function-advancing propositions in Sections 2.3.3. These lines are preceded by an earlier description of the city of Corinth.

> . . . .so all Corinth all. Throughout her palaces imperial,
> And all her populous streets and temples lewd,
> Muttered, like tempest in the distance brewed,
> To the wide-spreaded night above her towers.
> Men, women, rich and poor, in the cool hours,
> Shuffled their sandals o'er the pavement white,
> Companioned or alone; while many a light
> Flamed here and there, from wealthy festivals,
> And threw their moving shadows on the walls,
> Or found them clustered in the corniced shade
> Of some arched temple door, or dusky colonade. (350–61)

The opening description of Corinth contains a number of world-building elements, the metonymies of 'palaces imperial' (350), 'populous streets', temples lewd' (351), 'towers' (353) and 'rich and poor' (354) inhabitants of the city. The text world constructed through these referential elements is developed with the function-advancing proposition 'shuffled their sandals' and the descriptive-advancing function of the movement of the light, responsible for the shadows of the inhabitants being visible on the walls of the city or revealing small groups of people 'clustered in the corniced shade'. Diagrammatically, the text world presented in these lines would be shown as in Figure 2.3.

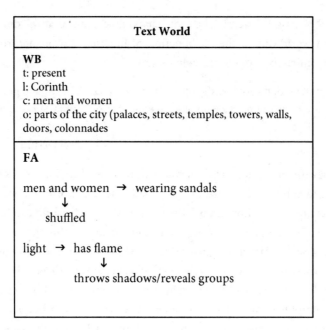

Figure 2.3 World-building elements and function-advancing propositions in lines 350–61 of *Lamia*

In context, lines 378–82 can therefore be seen as a return or re-evaluation of the description in lines 350–61, but from a different viewpoint: the emphasis is on the private world of Lycius and Lamia within the city. It should be noted that this is not a flashback or case of spatial alternation, since the landscape detailed in lines 378–82 is clearly part of the overarching panoramic sweep of the city of Corinth provided in the earlier lines. It can therefore be best thought of as an example of focus in Werth's terms: a re-evaluation of a previous description for closer and revised attention.

2.4 Gavins' reworking of Werth's model

The most significant work and revisions to text world theory has been undertaken by Gavins (2001, 2005a, 2007). Gavins suggests that there are inconsistencies in Werth's model of sub-worlds and in particular the hierarchical relationship that Werth proposes as existing between text world and sub-world. She suggests that the prefix *sub-* points to a subordinate relationship between worlds, which is not necessarily always the case. For example, she points out that in most literary fiction, the deictic make-up of the originating text world is prone to constant revision and the initial text world established may be departed from and never returned to again (Gavins 2005a: 82). In this way, she claims that it makes more sense to treat these deictic alternations by using Emmott's notion of the *frame switch* (Emmott 1997: 147) to explain how a reader might track temporal and spatial movement within a narrative, without necessarily seeing them as subordinate to a larger conceptual structure. For these reasons, Gavins suggests that the term *world-switch* (2005a: 82) replace Werth's notion of the deictic sub-world. In addition, Gavins adopts Emmott's notion of the *enactor* (Emmott 1997: 188), to replace Werth's *character* (and associated phrases), as a more explicit way of understanding entities as present, past and future conceptual realisations of a given referent.

Gavins proposes further modifications to Werth's attitudinal and epistemic sub-world categorisation. She criticises Werth's discussion of modalised propositions, suggesting that since anomalies exist in his attempts to classify modal constructions as part of both attitudinal and epistemic worlds, he fails to differentiate between 'the kinds of conceptual activity being expressed through such modalised propositions' (Gavins 2005a: 85). Using Simpson's (1993) classification of modality into the three main categories of *deontic, boulomaic* and *epistemic* modality, she proposes that Werth's original distinction between attitudinal and epistemic sub-worlds is replaced by a new taxonomy of *deontic, boulomaic* and *epistemic modal worlds*. Gavins' epistemic modal worlds include constructions concerned with knowledge and belief, such as hypothetical and conditional constructions, as well as examples of indirect and free indirect discourse, which represent speech or thought shaped in some way by a narrative voice, and consequently, unlike in Werth's original formulation, are viewed as departures from the text world. In a similar way, Gavins proposes that focalised narratives, representing one 'world view', form character-accessible epistemic modal worlds. In these cases, since 'the reader has no choice but to accept the contents of that world as reliable information if he or she is to construct a text-world of the discourse at all' (Gavins 2005a: 89), the epistemic modal world that structures the focalised narrative and is accepted by the reader as replacing Werth's original notion of the text world itself, which in Gavins' terms becomes 'redundant' (2001: 154). As there is no matrix world and all further deictic and modal movement automatically follows from the initiating modal world, Gavins again suggests that it is unnecessary to use the *sub-* prefix.

Gavins' revisions to the text world model provide a much neater way of considering world construction as either deictic movement (the world-switch) or some kind of attitudinal construction (the modal world). As such, I use these revisions in preference to Werth's original ideas and terms throughout the remainder of this book, except on those occasions where my own suggested modifications to text world theory support using alternative terminology.

2.5 Review

In this chapter, I have provided a summary of the basic theoretical principles underlying text world theory together with some practical applications of Werth's original model. In Section 2.1, I outlined the key principles underpinning the cognitive linguistic enterprise and explained text world theory's position as a cognitive discourse grammar, drawing on similarities it shares with other structured representation and discourse processing and tracking models. In the remaining sections of this chapter, I discussed Werth's text world model and drew attention to modifications to Werth's text world model suggested by Gavins, anticipating a further discussion of modality and text world theory in Chapter 4. This chapter has therefore provided a theoretical overview of text world theory in anticipation of my suggested additions to Werth's framework with regard to the notions of modality, dreams and desires that are the focus of this book.

3

Dreams

3.1 Introduction

In Book I of *Endymion*, Keats' eponymous hero is laid to rest by his sister Poena, before waking up 'calmed to life' (464) and with a 'healthier brain' (466). In this poem, the restorative, regenerative and revealing nature of the imaginative force represented in Keats' characterisation of Endymion is mirrored in the similar power of sleep and the dreaming process. The poem yokes together the concepts of the poetic imagination as the archetypal Romantic force and the mental state from which the dreaming process occurs, as a way of identifying the role each plays in the construction of poetic character and identity and the conceptualising and constructing of the self. Keats' narrator calls out to sleep as a

> . . . comfortable bird,
> That broodest o'er the troubled sea of the mind
> Till it is hushed and smooth! O unconfined
> Restraint! Imprisoned liberty! great key
> To golden places, strange minstrelsy,
> Fountains grotesque, new trees, bespangled caves,
> Echoing grottoes, full of tumbling waves
> And moonlight: ay, to all the mazy world
> Of silvery enchantment! Who, upfurled
> Beneath thy drowsy wing a triple hour,
> But renovates and lives? (453–63)

In this chapter, I seek to contextualise some of the central concerns that will form the basis of later work in this book, by considering how the notion of the dream and its associated mental states can be understood and explained by using the text world theory model. In Chapter 2, I provided a detailed overview of the influences on and architecture of Werth's text world theory model and in doing so, drew attention to the ways in which it made use of a broad range of theories and practices from a number of related disciplines. In this chapter, I develop a similarly eclectic approach and provide an overview of work in dream theory and the function of dreams to develop a definition and set of parameters for text world theory to use. In the following sections, I therefore draw on work in psychology, specifically cognitive psychology, and philosophy as a way of anticipating some of the additions I suggest to Werth's model in Chapter 4. However, since my central concern here is to provide a context for modification to the text world theory model and its subsequent use in the study of Keats' poetry, it is clearly beyond the scope of this chapter to provide a fully comprehensive overview of what is a considerable wealth of research within the fields of psychology, philosophy and neuroscience on dreams and the process of dreaming. The following therefore remains a necessarily selective account of some relevant key findings.

In the following sections, I begin by presenting a summary of definitions of dream and work within historical and present-day dream theory. In Section 3.3, I provide an overview of the common nineteenth-century view of the dream in the context of Romantic poetry. I explain Coleridge's fascination with and ideas on dreams and provide details of his meeting with Keats that influenced the younger poet. I complete the section by exploring Keats' treatment of dreams in his poetry with a particular focus on the Keatsian view of poetic imagination as a kind of dreaming. Finally in Section 3.4, I consider a cognitively plausible model for exploring notions of *dreaming* as one of a number of different 'mental acts' (Freud 1976: 169) and use Hartmann's (1998) waking-dream continuum as a model for proposing how these *mentation states* might be categorised as part of the text world theory model.

3.2 A definition of *dream*

In the fields of psychology, neuroscience and sleep medicine, definitions of the dream have all tended to centre on the notion of a *mental experience* occurring during a phase of sleep. So, for example, Hall (1973: 273) proposes that a dream is 'a succession of images, predominantly visual in quality, which are experienced during sleep', while Mahowald et al. (1998: 89) define dreams simply as 'experiences arising during sleep'. As might be expected, variations in definitions have tended to be controlled by researchers' own fields of study,[1] with a wide range of explanations for the phenomenon. These have included the dream as a by-product of REM sleep (Hunt 1991; Squier and Domhoff

1998), the representation of a dreamer's brain activity originating from neural sites during the sleep process and resulting in the offloading of bizarre yet ultimately meaningless fragmentary material (Hobson and McCarley 1977; Hobson 1988), or the dream as part of a larger cognitive-developmental process of maturation and consciousness (Foulkes 1985, 1990). More integrated studies have sought to take a 'neurocognitive' (Domhoff 2001a) approach combining research on specific neural networks within a developmental cognitive framework. These have acknowledged how the sleeping state deals with the dreamer's everyday emotional concerns and the complex set of phenomena that form part of broad dream-like experiences within and outside of the sleeping condition (Bosinelli 1995).

Perhaps more controversial has been the question of whether dreaming exists as a form or state of consciousness at all. The sheer volume of debate on either side[2] is made problematic by the fact that consciousness as a concept across various academic disciplines has proved to be notoriously difficult to define (Tassi and Muzet 2001). Kozmová and Wolman (2006: 196) take the view that consciousness is largely an issue of 'self awareness or subjective experience'. Their empirical studies show that the same perceptual, experiential, cognitive and recovery-based mental processes are used to define and preserve a sense of the self as those in waking thought. Bosinelli (1995) suggests that dream consciousness is of a particular type, governed by the same principles as those of waking cognition, but operating under the conditions of an alternative brain state (sleep). He distinguishes between three types of awareness: phenomenal and self- awareness, which can be found in the dreaming state; and a third, meta-awareness, more typical of waking cognition, and only to be found in lucid dreams. It has therefore become customary to speak of dream consciousness as defined by a particular set of features, distinguishable from waking cognition but operating using the same forms of mental process (Delacour 1995; Hartmann 1998; Tassi and Muzet 2001).[3]

3.3 Theories and functions of dreaming

3.3.1 Pre-scientific to modern thinking

The main shift from what can be generally termed pre-scientific speculation to modern thought has been that dreams are not transmitted from deities or other spiritual beings external to the dreamer but are the product of the self

(White-Lewis 2001). Classical approaches to the study of dreams were wide ranging and physiological in orientation, with both the Greek and Romans suggesting that dreams could be viewed as part of a broader physical medicine, related to states in the material world and to conscious thought (Ford 1998: 10–12). A number of studies of pre-scientific thought identify the importance of the dream as cultural practice (Shulman 1999; Packer 2002), as a shared religious experience, sometimes prophetic (Hermansen 2001; Young 2001), and as existing beyond human volition and control (Szpakowska 2001). In medieval literature, the poem based around a dream vision became a genre in its own right (Kruger 1992).

3.3.2 Modern thinking: Towards a more cognitive model of dreaming

Schwartz (2000) identifies three clear stages of research practice that have dominated research on dreams over the last 100 years. She suggests that research has centred on the working practices of: (a) experimentation, questionnaire studies and internal observation, (b) a psychoanalytical emphasis on the latent and manifest nature of dreams and (c) an integrated neurophysiological and cognitive approach to accounting for both the physiological and the phenomenological (Schwartz 2000: 56).

Whereas the first stage tends to be characterised by an approach that seeks to identify the factors responsible for dreaming rather than propose any sense of meaning from a dream's content, the second stage is characterised by psychoanalytical approaches that explain the dream image as a representation of the dreamer's dominant emotional state. In doing so, attention is shifted from a dream's explicit or *manifest dream content* on to that which is not explicitly stated: the dream's *latent dream thoughts* (Freud 1976: 381) as a way of uncovering both meaning and insight into the dreamer's psychology.

Freud's own work begins from the premise that the *interpretation* of dreams is a meaningful exercise; he sees dreams as containing important ideas from waking life which can be meaningfully analysed for the benefit of the dreamer. Consequently, the process of dreaming, as opposed to the content of the dream itself, represents an important 'mental act' (1976: 169):

> every dream reveals itself as a psychical structure, which has a meaning and can be inserted at an assignable point in the mental activities of waking life.
>
> (Freud 1976: 57)

However, as Freud views the dream content as 'completely severed from the reality experienced in waking life . . . . separated from real life by an impassable gulf' (1976: 67), the vast array of latent thought processes behind that content become the significant focus for the analyst. The central focus of Freud's work is therefore concerned with explaining the process by which latent thought becomes manifest content. This process of *dream-distortion* (1976: 216) occurs in a number of ways. First, the term *condensation* (Freud 1976: 383) is used to refer to the process whereby material from a variety of different sources becomes condensed into one central (or manifest) dream image. The act of compression that Freud suggests as taking place is representative of the gulf in richness between manifest content and latent thoughts. Condensation may be of two types: *identification*, where compression has already taken place in latent thought, and *composition*, where the compression occurs as part of the construction of manifest content itself. Secondly, *displacement* (Freud 1976: 414) is used to explain those occasions when there is a clear difference between the central image of a dream's content and the central concerns underlying latent thoughts. Finally, both *regression* (Freud 1976: 698), the recasting of thought processes into primary visual and sensory images, and sexual *symbolism*, which dreams make use of 'for the disguised representation of their latent thoughts' (Freud 1976: 469), account for the ways in which thought processes become explicit dream material.

Freud also claims that the dream represents 'a state of affairs as I should have wished it to be' (1976: 196). This view of dream as wish-fulfilment, as a '(disguised) fulfilment of a suppressed or repressed wish' (1976: 348) is held even for distressing dreams and those that on the surface appear not to have any wish-fulfilling function. These contain repressed wishes as the result of the mind blocking out material from reaching consciousness through the process of *censorship* (Freud 1976: 225).

Freud's ideas have been discredited in twentieth-century dream theory for their lack of supporting empirical evidence (e.g. Crews and Bulkeley 2001; Domhoff 2001b) and for the convoluted and unconvincing manner in which an argument is put forward for the dream as wish-fulfilment rather than simply showing the more general emotional concerns of a dreamer (Hartmann 1998: 176–7). This idea of the dream as wish-fulfilment is particularly problematic when the focus of attention is the bad, unpleasant dream or nightmare (see my discussion in Chapter 6). However, it is clear that Freud's emphasis on interpretation or *dream-work* (1976: 669), his ideas on dreams as a substitute for some other kind of thought process (1976: 169) and the 'loss of intentional guidance' (1976: 119), and his more general focus on the dream as image and therapy and on relaxation, psychosis and mental disease have formed the basis for more cognitive approaches to dream research.

The neo-Freudian work of Calvin Hall (1973) epitomises the way in which the cognitive processes involved in dreaming have been aligned to those of waking thought. Working from the premise that a dream is a 'world of pure projection', and 'thinking that occurs during sleep', Hall (1973: 362) likens dreaming to a transformative process in which conceptions become images and, consequently, the dream content. The interpretation of a dream consequently becomes a reversal of this process, with the analyst aiming to discover the conceptions behind the dream images. Hall demonstrates that these conceptions may be of the self, others, of the world, feelings and impulses, or problems and conflicts, and represent underlying structures in an individual's conceptual system, responsible for different kinds of behaviours. These ideas, while maintaining some of Freud's central concerns about the function of dreaming, importantly highlight the significant cognitive processing that must take place as part of a wider process of conceptualisation similar to that in waking cognition. This importance placed on the functionality of dreams and their relationship to general cognitive mechanisms (Foulkes 1990) is in sharp contrast to more neuro-scientific and biological focuses on the dream as nocturnal activity only, the by-product of sleep and the result of a dysfunctional brain activity in the absence of consciousness (e.g. Hobson 1988).

These proto-cognitive views become much more comprehensively developed towards the end of the twentieth century. Foulkes (1990) develops a cognitive model of dreaming, based on extensive research into the dreams of children, which shows that both dreaming per se, evident in the kinds of images described, and the ability to report those dreams in some coherent fashion is 'constrained by waking cognitive maturation' (1990: 43). In findings which are suggestive of a closer relationship between sleep states and waking cognition, Foulkes (1979) also proposes that most dreams are centred on the routine rather than on the strange and fantastical, and thus are closely linked to a dreamer's everyday concerns. Acknowledging this kind of continuity between waking and sleep states, Hartmann's (1998, 2007) 'contemporary theory of dreaming' synthesises a number of different approaches to dream theory to argue that the nocturnal dream is just one of a series of *mentation states* that exist as part of 'a continuum of mental functioning' (2007: 171). Hartmann's proposal of a wake-dreaming continuum, ranging from focused waking thought to dreaming, emphasises that dream-like phenomena are not exclusive to one particular kind of mental state. This has been supported in other work within sleep medicine that sees continuity between dreaming and waking state consciousness (Domhoff 2010). Nir and Tonini (2009: 88–9) provide details of research that highlights that modalities and submodalities dominant in waking states are also present in dreaming, and that sleep-dreams are characterised by an intensity and range of emotions that are experienced in waking states (Foulkes et al. 1988; Hartmann et al. 1999; Fosse et al. 2001; Hartmann et al. 2001). In addition, studies in neuro-imaging have shown that electroencephalograms (EEG) are similar in periods of REM sleep to certain waking states (Maquet et al. 1996; Hobson et al. 2000), suggesting similarities in brain mechanics and functioning. Pagel et al. (2001) draw attention to the fact that dream-like activity occurs in a range of different states, for example:

> during sleep onset (hypnogogic phenomenon), awakening (hypnopompic phenomenon), meditation, drug induced states, (anesthetics, sedatives, hypnotics), daydreaming, associated with hallucinations, and even during looser, less consciously structured waking thought.
>
> (Pagel et al. 2001: 198)

This broader, not sleep-exclusive model of dreaming is attractive as part of an attempt to provide a more extensive view of conceptualisation which acknowledges the clear continuity in the kinds of emotional concerns that are present in both waking thought and sleep-dreams. However, clearly some differentiation is needed between these various mentation states. I will therefore return to Hartmann's continuum of mental functioning in Section 3.4, where this is given more extensive coverage and discussion, and in Chapters 4 and 5, where, further developed, it forms an important component of a revised model of desire and dreams within the domain of boulomaic modality.[4]

In addition to a principle underlining the connections between dreaming and waking thought, the wider function of dreaming has also come under scrutiny and discussion. In contrast to the Freudian belief that once interpreted, the manifest dream content is no longer considered useful or functional, a cognitive or neuro-cognitive account of dreaming views the dream as the realisation of a conceptualisation and places value on the dream itself, highlighting its status as an important entity. Thus, the dream content becomes important in its own right in *dream content analysis* (Domhoff 1999), which uses quantitative techniques to account for categories occurring in dreams and in the identification of dominant central images in dream reports (Hartmann et al. 1999, Hartmann et al. 2001) as a way of accounting for the ways in which dreams provide a way of 'contextualising emotion' (Hartmann 1998: 4) through a dominant image that holds the dream's concerns open for analysis. Furthermore, States (2003: 8) suggests that dream content may be viewed in a similar way to literary fiction, having world-building properties and existing as kinds of archetypes that 'belong as much to our species as to individuals', often ending up having what Domhoff (2001a: 15) calls distinct 'cultural uses' among communities. States also suggests that dreams, like fictions, may well have an evolutionary role in updating schematic knowledge or 'personal survival equipment' (2003: 5) as part of a revamping of what Tooby and Cosmides (2001: 24) call 'mental organisation'. Much has also been written on the therapeutic function of sustained work on dream content (e.g. Cartwright 1991; Greenberg and Pearlman 1993, and the collection of papers in Barrett 1996) and on the identification and analysis of repetitive structures in dreams (Domhoff 1993) in those suffering from post-traumatic stress (Kramer et al. 1987; Hartmann 1998).

3.4 Nineteenth-century theories of dreaming

Ford (1998) draws attention to the vast range of often contradictory thinking on dreaming in the late eighteenth and nineteenth centuries.

> Some argued that they were miraculous, potentially divine events. Many believed that dreams revealed the powers of the imagination and that dreaming was a form of poetic inspiration. Others argued that they were entirely attributable to the dreamer's physical or psychological constitution. (Ford 1998: 9)

Lindop (2004: 20) argues that dreaming in the late eighteenth and nineteenth centuries was understood either as the result of the mind being overcome by a powerful spiritual, supernatural agency or else caused by ailments, particularly those of the stomach and the brain.[5] The separation of rational waking thought and irrational, chaotic dreaming is viewed by Erasmus Darwin (1796) as the difference between volition (waking) and lack of volition (dreaming). For Darwin, the unpredictable and random associations occurring in dreams must be the consequence of a distinct lack of dreamer control in comparison to the more rounded and well-formed ideas and associations existing in a waking state.

> The great novelty of combination is owing to another circumstance; the trains of ideas, which are carried on in our waking thoughts, are in our dreams

dissevered in a thousand places by the suspension of volition, and the absence of irritative ideas, and are hence perpetually falling into new catenations. (Darwin 1796: 158)

A kind of middle ground exists in the *reverie* (although the term does continue to be used interchangeably throughout the period with *dream*), which Darwin (1796: 160) defines as a state in which the experiencer, although not asleep and maintaining some degree of volition, becomes completely absorbed in the experience to the point of remaining 'inattentive to time and place'. Shelley, in his essay, *On Life*, remarks on the power of the state of reverie, occurring at moments of heightened intensity, to consume the experiencer, to break down any notion of boundary between the imagined and the real and to hold an intense and revelatory power:

> Those who are subject to the state called reverie feel as if their nature were dissolved into the surrounding universe, or as if the surrounding universe were absorbed into their being. They are conscious of no distinction. And these are states which precede or accompany or follow an unusually intense and vivid apprehension of life.
>
> (Shelley 1977: 477)

The emphasis on an imaginative, creative state equates to a belief in the more subjective, psychological character and function of dreams. As O'Connell (2006) suggests, the idea that dreams represent more than simply an irrational incoherence that can be explained simply through reference to thought residues or bodily sensations becomes attractive to Romantic poets who sought answers to the nature of dreaming and its relationship to the creative, transcendent poetic imagination. Indeed, as Tsur (2003: 56) explains, the very fact that Romantic poetry is ultimately concerned with the feeling of 'human limitness, being confined to the *here and now*' engenders the desire in the acts of imagining and writing to break beyond that limit into an alternative space or world and consequently an alternative state of consciousness as a form of secular mysticism. In Romantic writing, this transcendence is seen to occur in a range of imaginative states, not just dreaming. So, both Hazlitt's definition of poetry as 'the language of the imagination and passions' (1930: 8) and Shelley's assertion of composition in his *Defence of Poetry* as 'the expression of the Imagination' (Shelley 1977: 480) encompass the ability of the poetic mind to generate dream-like movement into bold new spatio-temporal parameters. The equating of the ability to dream with a powerful poetic imagination thus becomes a central concern of writers of the period. So, for example, Hazlitt (1931: 23) remarks on the power of the dream, where 'the imagination wanders at will' to 'discover our tacit, and almost unconscious sentiments, with respect to persons or things', and in his essay 'Witches and other night fears', Charles Lamb credits the ability to write poetry to a powerful imagination that manifests itself in the most vivid of dreams. For Lamb, the ability to create in the dream mode anticipates the ability to compose poetry itself:

> The degree of the soul's creativeness in sleep might furnish no whimsical criterion of the poetical faculty resident in the same soul waking.
>
> Lamb (1987: 80)

In a wide-ranging study of the poetry of Wordsworth, Wilson (1993) claims that there are three central beliefs about dreams, core to the vision held by those working within what is broadly known as Romanticism:

> They represent the waking world, they have a formative function upon daily life, and dream activity is analogous to poetic creation.
>
> (Wilson 1993: xiii)

The opening lines of Byron's 'The Dream' can be used to exemplify this viewpoint as well as providing a useful way of exploring some of the properties of the Romantic notion of dreaming:

> Our life is two-fold: Sleep hath its own world,
> A boundary between the things misnamed
> Death and existence: Sleep hath its own world,
> And a wide realm of wild reality.
> And dreams in their development have breath,
> And tears, and tortures, and the touch of joy;
> They leave a weight upon our waking thoughts,
> They take a weight from off our waking toils,
> They do divide our being (1–9)
>
> (Byron 1905)

In this poem, Byron dismisses the view that sleep is simply a passive, chaotic state and instead highlights its potential as both a powerful and mysterious entity. Here, dreaming is seen as distinct from waking consciousness as part of a 'two-fold' (1) human existence, similar to the creative imagination in holding world-building properties to produce 'a wide realm' (4), an alternative third state to that of 'death and existence' (3). Consequently, the dream has inherent world-building properties since it creates a richly conceived imaginative space, and is populated by a range of human attributes, emotions and experiences that mirror that of the waking state.[6] However, some of the random associations evident in dream construction mean that there is the potential to create an infinite landscape, with its 'wild reality' (4), untamed and chaotic. The dream is therefore an alternative mode of consciousness that paradoxically remains both powerful yet fearful. It also has an edge, the 'boundary' of the poem and the felt experience of moving across this edge, what Tsur (2003: 53) calls the 'limitness', is responsible for what might be considered the *texture* of the dream, experienced in 'the weight' (7) that is felt as impressed on the dreamer in the act of waking after the dream. Clearly here, Byron views dreaming as a unique world-building phenomenon, and the world-building potential of the dream experience is seen as analogous to imaginative creation in the ability of the dreamer to construct new, imaginative and intensely dramatic worlds.[7]

Of all the early nineteenth-century poets, Coleridge has the most engaged and comprehensive thoughts on the nature of dreaming and its relationship to other forms of imaginative thinking, including poetic creation. His notebooks and lecture materials show that he went to great lengths to investigate the origins and functions of the dream state, and he meticulously maintained records of his own dreams for later reflection on and analysis of their meaning. His initial interests, however, begin in the more supernatural, visionary nature of the dream, developed from his study of writers of the period such as Andrew Baxter (1733) who purported the dream to be some kind of spiritual visitation. Equally much of Coleridge's thinking arose as a result of his reading, attending lectures on, and engaging and often disagreeing with those working within the newer fields of medicine, such as the physiologist John Brown and the physician Thomas Beddoes (Ford 1998: 16ff). Miall and Kuiken (1997: 4–5) suggest that the range of Coleridge's influences and his careful, but at times inconsistent, early thinking on his dream experiences act as a precursor to his more developed views on the imagination as a modifying power. Ford (1998), in a comprehensive survey of dreaming in the context of Coleridge's work, discusses the poet's rapidly changing ideas on dreams as an attempt to formulate his own theoretical position as a result of his wide reading of contemporary philosophical and medical literature.

Coleridge was clearly interested in the range of states of minds that the term *dream* might cover, and its relationship and overlap with his notions of primary and secondary imagination (Coleridge 1906: 167). According to Keats, he classified sleeping states, nightmares and a variety of states of consciousness between sleeping and waking such as reverie, daydreams and visions as different 'species' of dream (*Letters* II, 89, n. 159). Although Coleridge believed that nocturnal dreaming took place on its very own spatial plane, distinct from other spaces in which conscious thought occurred (Ford 1998: 39), there is clear evidence that he saw continuities between waking and dreaming states, in particular, how daydreaming or reverie, under the control of the will, could facilitate poetic composition as a kind of 'waking dream' (Coleridge 1987: 425), an example of what he termed 'the power of acting on a delusion, according to the Delusion, without dissolving it' (Coleridge 1973: e.3280).

In viewing the writing of poetry as necessarily involving some loss of volition, yet controlled to the extent that it can be seen as a kind of 'rationalised dream' (Coleridge 1962: e.2086), Coleridge became fascinated by the more 'psychological, subjective processes of dreams and the complex links between subjective and physiological processes' (Ford 1998: 16) as a way of distancing himself from those theories of dreaming that emphasised its passive nature as his own practice moved towards a central concern of transforming 'the practice of reverie into a desire for making poetry' (Wilson 1997: 68). Coleridge's view of the dream as a form of imaginative construction also mirrors a more general shift among nineteenth-century writers and thinkers to use the term *dream* to refer to a much wider range of mental states beyond that of merely sleeping, encompassing not only sleeping dreams, but also hopes, ambitions and an array of imaginative states such as thought, and the creative acts of reading, writing and even acting (O'Connell 2006).

3.5 Keats, dreams and the imagination

Although there is little evidence to suggest that Keats was interested in the materialism of dreams as passionately or as systematically as Coleridge, he was probably influenced to some extent by the older poet's ideas. Keats' letters contain only minimal references to dreaming: the recount of writing a sonnet following a dream about Dante's meeting with Paulo and Francesca in canto V of Inferno (Letters II, 91, n.159), and a series of comments on sleep and dreaming as a result of his worsening tuberculosis (*Letters* II, 271, n.240; II, 277, n.247).

However, in the same letter as he recounts the dream of Dante, Keats recalls a meeting with Coleridge on the 11th April while walking towards Highgate:

> I met Mr Green our Demonstrator at Guy's in conversation with Coleridge – I joined them, after enquiring by a look whether it would be agreeable – I walked with him a[t] his alderman-after dinner pace for nearly two miles I suppose In those two Miles he broached a thousand things – let me see if I can give you a list – Nightingales, Poetry – on Poetical sensation – Metaphysics – Different genera and species of Dreams – Nightmare – a dream accompanied with a sense of touch – single and double touch – A dream related – First and second consciousness – the difference explained between will and Volition.
>
> (*Letters* II, 88–9, n.159)

Whether this meeting directly influenced Keats beyond the episode is unknown. However, it is clear from both his letters and poetry that Keats shared Coleridge's concerns with daydreaming, nocturnal dreaming, visions and fantasies in so far as they are related to the notion of the poetic imagination. In his verse letter 'To J. H. Reynolds, Esq.', Keats conflates the acts of dreaming and imagination at the opening of the poem into a visionary experience:

> . . . as last night I lay in bed,
> There came before my eyes that wonted thread
> Of shapes, and shadows, and remembrances,
> That every other minute vex and please. (1–4)

Like other writers and thinkers of the period, Keats clearly saw the term and notion of the *dream* as covering a range of mental imaginative acts from sleeping to focused waking speculation. In the same poem, he speaks of 'our dreaming all, of sleep or wake' (67). For Keats, the dream was an imaginative act and the imagination a kind of dreaming.

In a wide-ranging survey, Waldoff (1985: ix–xi) proposes three working models of the Keatsian imagination. The first emphasises its creative power, where imaginative states necessarily reveal a type of reality or truth previously undiscovered or else an individual is able to construct that reality simply through imagining or desiring it. This is exemplified in Keats' letter to Benjamin Bailey in November 1818:

> what the imagination seizes as beauty must be truth. . . . .the imagination may be compared to Adam's dream – he awoke and found it truth
>
> (*Letters* I, 184–5, n.43)

The choice of the verb 'seizes' represents the convinction with which an early Keats believed the imagination was able to work as an active maker of a desirable states of affairs. In the same letter to Bailey, Keats had posited the ability of the imagination to revivify any felt or living experience and to present it in a more powerful and intensely felt way:

> Have you never by being surprised with an old melody – in a delicious place – by a delicious voice, f[e]t over again your very speculations and surmises at the time it first operated on your soul – do you not remember forming to yourself the singer's face more beautiful that it was possible and yet with the elevation of the Moment you did not think so – even when you were mounted on the Wings of Imagination so high – that the prototype must be here after – that delicious face you will see.
>
> (*Letters* I, 185, n.43)

Keats often remarks on the imagination and various dreaming states as being both more dramatic and real than reality itself. In several letters, he stresses the ability of the imagination to affect him more urgently and with greater consequences than that of the actual world.[8] In his early poems, Keats emphasises the creative power of imaginative and dream states by presenting them as calming, liberating and overtly imaginative, sitting comfortably between the modes of reality and irreality, and synonymous with poetic composition. In 'Sleep and Poetry', which can be considered a kind of early, playful Keatsian manifesto, Keats stresses the power of poetic mind as an imaginative dream state to undertake the creative and restorative functions usually inherent in sleep. Similarly, sonnets such as 'Written on the day that Mr Leigh Hunt left prison' and 'On sitting down to Read *King Lear* once again' dramatise poetic imagination as a type of liberation, like dreaming, from the reality spaces of the external world.

Endymion, often read as the dramatisation of the poet's imagination in the quest for an ideal beauty, remains central to understanding the rest of Keats' work on imagination and dreams and begins to develop some of the tensions that become more pronounced in later poems. Early in Book I, the imaginative dream becomes a mode of transportation across boundary edges emphasising its own restorative nature, where the poem's speaker can 'send/My herald thought into a wilderness -/There lets its trumpet blow' (I, 58–60). In the same book, Endymion's recollection of his dream of the moon goddess in lines 612–30 is couched in a kind of language that demonstrates the powerful eroticism of imaginative desire, reverie and fantasy. Yet, in Book II, further imagined senses of physical desire (II, 707–35) are tempered by a realisation that those entities imagined and yearned for are in reality merely transitory and, unable to exist beyond the world of the imagination, leave the dreamer in a state of destitution:

> ... wherefore may I not
> Be ever in these arms? In this sweet spot
> Pillow my chin for ever? Ever press
> These toying hands and kiss their smooth excess?
> Why not for ever and forever feel
> That breath about my eyes? Ah, wilt thou steal
> Away from me again, indeed, indeed –
> Thou wilt be gone away, and wilt not heed
> My lonely madness. (740–8)

Later episodes in the poem mark the beginning of conflicting views on the validity of imaginative thought. In Book IV, Endymion, realising the illusory power of the imagination and the fact that he has been 'by phantoms duped' (IV, 629), proclaims that 'never more/Shall airy voices cheat me to the shore/Of tangled wonder, breathless and aghast' (IV, 653–5). However, the fact that the poem does allow for the fusion of the imagined-desired and the real at its climax in the appearance of Cynthia as the Indian maid is indicative of a complexity that Keats is unable to address at this stage.

Waldoff (1985: 18) suggests that in *Endymion*, Keats very quickly realised the limitations of the imagination in fusing together dream and desire states into a concrete reality, yet was unable to reconcile himself to them, attracted as he was by the potential of an imaginative force to bring into being the objects of the poetic mind. Waldoff's reading of Keats is inspired by Freud's (1985a) 'Creative Writers and Daydreaming', where the imaginative writer is seen as analogous to the fantasist daydreamer in the construction of 'egocentric stories' (1985a: 136), and centres on the power of the imagination in being able to recapture or rediscover that which has been lost yet remains desirable. In the case of Keats, Waldoff reads this loss and a subsequent separation anxiety as the consequence of a series of deaths within Keats' immediate family and views the death of his mother in particular, as disabling in that it initiates a more general concern about the maintenance of relationships with females and specifically with Fanny Brawne. With his final comment a reference to Keats' own letter to Bailey in which he had spoken of the power of the imagination, Waldoff explains that

> The real difficulty he faced in his preoccupation with the visionary imagination was not in recognising its limitations but in reconciling himself to them. He was all too aware that dreams don't come true, the "You cannot eat your cake and have it too" (the proverb he placed as an epigraph to the sonnet 'How fever'd is the man') and that "Things cannot to the will/Be settled" ('Dear Reynolds,' *Letters* II, 76–7, n. 159). But wish and will continually reasserted themselves, and one continued to form the singer's face as more beautiful than it had been.
>
> (Waldoff 1985: 18)

This difficulty that Waldoff suggests is addressed in later work, where mental states that form part of a dream or imaginative mode are carefully contrasted with those of waking thought at the other end of a continuum, often in a kind of reversal of consciousness. In 'Ode on a Grecian Urn', 'Ode to a Nightingale' 'Ode on Melancholy' and 'Ode on Indolence', imaginative states provide a sense of heightened emotional and physical sensation that contrast with those waking states that are more soberly presented yet are ultimately more convincingly real. In these cases, the imaginative/dream state retains all the power of its earlier incarnations but reveals itself to be transitory and merely part of an extended illusion. The traumatic nature of dreaming is also seen in poems which explore imagination alongside states expressing desire and both erotic and romantic love. In *The Eve of St Agnes* (discussed in Chapter 5), much of the literary texture can be understood through the interplay between the spiritual union Madeline seeks in her dreams and the physical desire of Porphyro. In *Lamia*, Lycius and Lamia's micro-world is destroyed by the figure of Apollonius, who 'haunting my sweet dreams' (387) reveals Lamia to be a serpent. And, in *Isabella; or, The Pot of Basil* (discussed in Chapter 7), Lorenzo's appearance in a dream to Isabella, following his murder, emphasises his existence as merely a 'pale shadow' (281) and highlights the divided nature of the lovers in an inverted form of the idealised presentation of love in *Endymion*.

Waldoff's second and third models of the Keatsian imagination can be viewed together as a more pragmatic take on the dream, a humanistic view of poetic composition and an emphasis on the functional design of the dream within Keats' poetry. So, imaginative states come to facilitate sympathetic identification, the ability of the poetic self to move beyond its own existence and world and to project itself into a sense of otherness or alternative consciousness. As Bate (1963: 259–60) suggests, much of Keats' thinking on this no doubt came from his attending Hazlitt's *Lectures on the English Poets* at the Surrey Institute, where he would have heard Hazlitt's comments on the absence of egotism in Shakespeare (Hazlitt 1930). In turn, these influence and generate Keats' own comments on the 'poetical character', which in contrast to the 'wordsworthian or egotistical sublime' is marked by the poet's conception of himself as 'camelion. . . .continually in for – and filling some other body' (*Letters* I, 387, n. 118). The explicit placing of the poet as a kind of dramatic creator in the mould of Shakespeare is also a feature of Keats' earlier notion of negative capability, which he defines as

> when a man is capable of being in uncertainties, Mysteries, doubts, without any irritable reaching after fact & reason.
>
> (*Letters* I, 193, n. 45)

Additionally, the imagination and dreaming may be considered as operators of self-deception both in their ability to present false hopes and dreams and in disguising potentially harmful and dangerous situations. In this instance, imaginative, dreaming states leaning inwards in what Bloom (1970: 6) terms an 'acute preoccupation' painfully reveal the isolated self. In Keats, this becomes evident in the disorientation felt by the speaker at the end of 'Ode to a Nightingale', the bitter pain expressed in late letters to Fanny Brawne and noticeably in the fragment 'This living hand, now warm and capable', which I explore as a composite nightmare experience in Chapter 9.

3.6 Towards a definition of the dream for text world theory

3.6.1 Dreams in Werth's text world theory model

The categorisation of dreams, prevalent in modern dream science, as distinct conceptual structures yet operating as part of a continuum of mental states has yet to be fully developed in text world theory. In Werth's original model, dreams might initially appear to be examples of deictic sub-worlds, since they represent variations in and modifications to an original text world's internal structure in terms of either space, location, time or entity (a dream will necessarily contain a different enactor of a character from that of the matrix world). However, in his discussion, despite admitting that 'a dream world is in general one in which the normal "laws" of space and time have been suspended' (1999: 231), Werth does not commit himself to explicitly categorising a dream world as part of an altered deictic space. Instead, his reference to 'dream sub-worlds' is part of a larger discussion on desire worlds (Werth 1999: 227–33). Indeed, Werth pays no attention to how the explicit notion of a dream per se fits into text world theory. Equally, Gavins (2005a), in reconfiguring Werth's sub-world system, does not discuss in any real detail notions and forms of dreaming, and does not explore the various mental acts that might constitute dream-like states.[9] I return to these in more detail in Chapter 4 on modality, which offers suggestions for a revised model for dreams and desires within text world theory. However, the sections below offer a starting point for some preliminary discussion.

3.6.2   A 'wake-dreaming' continuum

In arguing for poetic conception as a form of psychoanalytic practice, Easthope (1989) differentiates between the kinds of *phantasies* that exist in night-dreams, the 'discourse of the unconscious and those that exist in daydreams or inner discourse' (1989: 19). This primary difference between a full dream state represented by sleeping and a more subtle imaginative sense of dreaming is also present in Bachelard's distinction between dream and reverie. For Bachelard, a dream represents a passive nocturnal state (1969: 11), while reverie, a fully enriched and predominantly poetic kind of daydreamings, provides an opening to an as yet undiscovered world, serving as a 'useful irreality function' (1969: 13). This distinction between states of dreaming is one that treats reverie as a more wilful, imaginative state, closer to conscious thought while still holding the kind of an imaginative power seen in the work of nineteenth-century poets.

As I discussed in Section 3.2, Hartmann (1998) suggests that a state continuum running from focused waking thought to dreaming is useful in describing the range of dream-like states that may exist across a number of sleep and waking mental acts. This is shown in Figure 3.1.

Hartmann likens the functioning involved in mentation states to a net of interconnected units existing across the cerebral cortex of the brain (1998: 78). This connectivity between units takes place during both waking and dreaming

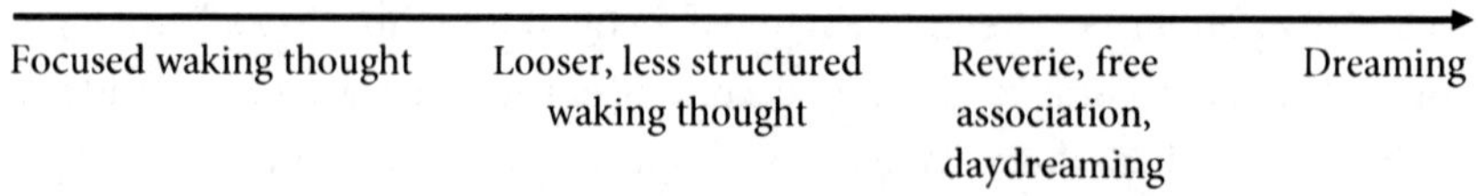

Focused waking thought	Looser, less structured waking thought	Reverie, free association, daydreaming	Dreaming

Figure 3.1 A 'wake-dreaming' continuum, adapted from Hartmann (1998: 90)

states. During waking, connections tend to be more linear and 'guided by a specific task or goal' (1998: 80), while dreaming has more random, widespread and less specific connections. Thus, waking nets are more tightly woven, rely on rapid sensory input-motor output processing in a feed-forward mechanism, and tend to follow a straightforward logical sequence, while dreaming has looser nets with no rapid processing, and is formed of auto-associative exploratory patterns that avoid logical and direct structures. This accounts for the ways in which dreaming states tend to be more fantastical and contain more bizarre and literal imagery (Hartmann 1998: 84). Clearly, the continuum model suggests that dream-like experiences can occur across a range of mentation states. In each case, degrees of the characteristics of those states at the poles of the continuum would be evident.

Using the continuum model as a starting point for further exploration of the dream phenomenon within text world theory has the following advantages. First, it allows for a broader discussion of the term *dream* to incorporate imaginative states, the *reverie* of Shelley and Bachelard, as well as those nocturnal states associated with sleep. Secondly, its commitment to continuity between dreams and waking thought aligns it clearly to Lakoff's generalisation commitment (1990: 40) by proposing a way of understanding the continuum of dreaming as a continuum of *cognition*. Thirdly, it allows for a more developed discussion of the explicit characteristics of states along the waking-dream continuum within the text world theory model than originally allowed by Werth.

With this in mind, it should now be possible to speculate as to the kinds of text world structures represented by states along the wake-dreaming continuum. On the surface, any kind of mental act would appear to initiate a structure similar to a deictic sub-world (Werth 1999: 216) since it involves movements into different and distinctive deictic spaces from the matrix world. However, clearly this is not always necessarily the case. Moreover, the kinds of reflective and speculative acts, typified by predicates such as *recall, remember, wonder* and *imagine*, are concerned as much, if not more, with attitudes as they are with actions and could arguably be better served by Werth's attitudinal sub-worlds of desire, belief and purpose (Werth 1999: 216). The range of mental states represented along the continuum line from focused goal-driven thought to nocturnal sleep clearly do not fit well into Werth's model, evident in his difficulty in convincingly accounting for these types of worlds.

Gavins' (2005a) reconfiguration of sub-worlds into world-switches and boulomaic, deontic and epistemic modal worlds appears better placed to account for dream worlds. Although again, these could be considered in terms of their temporal or spatial deictic movement, their existence as attitudinal acts marks them as best conceived of as examples of *modalised expressions*. Of the three modal worlds proposed by Gavins, the mental acts represented by dreaming would appear to fit most appropriately into either the epistemic or boulomaic domains since these mental states all represent degrees of perception or of volition. As part of the boulomaic domain, this assumes clear movement along the continuum from the essentially volitive and self-directed nature of focused waking thought to a less intentionally activated dreaming (outside of any Freudian notion of wish-fulfilment). Although I return to a more developed discussion of Gavins' work, modality and degrees of volition in Chapter 4, it is now possible to propose the following as the beginnings of a more cognitively plausible notion of the dream for text world theory:

1. dreams are best considered as part of a waking thought-dream continuum of mental states and functioning, covering different types of mental process;
2. there is a continuity principle that runs along these states, meaning that the same systems are responsible for providing structure to each state along the continuum;
3. these states are best understood when realised linguistically as types of modalised constructions since dream states are representative of the emotional concerns of the dreamer;
4. it is possible for 'dream-like' phenomena to occur outside of pure dreaming, characterised as nocturnal sleep on the right hand side of the continuum, in other mental states such as reverie and fantasy; and
5. in the light of its claims as a model for explaining how readers organise, monitor and track textual information, the text world theory model as it currently stands needs to be re- evaluated and developed to account for these specific kinds of conceptualisation.

3.7 Review

Since subsequent chapters use text world theory to explore prominent stylistic effects created by Keats' use of both dream and waking states, the aim of this chapter was to provide a broader context for this study beyond that of the focus in Chapter 2 on text world theory. In Sections 3.2 and 3.3, I provided a brief summary of the notion of dream, suggesting that most recent work has sought to define the dream as one of a series of linked mentation states. I discussed a more cognitive approach to the dream phenomenon and dreaming, where I showed that cognitive models have sought to build on existing and mainly Freudian psychoanalytical models of dreaming, maintaining the therapeutic and revelatory nature of sleep-dreams but emphasising their position as continuous to waking cognition. Here, I explained that these models have also stressed the individual's dreaming capacity as part of a more general developmental cognition. In Section 3.4, I focused on nineteenth-century notions of the dream within the context of Romantic poetry, providing a summary of the interests of Coleridge and the importance of the dream as an imaginative force by the period's major writers. In an overview of Keats' use of dreams in his poetry in Section 3.5, I argued that his shifting attitudes to dream states form important thematic concerns in his poetry. These will form the basis of more extensive discussion on dreams and imaginative states in Chapter 5 and on nightmares in Chapters 6, 7, 8 and 9.

Finally, I anticipated more detailed discussion in Chapter 4 by arguing that Hartmann's (1998) wake-dreaming continuum provides a more useful way of approaching the range of mental states in which dream-like mentation occurs. This distinguishes pure focused waking thought from more dream-like imaginative states from pure sleep-dreaming in a way that admits to a more layered and textured approach to cognition and is clearly suited to the analysis of states of poetic dreaming and imagination. In this final section, I suggested that the text world theory models proposed by both Werth and Gavins do not set out to develop the notion of the dream and associated states, and are therefore unable to fully explain the conceptual spaces that these kinds of structures initiate. In suggesting that mental states running along a continuum might best be considered modal constructions, I anticipate a detailed discussion of modality and its place in text world theory that I began in Chapter 2, and which will form the basis for Chapter 4 to follow. Chapter 4 in turn provides a model for the analysis of *The Eve of St Agnes* in Chapter 5, and for my discussion of nightmares in three poems in subsequent chapters.

Modal Worlds

4.1 Introduction

As I explained in Chapter 2, Werth originally accounts for modal propositions as either attitudinal or epistemic sub-worlds. These were reconfigured in Gavins (2001, 2005a), following Simpson (1993), to form deontic, epistemic and boulomaic modal worlds. However, as I explain in Chapter 3, Werth and Gavins do not substantially develop the notions of desire and dream within their text world theory models. In this chapter, I therefore suggest an augmented model of modality for text world theory, and subsequently develop the notions of *desire* and *dream worlds*.

In Section 4.2, I aim to contextualise my reworking of boulomaic modal worlds within the text world theory framework by discussing modality per se, drawing on research and literature in generative and cognitive linguistics. Consequently, I review approaches to the study of modality which have placed the phenomenon as a way of exploring speaker attitude or drawing attention to a state of affairs as yet unrealised. This is then further developed to explore the ways in which modality has been broadly categorised as one of the two domains of root and epistemic modal forms and to summarise attention that has been afforded to boulomaic modality. Finally, I look at work that has been completed on modality and gradience.

In Section 4.3, I look at significant work in modality within the field of cognitive grammar. In Section 4.3.1, I use Langacker's (1987, 2008) notions of clausal grounding, conceived reality and projected and potential reality to explain the potency inherent in modalised propositions. Then, in Sections 4.3.2, I refer to work that views modality as structurally underpinned by a FORCE metaphor that allows for the understanding of the psychological in terms of the physical. In Section 4.4, I aim to develop the treatment of modality in the text world theory framework, drawing together some of the key issues that I discuss in previous sections to propose a cognitively plausible model for accounting for desires and dreams as modalised expressions. Following my discussion in Chapter 2 where I explained Gavins' revisions to Werth's original model, I provide further details of Gavins' objections to Werth's attitudinal and epistemic sub-worlds, and outline her reconfiguration of modality into three modal worlds. In Section 4.4.3, I build on Gavins' welcome reworking of Werth's original ideas to propose a desire-dream continuum in order to distinguish between desire and dream worlds. This chapter forms the basis for the four analysis chapters in this book and also provides the background for my examination of nightmares in Chapter 6.

4.2 Modality as a linguistic phenomenon

4.2.1 A definition of modality

Modality is the term used to describe what Lyons (1977b: 763, 808–9) calls 'non-categorical language', and is marked by the use of modal lexical verbs such as *believe*, modal auxiliary verbs such as *will* and modal adverbs and adjectives such as *possibly* and *possible*. Modality may also be expressed through mood, modal tags such as *I guess* and modal affixes and particles. It has been argued that these linguistic forms constituting the domain of modality share certain semantic properties, such as an attitudinal status and values of necessity and possibility status (Nuyts 2006). Modality has been defined in very broad terms firstly as referring primarily to a speaker's attitude to, confidence in, perception of or subjective modification of a particular speech act, state of affairs or proposition (e.g. Lyons 1977b; Coates 1983; Bybee et al. 1994; and Evans and Green 2006). I term this the *'attitude' definition*. Alternatively, it has been seen primarily as a phenomenon which refers to a state of reality or factuality: a modalised proposition is one that refers to a non-factual state rather than an actualised or factual one (e.g. Palmer 1979, 1986, 2001; Chung and Timberlake 1985; Mithun 1999). I term this the *'factuality' definition*.

4.2.2 Categorising modality

Following early attempts at classification of modal categories or types (e.g. von Wright 1951 and Rescher 1968), researchers working within the field of modality have generally favoured either a 'narrowing' approach to limit the range of modal categories or a 'widening' one to maintain as many types of modality as is possible.

The common bipartite method of classifying modality can be seen in Coates (1983), who makes a distinction between *epistemic* and non-epistemic or *root modality* (Coates 1983: 18–20). Coates defines epistemic modality as relating to the 'speaker's confidence (or lack of confidence) in the truth of the proposition expressed' (1983: 18). In comparison, the agency involved in root modality is more forceful and concerned with bringing about the event itself rather than presenting a speaker's attitude towards a particular event. Coates therefore defines root modality in terms of its syntactic patterns, stating that its examples will typically contain animate subjects acting as agents in verb processes that exist as the focus of the modal expression. In addition, she widens the range of root modal propositions to cover all aspects of obligation, permission, ability and desire. This distinction based on force has been adopted by those focusing on the agency inherent in modalised propositions.[1] Coates' decision to maintain a narrow bipartite structure of root and epistemic modality is, according to her, on the basis that these types have an 'essential unity' (1983: 21) although she later confesses that the root modals have 'a range of meaning' (1983: 21) and that their unity is confirmed only by their syntactic patterns. This throws some doubt on Coates' distinction in so far as it fails to account for the whole range of possible meanings or *senses* (Collins 1974: 154) covered by these kinds of modal forms. Clearly, to say that a formal grammatical unity exists is not enough to account for the rich range of interpretations attached to modal forms and indeed Coates' own example of the subtle difference between meanings of *must* suggests that a narrow category of non-epistemic forms as root modals may not necessarily be a helpful one (Coates 1983: 21).

Others have discussed a bipartite model of classification. Palmer (1976) begins with a tripartite system of *epistemic, subject oriented* and *discourse oriented* modality before refining this to *epistemic, deontic* and *dynamic* modality (Palmer 1979). He then switches to a bipartite system similar to that of Coates (Palmer 1986) before finally reverting to and developing this to cover *propositional* modality (*epistemic* and *evidential* forms) and *event* modality (*deontic* and *dynamic* forms) (Palmer 2001). This new structure offers the clear bipartite structure while acknowledging, unlike in Coates' work, that there is sufficient variation in meaning within the traditional root category to warrant further sub-categorisation and definition of discrete modal entities.

Palmer's system for categorising modality clearly differentiates between those kinds of modal expressions that are concerned with a speaker's attitude to the factual status of the proposition and those that are concerned with potential events that have yet to be actualised, yet are potential or possible. In this way, although Palmer himself prefers the terms *realis* and *irrealis*, it is a model of modality that acknowledges both subjectivity and factuality. He also clearly differentiates between types of traditional root modality.

Palmer's main distinction is between *propositional* and *event* modality. Propositional modality is concerned with a speaker's judgement of a proposition, whereas event modality is concerned with a speaker's inclination towards an as yet unactualised event. He illustrates this basic difference with the following two examples:

> (1) Kate may be at home now/Kate must be at home now = propositional modality
> (2) Kate may come in now/Kate must come in now = event modality.
>
> (Palmer 2001: 7)

Palmer explains these examples by paraphrasing them to show how when fronted with the clause 'It is possible/it is necessary', the first pair is concerned with a belief, thought or possibility and the second pair with permission or obligation. In both sets of examples, there are clearly degrees of belief, permission and obligation, so that 'It is necessarily the case that Kate is at home now' is more assertive and shows a greater degree of *speaker affinity* (Hodge and Kress 1988: 123) than 'It is possible that Kate is at home now':

> 1. It is possible that Kate is at home now/It is necessarily the case that Kate is at home now
> 2. It is possible for Kate to come in now/It is necessary for Kate to come in now.
>
> (Palmer 2001: 7)

In addition, Palmer extends his model to account for different types of propositional and event modal forms. Within the system of propositional modality, he distinguishes between epistemic and evidential modality, the former being concerned with speaker judgement towards a particular event and the latter existing as evidence in itself for the event's factual status (Palmer 2001: 8).

Within the epistemic domain, Palmer distinguishes between a judgement that 'expresses uncertainty, one that indicates an inference from observable evidence and one that indicates inference from what is generally known'

Speculation	Assumption	Deduction
MAY	WILL	MUST
Possible	Most Possible	Only Possibility

Figure 4.1 A continuum of epistemic forms, after Palmer (2001)

(2001: 24), calling these types of *speculative, deductive* and *assumptive* epistemic modality. The three types may be seen to form a continuum of epistemic forms as illustrated in Figure 4.1.

The continuum shows that there are contrasts that can be made between the degrees of closeness to reality that can be attached to a speaker's judgement based on the particular modal expression chosen. These degrees of closeness can be viewed as examples of *graded epistemic sense.*

Palmer categorises evidential modality as falling into one of two types: *report*ed and *sensory.* Sensory modality incorporates aspects of visual and auditory evidence on the part of a speaker, while reported evidential modality is likely to include evidence from either a direct or indirect witness to an event, distinguished by Willet (1988: 57, 96) as *second-hand evidence* and *third-hand evidence.*

Palmer's second modal system aims to provide a way of distinguishing between types of root modality in more detail. He proposes a distinction between *deontic* and *dynamic* modality with further differences identified within these two domains. The deontic domain covers aspects of either permission or obligation in line generally with other studies of deontic forms, while the dynamic domain covers aspects of ability and willingness (2001: 75–6).

4.2.3 Boulomaic modality

Although it is often not mentioned explicitly within traditional surveys of modality, boulomaic modality can be defined as 'the degree of the speaker's (or someone else's) liking or disliking of the state of affairs' (Nuyts 2006:12), 'the wishes and desires of the speaker' (Simpson 1993: 48) and 'relating to desire' (Rescher 1968: 24 ff). Very little work has been explicitly undertaken within the field of boulomaic modality, which for some researchers is simply incorporated into a broader category of modal systems. For example, Hengeveld (1988: 139) includes it as a subtype of what he calls *subjective modality* defining the speaker's commitment to degrees of wishing and hoping within his epistemological system and Nuyts (2001: 6; 2006: 12) who in referring to it as *emotional attitude,* recognises its similarities to epistemic forms, marking forms expressing volition as members of the boulomaic category. Although Nuyts (2005) places boulomaic modality as one of four attitudinal categories together with *epistemic, evidential* and *deontic* modality, he later draws attention himself in what he terms the 'modal confusion' (2005: 5): the difficulty in accounting for forms of desire within a modal framework. He also acknowledges the similarity between forms of desire and a type of obligatory modal force by remarking that 'it is not always easy to draw a precise line between this category (volition) and deontic modality' (2006: 12).

Simpson's 'modal package' (1993: 47) offers some developed discussion of boulomaic modality in the context of his work on narrative point of view. Simpson follows Perkins (1983: 11, 14–15) and Lyons (1977b: 826) in suggesting that the boulomaic system is more related to the deontic domain than the epistemic one, given that they are in Bybee and Pagliuca's terms essentially agent-oriented (1985: 63–4) and their respective desiderative and instrumental Hallidayan functions are clearly 'very closely connected' (Lyons 1977a: 286). Simpson uses his modal grammar through the identification of *epistemic, deontic, boulomaic* and *perception* modality (Perkins 1983) to distinguish between different narrative types of developing work by Fowler (1986) and Genette (1980). Thus, foregrounded boulomaic modality along with deontic modality is said to characterise positively shaded *homodiegetic* and *hetereodiegetic* narratives, or in Simpson's terms Category A and Category B (*narratorial* and *reflector* mode) narratives. These distinctions are used to explore focalisation and stylistic effect in a range of literary texts (Simpson 1993: 51–83).

4.2.4 Gradience

One of the defining features of Coates' work is her discussion (1983: 9 ff) of approaches to modality as either *monosemantic*, identifying a basic meaning for each modal construction, or *polysemantic*, using a discrete system of categorising to account for specific uses of modal expressions. In doing so, Coates highlights the indeterminacy of natural language, following her own data, which showed that examples of modal propositions covered a range of different meanings that exhibited gradience (1983: 10).

Coates' initial work on gradience (Coates and Leech 1980; Leech and Coates 1980) is rejected in favour of a model based on *fuzzy sets theory* (Zadeh 1965, 1970, 1971, 1972) which has the most frequently used modal

Figure 4.2 The dimension of volitivity, from Narrog (2005: 685)

forms defined as *core* examples. In these terms, a core example is what Coates describes as

> the cultural stereotype, that is if you stopped people at random and said 'Give me an example of MUST/MAY/CAN. . .' they would respond with a core example.
>
> (Coates 1983: 13)

In addition to core examples, modal forms in *the periphery* are more remote and consequently less prototypical, while intermediate examples sit in *the skirt* (1983: 13).[2] Another model of gradience is that suggested by Narrog who develops his model of volitivity, following Coates (1983) and Nuyts (2001) by emphasising 'degrees of gradience' (2005: 685). Narrog's 'dimension of volitivity' (2005: 685) understands deontic and epistemic forms of the modal auxiliary verb 'must' as polarised with given instances of their use resting somewhere between the two poles. Figure 4.2 shows Narrog's 'dimension of volitivity' that places deontic and epistemic forms of the modal auxiliary verb 'must' as polarised with given instances of their use resting somewhere between the two poles.

Radden and Dirven offer a similar model in their 'scales of epistemic assessment and deontic attitude' (2007: 239), which follows Palmer (2001) in its continuum-based approach. Equally, Hodge and Kress's notions of 'degrees of affinity' (1988: 123), Halliday and Matthiessen's three 'values of modality' (2004: 620) and, from a stylistic perspective, Simpson's 'strong, medium and weak commitment' (1993: 50), which form the basis of his model of positive, negative and neutral shading (1993: 75), all emphasise a focus on gradience as a central feature and concern of modalised propositions and modality in general.

4.3 Cognitive grammar and modality

Ronald Langacker (1987, 1991, 2008) claims that the modal system with its emphasis on speculation, imagination and projection into future events offers a way of contrasting present time with that of the future. Langacker's equal focus on how modalised propositions draw a distinction between the real and the unreal, and are reliant on agentive force in terms of desire and attitude, offers a neat way of drawing together the two traditionally contrasting ways of considering modality in terms of attitude and factuality.

4.3.1 Clausal grounding and the conception of reality

Langacker's ideas on modality are inherently tied to his model of *grounding*. In cognitive grammar, the notion of *ground* refers to 'the speech event, its participants, their interaction and the immediate circumstances' (Langacker 2008: 259), and *grounding* is the process whereby a phrase or clause is given status within the ground through the use of *grounding elements. Nominal grounding* occurs when a hearer/reader is directed towards a nominal referent through the use of the determiner system, whereas *clausal grounding* establishes through the addition of bound morphemes or designates modality through modal auxiliary verbs.[3]

As an example, Langacker offers the string 'girl like boy', which presents only types of nouns 'boy' and 'girl' rather than actual instances of them and a verb 'like' that represents a schematic *type* of process rather than stressing the relationship between the two.[4] Although the schematic type for *'like'* is a fairly rich one, we could still imagine countless possible examples involving different instances of the process itself and different girls and boys (2008: 265). The example given therefore merely presents a type of situation as opposed to a specific *instance* in the grounded clause 'the girl likes this boy'. In cognitive grammar terms, this specificity is an example of *instantiation*, where instances of the nouns 'girl' and 'boy' have been selected and identified. Here, the linguistic mechanism through which this occurs is the use of the grounding elements 'the' (determiner), and 's' (bound morpheme). Grounding, then, can be viewed as the difference between *actualising* and mere *contemplation* (Langacker 2008: 259).

Unlike nominal grounding, which serves to instantiate nouns, clausal grounding makes some comment on the likelihood of a verb process occurring, in order to determine the 'epistemic status . . . in relation to what we currently know and what we are trying to ascertain' (Langacker 2008: 297). Clausal grounding therefore is concerned with the *conception of reality*.

Langacker calls reality 'the history of what has occurred up through the present moment' (2008: 297) and later 'what a speaker conceives as being real' (2008: 297).[5] Langacker's model of reality has a *conceptualiser* (C) moving through time. What he terms *conceived reality* (R_C) represents what C conceives

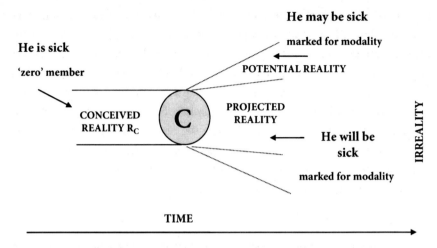

Figure 4.3 A model of reality, adapted from Langacker (2008: 306)

and accepts as being real at any given moment as part of a larger space of *actual reality*. It is the *absence of modality* that marks a process as being conceived inside this space marked as R_C. In contrast, a modal expression places a process as outside of R_C and therefore part of *irreality*. This is accounted for by highlighting the general grounding system as a binary pair, with one member marked as the *zero member* and the other overtly marked for modality. In the case of the modal expressions, the *zero member* is the absent modal expression which sits at less of an epistemic distance to the conceptualiser. In contrast, the marked modal forms 'He may be sick' and 'He will be sick' are more remote in terms of distance as they have yet to be actualised and are not part of the R_C; they instead represent current *irreality* and either *projected* or *potential reality*. These are shown in Figure 4.3.

As R_C evolves through time, certain pathways are rejected and remain part of irreality. However, modalised propositions mark others as having greater proximity to conceived reality as part of either projected or potential reality. Langacker uses these two domains to distinguish between the main types of epistemic forms:

(A) This election may be close
(B) This election will be close.

(Langacker 2008: 307)

The difference between the epistemic forms 'may' and 'will' defines the difference between potential and projected reality. Clearly, 'will' has stronger epistemic power and is therefore at less of an epistemic distance to current conceived reality than 'may'. Consequently, the evolution of R_C is conceptualised as being more likely to follow the process grounded by 'will' than by 'may', or in basic terms, the conceptualiser projects the process as being more likely to occur. Langacker does not include the third epistemic form 'must' (cf. Palmer 2001) as part of his brief discussion, although he does admit to 'must' having epistemic uses, instead suggesting that only 'will' and 'may' are used in this manner, since 'must' only pertains to the future when it has a root sense. Yet as a more potent grounding element than 'may' or 'will', 'must' clearly does have elements of futurity in terms of the speaker's acceptance of a proposition as factual. For example, we could add (C) to the examples using 'may' and 'will':

(C) This election 'must' be close

In this example, the use of 'must' suggests that the speaker has yet to accept the proposition as being factual. In its epistemic sense then, 'must' indicates that the proposition has yet to become part of the R_C, although it is a stronger candidate for doing so than both 'may' and 'will'. In fact, as Langacker later admits, 'must is stronger (as a modal grounding element) because it suggests that evolutionary momentum makes this inevitable' (2008: 308). In essence, a cognitive approach to the epistemic modals sits neatly with Palmer's (2001) continuum of epistemic forms.

Langacker uses this model to classify modal expressions as either root (covering deontic and boulomaic forms) or epistemic. For both kinds, we can say that they contain a *potency* that is responsible for the undertaking of an action and which becomes central in the grounding process. Root modals work to *effect the grounding process* (2008: 306) in so far as they aim to cause the process to take place or become actualised as part of conceived reality. On the other hand, epistemic forms do not work to actualise a process but rather to assess its position as either projected or potential reality. In this way, the force or power is not located in the grounding itself but rather is internal to the conceptualiser, referring as it does to the speaker's attitude or belief about how a state of affairs might evolve. It is in this way that we can see how cognitive grammar neatly draws together the 'attitude' and 'factuality' definitions of modality.

4.3.2 Modality as 'force'

Other key work and approaches in cognitive linguistics equally argue that modalised propositions inherently exhibit potency. Sweetser draws on the notion of embodied cognition in suggesting that a pervasive and coherently structured system of metaphors underlies our tendency to use vocabulary from the external (sociophysical) domain in speaking of the internal (emotional and psychological domain).

(Sweetser 1990: 49)

From this, Sweetser first argues that root (deontic) modality developed from non-modalised meanings related to physical strength, and that secondly, this mapping was then extended across to more psychological epistemic senses. Consequently, both modal functions display types of mental force, which are originally dependent on our understanding of 'real-world forces' (Sweetser 1990: 51).

Johnson (1987) also argues that this metaphor, where the force is psychological, mental and rational rather than physical (1987: 55), is responsible for understanding epistemic modality through a series of *image-schematic patterns* and structures based on human experience. *Image-schemas* are what Ungerer and Schmid (1996: 160) call 'simple and basic cognitive structures which are derived from our everyday interaction with the world'. These act as building blocks of the conceptual system, which ultimately are responsible for larger order knowledge structures (Evans and Green 2006). Johnson argues that modalised propositions are understood with reference to a *force* image-schema, which he claims plays a crucial role in understanding our experience as human beings. Johnson summarises the features that form our understanding of the sense of force:

> forces as experienced through *interaction*, for example when we are in a dark room and bump into a table, we experience the interactional nature of force;
>
> force as a *movement through space of an object*, for example a thrown ball or the movement of a hand towards something;
>
> force as a *single path of motion* from a *source* to a *target* or *goal* due to the power of an *agent*;
>
> forces as having *degrees of power and intensity*, which are *measurable*;
>
> force as having an underlying *structure* or *sequence of causality*.
>
> (Johnson 1987: 143–4)

In turn, these give rise to these more specific image-schematic gestalts COMPULSION, BLOCKAGE, COUNTERFORCE, DIVERSION, REMOVAL OF RESTRAINT, ENABLEMENT and ATTRACTION, whose structures underpin a whole range of modal forms.[6]

Talmy (1988) highlights this force-oriented nature of modalised propositions through his *force-dynamic* system, which identifies different types of participant and process forces acting on a given entity. Talmy argues that two entities are profiled: *the agonist*, who is the subject of focus; and the *antagonist*, which represents an oppositional force (the terms are from the physiological use of opposing muscle pairs). Talmy (1988: 55) suggests that there are four basic 'steady-state' patterns that represent the agonist in relation to the force applied by the antagonist:

> The ball (ago) kept rolling because of the wind (ant) blowing on it
> *The ball's tendency towards rest is opposed by the stronger wind*
> The shed (ago) kept standing despite the gale wind (ant) blowing against it
> *The shed's tendency towards rest is stronger than the wind's force and so resists it*
> The ball (ago) kept rolling despite the stiff grass (ant)
> *The ball's tendency towards movement is stronger than the grass's force and attempt to restrict*
> The log (ago) kept lying on the incline because of the ridge there (ant)
> *The log's tendency towards movement is opposed by the stronger force.*
>
> (Talmy 1988: 55)

Talmy dedicates a significant part of his work to modal forms, arguing that the defining feature of force oppositions 'appears to lie at the core of their meaning'. So, he suggests that deontic forms can be understood as one of his four basic 'steady-states'[7]:

> I (ago) can leave the house (ant is undefined force)
> *The subject has a tendency to movement and this occurs despite any force and attempt to restrict*
> I (ago) may leave the house (ant is undefined force)
> *The subject has a tendency towards movement and this occurs because an opposing force allows it*
> I (ago) must leave the house (ant is undefined force)
> *The subject has a tendency to rest (remain) yet this is opposed by an authoritative force*
> I should (ago) leave the house (ant is an undefined force)
> *The subject has a tendency to either move or rest, which is either opposed or allowed by an opposing force*
> I will (ago) leave the house (ant is undefined force)
> *The subject has a strong tendency to movement and this occurs despite any opposing force.*
>
> (adapted from Talmy 1988: 79)

From the above, we have built up a view of modality that emphasises its inherent potential for conveying force of either a physical or a psychological kind, and identified differences between functioning within the deontic and epistemic domains. It is now possible to return to Werth's original model to consider the extent to which this may help develop certain aspects of the framework.

4.4 Text world theory and modality

4.4.1 Werth's original text world model

As I explained in Chapter 2, Werth's model deals with modality at the level of three types of sub-world: *deictic sub-worlds* that mark a movement in spatial or temporal terms from the deictic parameters of the matrix world; *attitudinal sub-worlds* that represent the beliefs or desires of the participants or characters rather than any explicit actions carried out by them and *epistemic sub-worlds* that come into being through modalised propositions (Werth 1999: 216). Of these three types, epistemic and attitudinal sub-worlds are concerned with modal propositions, and were summarised in Section 2.3.5.

Werth's treatment of epistemic sub-worlds focuses on the notion of *remoteness* or movement away from the existing text world in the form of reported speech, politeness, tentativeness, conditionals and narrativised accounts. In addition, Werth lists examples of hypothetical propositions and probability and possibility worlds as components of epistemic sub-worlds. Although Werth admits that 'there are many possible propositional attitudes', he limits his attention to those covering *desire* (want worlds), *belief* (believe worlds) and *purpose* (intend worlds) (1999: 227).

Werth's treatment of desire worlds acknowledges that predicates such as 'wish', 'want', 'hope' and 'dream', all of which he considers as prototypical world-building elements of a desire world, draw attention to 'a set of conditions not fulfilled in the current text world' (1999: 230). These make up *stipulative* as opposed to *existential* contexts that set up either simple desires or more complex situations with layers of stipulations.[8] Werth defines a belief world as existing whenever participants or characters express belief in a set of propositions, which are then judged with reference to the relative credibility of the speaker responsible. Werth treats purpose worlds as similar to desire worlds since they represent 'promises, offers, commands and requests ... all of them postulate future action' (1999: 238) yet draws a distinction between them by stating that in desire worlds 'there is no intention to carry out the action' (1999: 237).

4.4.2 Adapting Werth's model

Gavins (2005a) offers the major critique of Werth's model of modality in her re-evaluation of Werth's distinction between attitudinal and epistemic sub-worlds. She notes that 'important inconsistencies begin to emerge in his (Werth's) taxonomy of sub-worlds' (2005a: 83), mainly in his use of a further category of 'modal worlds' (Werth 1999: 244), which seems to overlap with his previous comments on belief and epistemic modality and conflates root and epistemic modality into one. As Gavins suggests,

> Werth does not appear to be making any differentiation between the kinds of conceptual activity being expressed through such modalised propositions. He provides no explanation of the apparent switching of epistemic modality from attitudinal sub-worlds to the epistemic category or any further clarification of whether root modals are to be considered as epistemic sub-world forming also.
>
> (Gavins 2005a: 85)

In its place, Gavins adopts Simpson's (1993) modal grammar model, which identifies three domains of modality, *deontic*, *boulomaic* and *epistemic*, to reconfigure Werth's original account of modality. She places intend worlds primarily into the deontic domain and sees want worlds as fitting neatly into the boulomaic category (2005a: 85–6). It is however with the final modal category that Werth's original model is most challenged. Defining the epistemic modal system under Simpson's modal grammar as reflecting a 'speaker's confidence or lack of confidence, in the truth of a particular proposition' (2005a: 86), Gavins reclassifies notions of belief, possibility, probability and perception modality (Perkins 1983; Simpson 1993) into an overarching system of epistemic modality, which represents a 'degree of psychological distance' (Gavins 2005a: 86) between speaker attitude and proposition. This reconfiguration is shown in Table 4.1.

4.4.3 Rethinking boulomaic modality: Desire and dream worlds

Gavins' (2005a, 2005b, 2007a, 2010) reconfiguration of Werth's original ideas is welcome and sensible, given the clear inconsistencies in Werth's model (see Chapter 2 for a summary of these). However, she only really begins to explore the potential subtleties of the boulomaic domain. Her discussion of attitude and

Table 4.1 The reconfiguration of Werth's original text-world modal system, from Gavins (2005a)

Werth (1999)	Gavins (2005a, 2007a)
Attitudinal sub-worlds	**Boulomaic modal worlds**
• Want worlds	desire
• Intent worlds	
• Belief worlds	
Epistemic sub-worlds	**Epistemic modal worlds**
• Reported speech	confidence or lack of confidence in a
• Politeness and tentativeness	proposition
• Conditionals	
• Narrativised accounts	
Modal worlds	
• Epistemic	
• Root (deontic)	**Deontic modal worlds**
	permission, obligation, requirement

desire, in an extract from *OK* magazine focusing on the wedding plans of two British pop stars, Michelle Heaton and Andy Scott-Lee (Gavins 2007a: 92 ff), identifies several boulomaic modal worlds relating to the wishes that Heaton has regarding her wedding. In her analysis, Gavins identifies an important distinction between two kinds of boulomaic world that are constructed in the process of reading. The first, initiated by Heaton's words 'I'd really like to have diamonds down my spine and for it to be really tight at the top but to have a floaty skirt' (2007a: 92), relates to *actual* wedding plans that Heaton has made. This boulomaic world is built from an initial temporal world-switch to a time before the matrix text world of the wedding in Dubai, and consists of an expression of desire towards what she and the groom will wear, which we expect will actually be the case. The second boulomaic world conceptualises a more 'abstracted "ideal wedding day"' (2007a: 95) in which Heaton comments on what her fantasy wedding would appear like: 'My ideal wedding would be a total fairy tale' (2007a: 92). I would suggest that here the difference between these two types of boulomaic world can be seen as a difference between an actual *desire* and a less developed *dream*. Or, in Gavins' words,

> What she describes rather fleetingly here is a vague fantasy situation which exists at a greater conceptual distance from her real world than her more concrete plans for a particular style of wedding dress, mode of arrival at the ceremony

and so on. The text-world Heaton creates to explain what she would like at her real-life wedding is still a boulomaic modal-world, but there is an added sense that *she has some intention to carry out her plans in reality.*

(Gavins 2007a: 96, added emphasis)

Despite the acknowledgement that the interplay of these two kinds of boulomaic modality has 'an interesting effect on the conceptual structure of the discourse' (2007a: 95), Gavins does not develop the crucial difference between these two kinds of modal construction. This first structure, with its clear emphasis on intention, can be seen to be close to a deontic construction since the realisation of the intention depends on its speaker (in this case Heaton) being obliged to undertake some additional act; the desire therefore leads to a kind of *obligation* on the part of the speaker. The expression here is close to Langacker's treatment of root modal propositions that have an inherent power to bring about grounding. So, in this example, Heaton's words have a strong intention attached to them and consequently there is an understanding that the content of the world is projected to be actualised.

In contrast, the second boulomaic world is less concrete, representing a more epistemically remote set of circumstances in imagining the ideal wedding. In this case, its propositional content is part of a less potent potential reality, and the force or power remains internal to the conceptualiser. The modalised content is attitudinal but clearly not deontic since there is no strong desire or obligation for the 'fairy tale' wedding to come true. In fact we could begin to differentiate within the boulomaic domain by suggesting that the difference between the two is the difference between a *desire* (obligation) and a *dream* (non-obligation).

In his own treatment of attitudinal sub-worlds, Werth does provide some mention of a *dream world* although unhelpfully he also lists *dream* as a prototypical *desire world* predicate. His brief focus on what he calls 'dream sub worlds' (1999: 231) highlights some confusion in an attempt at classification, for he admits that

I am uncertain whether dream sub-worlds are special cases of desire sub-worlds or whether they should be considered as totally distinct. Generations of soothsayers aside, dreams do not have to represent the dreamer's wishes. On the other hand, the parameters of the dream world are clearly not those of the current text world. It seems to me that including worlds explicitly built with the predicate *dream*, a dream world is one in which the normal 'laws' of time and space have been suspended.

(Werth 1999: 231)

Although he draws attention to the problem, Werth misses the opportunity to develop the important distinction between the notions of *desire* and *dream*. As an example of a dream world, Werth offers a short analysis of the opening of Emma Tennant's (1983) *Hotel de Dream*, in which the reader is asked to monitor the enactor-accessible dream sub-world of a Mr Poynter, marked explicitly through the dream world-building predicate 'dreamed', which over time moves back into the originating text world which until this point has been denied to the reader. In this example, the dream world clearly designates an unknown temporal shift (the time is undisclosed) and a known spatial shift (his city as opposed to the Westringham hotel in which he is staying). In this dream world then, where there are clearly deictic shifts, the movement from existing deictic centres, both temporally and spatially, sets up different world parameters. We might therefore suggest that dream worlds necessarily also rely on a kind of deictic movement, away from an originating deictic space. In contrast, a desire world, I would suggest operates within a different set of deictic parameters. Although a desire world will still be stipulative in the sense that it has a set of as yet unfulfilled conditions, it does not necessarily have the same kind of deictic movement as a dream world does.[9]

It is clear that both Werth and Gavins see the notions of dream and desire as similar conceptual structures. The issue for text world theory is that not enough has been made of the subtle but significant differences that exist between the two.[10] I would argue therefore that an augmented text world model therefore needs to take account of the continuities in meaning between desires and dreams, while acknowledging both that there are clear differences in the types of experiences that they represent, and that there are equally a wide range of potential states suggested by the idea of dreaming. In Chapter 3, I discussed Hartmann's (1998) wake-dreaming continuum to differentiate not only between waking cognition and sleep-dreams but also between the range of mental states that dreaming can occur in. The continuum is reprinted again as Figure 4.4.

| Focused waking thought | Looser, less structured waking thought | Reverie, free association, daydreaming | Dreaming |

Figure 4.4 A 'wake-dreaming' continuum, adapted from Hartmann (1998: 90)

It now becomes possible to map out desire and dream states across this continuum. The left-hand pole incorporates desire states that as I suggest, have a strong modal grounding force attached to them: their boulomaic status is more clearly aligned to the deontic domain. Equally, along Narrog's 'dimension of volitivity' (2005: 685), desire states are highly volitive, representing a strong degree of intention on the part of the speaker. Alternatively, movement towards the right hand pole can account for a range of dream-like states, including states of imagination, fantasy and sleep-dreaming. All of these can be considered kinds of dream worlds with the difference between them being one of boulomaic/epistemic degree. So, the lack of volitivity found at the right-hand pole in sleep-dreaming reflects beliefs in dreaming as a non-volitive state (Macario 1978; Hartmann 1996; Kahan 2001; Hobson 2005), which increases with movement towards the middle of the continuum to allow for increased volition for imaginative and fantastical thought. Although the whole continuum when used specifically to analyse notions of desire and dream can be seen as part of the boulomaic domain, it is clear that while boulomaic desire states/worlds have a deontic function, boulomaic dream states/worlds are closer to having an epistemic one.

The difference in modal force can also be explained by using the concepts of *thick and thin boundaries* (Hartmann 1991, 1998; Hartmann et al. 2001). Although Hartmann originally uses the terms in the context of his work on personality types, he suggests that mental states themselves can be seen as exhibiting degrees of *boundary thickness* (Hartmann 1998: 220). As we move from left to right along the wake-dream continuum, we move from thick functioning boulomaic states with well-defined goal-driven boundaries that are more likely to be both realised and maintained, to thinner dream-like states where thinner boundaries are representative of a more auto-associative 'merging mode', prone to dissolution (Hartmann 1998: 89–90). Using this notion, it is possible to identify the more likely potential for dream worlds to *decompose* (Stockwell 2000: 150). In Chapter 5, I explain how this distinction between desire (thick boundary state) and dream (thin boundary state) becomes important as part of an analysis of the interplay of modal worlds in Keats' *The Eve of St Agnes*.

Although it is clearly useful to consider dreaming in this way, attaching degrees of volition or intent to sleep-dreaming is problematic. Some dreams are clearly non-boulomaic (at the extreme end are traumatic dreams or nightmares, which are dealt with in Chapter 6) and any revised notion of a desire-dream continuum should take this into account. I suggest therefore that it is useful to

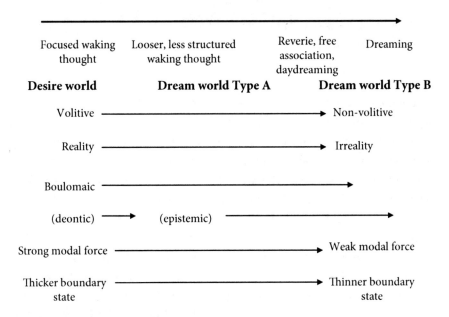

Figure 4.5 A 'desire-dream' continuum

differentiate between two kinds of dream states: *type A dream worlds*, which sit towards the middle of the continuum and are still driven by a dreamer's wishes or desires; and *type B dream worlds* that sit at the extreme right end of the continuum, are typically non-volitive, remain closer to a state of irrealis and have thinner, less-defined boundaries with a weaker degree of modal force. At this end of the continuum, dream states are essentially non-boulomaic; the increased epistemic sense of type A dream worlds develops into a fully epistemic world, close to Simpson's (1993) notion of perception modality. Finally, although there are no strict cut-off points as to when a type A world becomes a type B one, it is clearly possible to differentiate between them to some degree. This model can be shown as in Figure 4.5 as a *'desire-dream' continuum*.

Figure 4.5 shows that there is clearly a degree of force evident in the types of predicate that can act as world-building elements in a boulomaic modal desire world that does not appear to be the case with boulomaic modal dream worlds. In the three examples below, there is a difference in force between the predicates 'hope', 'wish' and 'want', which can be demonstrated with reference to Talmy's notions of agonist and antagonist.

I (ago) hope I win the race (ant is undefined force)

The subject has a tendency towards winning the race which is either opposed or allowed by an opposing force

I (ago) wish I was rich (ant is undefined force)
The subject has a tendency towards being rich which is either opposed or allowed by an opposing force
I (ago) want that car (ant is undefined force)
The subject has a strong tendency towards obtaining the car which is either opposed or allowed by an opposing force.

In the first, the undefined force that is the antagonist is arguably more of a threat than in the second example and even more so than the final one where the tendency of the agonist towards obtaining the car is stronger, therefore suggesting that the conceptual standing of the utterance is closer to that of a deontic form. The difference between these three types of desire provides an additional layering to how modal desire worlds operate (see also Lyons (1977a: 278) and Simpson (1993: 51) for how prototypical boulomaic forms mirror deontic ones, Palmer (2001: 134) for how 'wish' and 'want' modal operators should be treated as closer to epistemic and deontic forms, respectively, and Givón (1984: 317–8) for how strong boulomaic verbs such as 'want' are grouped with deontic forms as *manipulative verbs*, while weaker forms such as 'hope', 'fear' and 'wish' are grouped with epistemic forms as *non-manipulative*). We can therefore summarise the range of desire/dream boulomaic operators as follows in Figure 4.6.

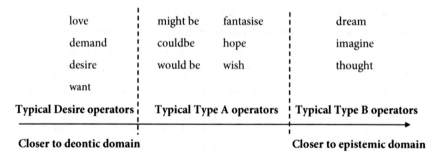

Figure 4.6 A continuum of boulomaic forms

4.5 Review

In this chapter, I have attempted to develop the notion of boulomaic modality following Werth's original text world model and revisions suggested by Gavins (2005a, 2007a). In Section 4.2, I explored the linguistic phenomenon of modality, drawing attention to how broadly speaking, it has been suggested that modality is concerned with a speaker's attitude towards a particular state of affairs or distinguishing the factual from the non-factual. In addition, I surveyed the ways in which modal forms have been categorised, in particular, drawing attention to deontic and epistemic modal domains as a common form of categorisation. In this section, I also explored boulomaic modality, which has often been incorporated into epistemic or deontic modality. A model of modality that focuses on attitudes clearly has a need for a discrete domain concerned with boulomaic forms. Equally, there is clear overlap in places between the domains.

In Section 4.3, I explored Langacker's (1987, 2008) notion of clausal grounding to highlight a crucial difference between epistemic and deontic forms. I explained in terms of the difference between a modal force designed to bring about the grounding process (the deontic domain) and that where the force is more internal and psychological to the conceptualiser (the epistemic domain). Here, I suggest that this distinction is not just useful for distinguishing between deontic and epistemic forms but also for drawing attention to elements of deontic and epistemic modality within the boulomaic domain. This was supported by reference to the work within cognitive linguistics that views modalised propositions as exerting degrees of force.

In Section 4.4.3, I used Hartmann's (1998) wake-dream continuum to propose a desire-dream continuum to account for boulomaic modal forms. Here, I suggested that boulomaic modal desire worlds hold the kind of modal force associated with deontic forms, while boulomaic modal dream worlds are closer to epistemic forms. In addition, I used Hartmann's (1991, 1998) notion of thick and thin boundaries to suggest that desire worlds have necessarily stronger world edges and are less prone to world decomposition.

This chapter is an important one in the context of this book since it provides the theoretical basis for my analysis of Keats' *The Eve of St Agnes*, where I explore the interplay of desire and dream worlds as a key stylistic component of the poem, and for my treatment of nightmares and the *nightmare world* in Chapter 6 and subsequent analyses of a further three poems in later chapters.

The Eve of St Agnes

5.1 Introduction

In this chapter, I build on my suggested developments to text world theory and the distinction I made between boulomaic desire and dream worlds in Chapter 4 to provide a text world account of Keats' *The Eve of St Agnes*. In a wide-ranging and comprehensive account of the poem's composition, reception and shifting interpretations, Stillinger (1999: 39–77) provides a 'token fifty-nine interpretations' of the poem, placing both individual idiosyncratic readings alongside more general critical ones from a range of theoretical positions in groups covering similar themes. Of these fifty-nine and four in particular form readings that are concerned with the 'notions of desire, fantasy and romance' (1999: 55). In this chapter, I use this cluster of readings as the basis for exploring boulomaic desire and dream modal worlds in *The Eve of St Agnes*, arguing that the power of the poem arises from the edgework required on the part of the reader to negotiate and navigate contrastive world edges that are created through the initiating of boulomaic modal worlds.

In Sections 5.2 and 5.3, I provide an overview of the poem's origins and conception and summarise critical response relevant to my discussion. In Section 5.4, I suggest that the opening of the poem, which has variously been credited with having cinematic qualities, is best thought of as a particular kind of text world, that I term an *establishing world*. In Section 5.5, I also suggest an addition to text world theory in the form of a *world zoom*, building on Werth's original notion of focus and drawing on work in attention studies. In this section, I also comment on the emerging pattern of dream worlds that mark Keats' characterisation of Madeline. In Sections 5.6 and 5.7, these are contrasted with the stronger modal force of boulomaic modal desire worlds that form a significant aspect of the characterisation of Porphyro. In the final sections, I suggest that a reading of the poem relies on navigating a sustained interplay of characters' boulomaic modal desire and dream worlds. In Section 5.8, I draw attention to these demands with a focus on edgework and, in Section 5.9, explore how text world theory can account for a particular kind of incrementation in the tracking of character across the narrative and its world edges. Here, I explain how the potential for prominence afforded to different enactors in updating the text world can account for varying critical responses to the poem.

5.2 Origins and conception

The Eve of St Agnes was published in Keats' final, 1820 volume *Lamia, Isabella, The Eve of St Agnes, and Other Poems*. Keats first mentions the poem in a letter to his brother and sister, where he recounts writing 'a little Poem call'd St Agnes Eve' during trips by visiting friends in Chichester and Bedhampton (*Letters* II: 58, n.159). His main biographers, Bate (1963: 440–51), Gittings (1968: 404–23) and Motion (1997: 338) all suggest a range of influences for the poem: encouragement from a female acquaintance, the mysterious Mrs Isabella Jones, to write a poem based on *John Brand's Popular Antiquities*; a French romance by de Tressan; the fourteenth-century fresco *The Triumph of Death*; and Keats' own reading of Spenser and Shakespeare (especially *Romeo and Juliet, Cymbeline* and *King Lear)*. In addition, Lau (1991: 70) draws attention to Keats' reading of Coleridge as an influence for the poem, Finney (1964: 691–2), suggests that Keats' reworkings of the poem were both directly influenced by and an attempt to emulate in his own writing, Byron's own ironic cynicism, and both de Selincourt (1926: 398) and Stillinger (1971: 163) point to Wordsworth's influence on vocabulary choices.[1]

5.3 Thematic concerns and critical response

The Eve of St Agnes has two central characters: Madeline, who believes in the superstition that on St Agnes Eve, a young virgin would dream of her future husband; and Porphyro, her admirer-lover, who enters the castle secretly during a party held by her family, and is helped by Angela, a maid, into Madeline's bedchamber. Here, Porphyro, concealed from Madeline and driven by his own fantasies, watches her undress and fall asleep before moving himself to her bedside. The awakening Madeline is initially disappointed by the living Porphyro and of the difference between her dream and reality. The lovers eventually escape into the liberating yet dangerous outside world, symbolised by the storm into which they turn.

Keats himself documents very little of his own feelings towards the poem, apart from requesting that it appear first in the 1820 volume (*Letters* II: 276, n.245) (it eventually was published in third place) and suggesting that he had placed too much emphasis on character rather than on poetic form (*Letters* II: 174, n.194). Contemporaneous reviews, although focused mainly on aspects of characterisation and plot, were generally positive. Charles Lamb, in line with common nineteenth-century reviews, focused on the poem's visual aspects and qualities, and described it as 'the almost Chaucer-like painting, with which this poet illuminates every subject he touches' (Schwartz 1973: 211), while Leigh Hunt commented on the poem's 'remarkable' portrayal of Madeline (Schwartz 1973: 223). Since the beginning of the twentieth century, the poem has attracted as much critical attention as Keats' other major poems and has been read variously as an allegory charting Keats' relationship with Fanny Brawne (Murry 1925; Bush 1966; Levinson 1988), as showing his central concerns with celebrating sexual awakening and union, evidenced in the interactions between Madeline and Porphyro (Fogle 1945; Bloom 1961; Enscoe 1967), and as a more sinister portrayal of male-as-subject, female-as-object voyeurism (Stillinger 1971; Ricks 1974; Levinson 1988). These latter readings have presented varying considerations of Porphyro as the embodiment of Keats' romantic imagination (Wasserman 1953; Sperry 1973; Waldoff 1977, 1985; Hall 1991), or as a fictional representation of his immaturity and feelings of inadequacies around women (Turley 2004), and of Madeline as victim (Stillinger 1971) or seducer (Arseneau 1997). Turley (2004: 26) suggests that the poem becomes a kind of therapy for Keats in his use of a disengaged narrative voice to recount the seduction of Madeline by 'his alter-ego, his manly Doppelganger'.

Writing from a historical-materialist perspective, Leader (1996: 299–301) suggests that Keats' initial concerns for writing the poem were more commercial, in that following the failure of Hyperion and the poor sales of Endymion, he was aware that his writing needed to attract a larger audience of poetry readers that at the time largely consisted of women.[2] McGann (1993: 452) suggests that Keats also remained anxious about his earlier failure with *Endymion* and being viewed as a weak poet, while Homans (1990: 346) claims that he had reservations about catering for female readers, for as Leader (1996: 301) points out, accommodating them would open him up to further accusations of weakness and effeminacy.[3] In all respects, it seems that he was faced with 'multiple and conflicting' (Leader 1996: 301) concerns in the writing of the poem.

5.4 The establishing world of *The Eve of St Agnes*

I

St Agnes' Eve—Ah, bitter chill it was!
The owl, for all his feathers, was a-cold;
The hare limp'd trembling through the frozen grass,
And silent was the flock in woolly fold:
Numb were the Beadsman's fingers, while he told   5
His rosary, and while his frosted breath,
Like pious incense from a censer old,
Seem'd taking flight for heaven, without a death,
Past the sweet Virgin's picture, while his prayer he saith.

II

His prayer he saith, this patient, holy man;   10
Then takes his lamp, and riseth from his knees,
And back returneth, meagre, barefoot, wan,
Along the chapel aisle by slow degrees:
The sculptur'd dead, on each side, seem to freeze,
Emprison'd in black, purgatorial rails: 15
Knights, ladies, praying in dumb orat'ries,
He passeth by; and his weak spirit fails
To think how they may ache in icy hoods and mails.

III

Northward he turneth through a little door,
And scarce three steps, ere Music's golden tongue   20
Flatter'd to tears this aged man and poor;

But no—already had his deathbell rung;
The joys of all his life were said and sung:
His was harsh penance on St. Agnes' Eve:
Another way he went, and soon among   25

Rough ashes sat he for his soul's reprieve,
And all night kept awake, for sinners' sake to grieve.

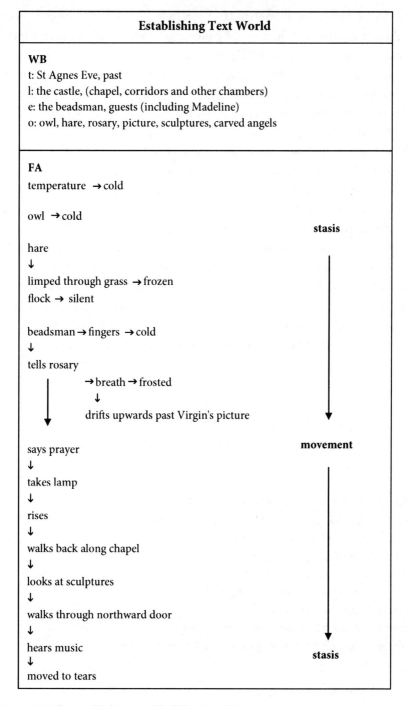

Figure 5.1 The establishing world of *The Eve of St Agnes*

Stanzas I, II and III have an intense focus on the cold, deathly spatial parameters of the castle, presented through the patterning of referential and deictic lexical choices 'bitter chill' (1), a-cold' (2) and 'frozen grass' (3). The poem begins with a lengthy description of the beadsman, an early yet much less physical version of Porphyro's worshipping of Madeline, praying before the sweet virgin's picture. He is represented as a figure devoid of warmth and vitality, shown through Keats' vivid choices making up a lexical field of physical poverty such as 'numb' (5), 'frosted breath' (6), 'meagre' (12), 'barefoot' (12), 'wan' (12), 'weak spirit' (17), 'aged man' (21) and 'poor' (21). These precise details are supported through Keats' heavily synaesthetic lines focusing on feeling (numbness), hearing (the telling of the rosary), sight (Mary's portrait and the beadsman's breath) and smell (the figurative use of incense). The patterning of stasis (stanza I) –movement (stanza II) – movement ending in stasis (stanza III) projects a rich detailed matrix world, which undertakes largely the same function as the cinematic *establishing shot* (Rowe and Wells 2003: 54).[4] Since the function of the first three stanzas is to establish a sense of background and to foreground the sense of danger through its detailing of the physical landscape, we might suggest that this particular type of text world be termed an *establishing world*. This is shown in Figure 5.1.

5.5 The *world zoom* and passive dreaming: The representation of Madeline in stanzas IV–VII

IV

That ancient Beadsman heard the prelude soft;
And so it chanc'd, for many a door was wide,
From hurry to and fro. Soon, up aloft,   30
The silver, snarling trumpets 'gan to chide:
The level chambers, ready with their pride,
Were glowing to receive a thousand guests:
The carved angels, ever eager-eyed,
Star'd, where upon their heads the cornice rests,   35
With hair blown back, and wings put cross-wise on their breasts.

V

At length burst in the argent revelry,
With plume, tiara, and all rich array,
Numerous as shadows haunting fairily

The brain, new stuff'd, in youth, with triumphs gay   40
Of old romance. These let us wish away,
And turn, sole-thoughted, to one Lady there,
Whose heart had brooded, all that wintry day,
On love, and wing'd St. Agnes' saintly care,
As she had heard old dames full many times declare.   45

VI
They told her how, upon St. Agnes' Eve,
Young virgins might have visions of delight,
And soft adorings from their loves receive
Upon the honey'd middle of the night,
If ceremonies due they did aright;   50
As, supperless to bed they must retire,
And couch supine their beauties, lily white;
Nor look behind, nor sideways, but require
Of Heaven with upward eyes for all that they desire.

VII
Full of this whim was thoughtful Madeline: 55
The music, yearning like a God in pain,
She scarcely heard: her maiden eyes divine,
Fix'd on the floor, saw many a sweeping train
Pass by—she heeded not at all: in vain
Came many a tiptoe, amorous cavalier,   60
And back retir'd; not cool'd by high disdain,
But she saw not: her heart was otherwhere:
She sigh'd for Agnes' dreams, the sweetest of the year.

The establishing world follows the beadsman's movement in stanza IV to the castle's 'level chambers, ready. . . ./to receive a thousand guests' (31–2). At this point, a spatial world-switch occurs from the establishing world to the hall into which the guests arrive. This has considerable referential detail in the form of the 'snarling trumpets' (31) and 'carvèd angels' (34), and the function-advancing proposition of the 'argent revelry' (37) bursting into the empty room. This world-switch reconfigures the reader's conceptual tracking of the narrative so that it takes the place of the establishing world as the central matrix world of the poem. The establishing world by contrast, since it is no longer the centre of attention, begins to *decompose* (Stockwell 2000: 150).

The movement from the broader landscape to a single, intense focus on Madeline, is marked by the participant-accessible boulomaic world forming clause 'These let us wish away', which initiates a shift from the matrix world to one that is more concentrated on an entity within that world, namely Madeline. In Chapter 2, I explained Werth's term *focus* as movement inwards to 'an earlier viewpoint at a later stage' (1995b: 194) and exemplified this notion by looking at an example from the end of Book I of *Lamia*. I now briefly return to that notion here.

Focus can be compared to the movement of a camera inwards in a frame containing many separate details to one that is focused on one entity in particular. The shift in perception must of course be a shift to a part of the preceding whole, since in the text world model, the movement is to an earlier viewpoint. This mirrors the camera zoom shot, a technique 'whereby the image appears to advance towards or recedes away from the viewer' (Nelmes 2003: 467). The zoom technique thus provides a mechanism for *attention*, of placing one entity or object as a prominent figure against the background of the wider originating frame. In his discussion of attention, Carstensen suggests that there are

> two general types of operations transforming one visuo-spatial attentional state into another: attention can either be shifted, or it can be zoomed. Whilst most locative prepositions express attention shifts, *in*, *between* and *among* express zooming.
>
> (Carstensen 2007: 8)

To this we can add the preposition *to* since it can be understood schematically as momentum along a PATH image schema (Lakoff 1987: 441) to an end focus of Madeline, directed by the spatial deictic 'there' but already present in the matrix world or frame. So, the world movement initiated by 'turn . . . .to one lady there' is zoomed since there is no modification of deictic detail but rather a reformulation of focus inwards. Madeline is already an entity in the matrix text world and the pointing is inwards towards a finer granularity rather than towards a different set of spatio-temporal co-ordinates.

Stockwell (2009: 20) defines those elements that demand attention as *attractors*, providing the following checklist of features that will be typically present in good examples of them:

- *newness* (currency: the present moment of reading is more attractive than the previous moment)
- *agency* (noun phrases in active position are better attractors than in passive position)
- *topicality* (subject position confers attraction over object position)

- *empathetic responsibility* (human speaker > human hearer > animal > object > abstraction)
- *definiteness* (definite ('the man') > specific indefinite ('a certain man') > non-specific indefinite ('any man'))
- *activeness* (verbs denoting action, violence, passion, wilfulness, motivation or strength)
- *brightness* (lightness or vivid colours being denoted over dimness or drabness)
- *fullness* (richness, density, intensity or nutrition being denoted)
- *largeness* (large objects being denoted, or a very long elaborated noun phrase used to denote)
- *height* (objects that are above others, are higher than the perceiver, or which dominate)
- *noisiness* (denoted phenomena which are audibly voluminous)
- *aesthetic distance from the norm* (beautiful or ugly referents, dangerous referents, alien objects denoted, dissonance).

Stockwell (2009: 25)

In the context of the stanza so far, the reader's attention has been focused on the collective: the thousand guests and the argent revelry. The shift in attention, marked by the syntactic deviation of imperative forms following declarative clauses, and the definiteness of the determiner-noun-spatial deictic phrase 'one lady there' (42), represents using the camera analogy, a zoom-in, since the movement is to both provide a conceptual decay of previous frame material (the desired result of wishing away) and increase the size of Madeline within the frame, and place her as the figure of attention against the ground of the establishing world. Since all of this reconfigures the deictic make-up of the establishing world, I suggest the term *world zoom* to describe this inwards focus of attention to Madeline, which stylistically remains as the central concern until the arrival of Porphyro in stanza IX.

Following this attentional zoom, the reader is required to track a quick and complex series of conceptual movements. First, there is an immediate switch to a boulomaic modal world, removed to a set of anterior deictic parameters introduced by 'all that wintry day' (43), which details Madeline's interior thought processes as she 'brooded. . . . on love' (43). This represents a type A boulomaic dream world with the conceptual structure representing Madeline's imaginative, fantastical yearning, and its modal force remaining fairly neutral. Her thoughts, informed by the stories heard from 'old dames'

(45), are marked by a temporal world-switch and initiate a further chain of conceptual structures, beginning with a world-switch outlining the dames' tales and a further deontic modal world, detailing the obligations that Madeline has to fulfil should she wish her dream to become reality. Since the boulomaic modal world Keats utilises to describe Madeline's state of mind is more attitudinal than state-effecting (the lack of inherent force or power is also evident in Keats' lexical choice 'whim' (55) in stanza VII), it quite clearly represents a dream rather than a desire world. Equally, this whimsical nature of Madeline's dreaming is emphasised by the fact that her boulomaic dream world is dependent on three conditions (lines 51–4) for it to become reality. These form part of a deontic modal world feeding back into the matrix world space, in image-schematic terms representing a type of COMPULSION on the part of Madeline. Consequently, it is an undeniably more powerful conceptual space than the relative weakness of Madeline's thoughts, which evident in their status as type A boulomaic modal worlds are marked as having thinner world boundaries.

Within the world zoom, function-advancing propositions ('the music, yearning like a God in pain,/She scarcely heard' (56–7) and 'in vain/came back many a tip-toe, amorous cavalier,/and back retired – not cooled by high disdain' (59–61)) propel the narrative forwards and emphasise Madeline's remoteness from the events in the castle. A negative modal world initiated by the negatively framed constructions 'she heeded not at all' (59) and 'but she saw not' (62) demands that the reader conceptualise Madeline, free of her whimsical dreaming, and responding to her suitors. In short, the fact that she does not, and indeed is represented as dependent on a series of obligations and old dames' tales, represents her as 'hoodwinked with faery fancy' in line with those readings of her that see her as either passive in the poem (Stillinger 1971) or symbolic of the disappointing nature of the imagination (Rosenfeld 2000). In both cases, in contrast to the grounding-effecting boulomaic modal desire worlds constructed around Porphyro later in the poem, this passivity is inherent in the subordinate dream worlds that Keats uses to frame her characterisation. The relationship between worlds in stanzas V–VII is shown in Figure 5.2. The attention afforded as part of the world zoom is shown through the use of a shaded text world. The bold line outlining the deontic modal world indicates its thicker boundary and consequent stronger modal force.

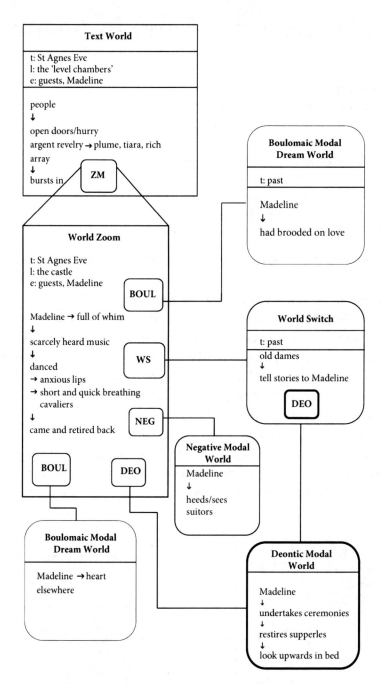

Figure 5.2 World conceptualisation in stanzas V–VII of *The Eve of St Agnes*

5.6 Desire worlds: The arrival of Porphyro in stanza IX

IX

So, purposing each moment to retire,
She linger'd still. Meantime, across the moors,
Had come young Porphyro, with heart on fire   75
For Madeline. Beside the portal doors,
Buttress'd from moonlight, stands he, and implores
All saints to give him sight of Madeline,
But for one moment in the tedious hours,
That he might gaze and worship all unseen;   80
Perchance speak, kneel, touch, kiss—in sooth such things have been.

In stanza VIII, the narrative focus remains on Madeline and her dream of the St Agnes Eve superstition. At the beginning of stanza IX, a boulomaic modal desire world is activated by 'purposing each moment to retire' (73). Mirroring Keats' presentation of Madeline as passive in the previous stanzas, we can view this in force dynamic terms as an example of an agonist (Madeline) and an antagonist (undefined force although assumed to be the guests at the party). In this instance, the main clause 'she lingered still' (74) explains that this intention is unfulfilled as a result of the antagonist's opposing force (despite the fact that the poem does not explicitly state what this might be, again we assume it to be some kind of pressure from the guests at the party).

In Johnson's (1987) image-schematic terms then, this represents an example of a BLOCKAGE schema; the desire world, though innately powerful, becomes nullified as a result of external forces. The opening of stanza IX can

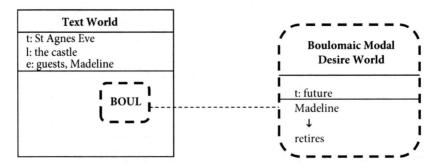

Figure 5.3 Nullified boulomaic modal desire world in stanza IX of *The Eve of St Agnes*

be diagrammatically shown in Figure 5.3, the dotted line marks the world as unrealised.

At this stage of the poem, the temporal and spatial alternation, evident in the clause 'Meantime, across the moors,/had come young Porphyro' (74–5), marks an attentional shift and a deictic world-switch through the introduction of a new character, Porphyro. Two rapid deictic temporal shifts first describe Porphyro's simultaneous movements, marked by the temporal discourse marker 'meantime' and the use of the past perfect tense 'had come young Porphyro' (75) before reverting to the present tense 'beside the portal doors ... stands he' (76–7). This takes us back to the original level of the text world although its conceptual organisation is best understood as a spatial deictic world-switch from this matrix world: we are spatially apart from the text world inhabited by Madeline at the beginning of the stanza, and Porphyro is essentially in a different part of the castle.

The perceptual deictic centre moves at this stage of the stanza from Madeline to Porphyro. First, the verb 'implores' acts to set up a boulomaic modal desire world, presenting a strong wish for an event (Porphyro seeing Madeline) to be actualised. Echoing Porphyro's sexual energy and appetite (he is described as having a 'heart on fire' (75)), this also stands as an example of a *strong* boulomaic modal desire world. Secondly, another boulomaic world, this time marked by the modalised construction 'that he might gaze and worship all unseen' (80), is a sign of Porphyro's fanciful imagination, and exists as an example of a type A boulomaic modal dream world. In this case, the force of the utterance remains internal to Porphyro himself and these fantasies are understood as far removed from the reality of the cold castle and 'tedious hours' (79) Porphyro endures. The final line of the stanza with its staged and increasingly eroticised movements towards Madeline, 'speak, kneel, touch, kiss', prefaced by a marker of epistemic distance, 'perchance' (81), draws further attention to this fantasy aspect of Porphyro's second boulomaic world, which is not just marked as a contrast to the stronger modalised desire world but is now shown as both more fanciful, less prone to realisation and consequently at a greater distance from reality. Its thinner boundary marks it as more prone to decomposing; it remains as a distinctly less powerful modal force. The conceptual structure of the final half of the poem can be shown diagrammatically as Figure 5.4.

These modalised constructions generate particular effects. The ambiguous line 'in sooth such things have been' (81) could well refer to a previous similar encounter between the pair (remembered by Porphyro).[5] Or, it could simply

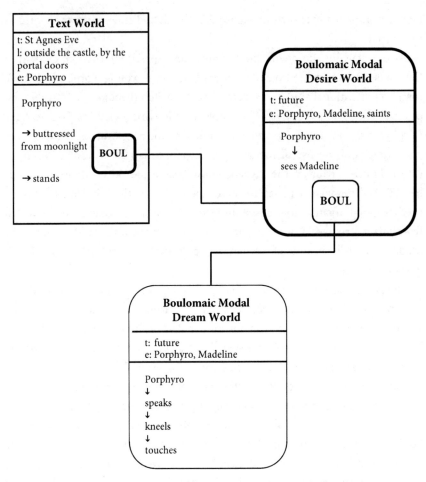

Figure 5.4 Text worlds in the second half of stanza IX of *The Eve of St Agnes*

point to the as yet unrealised situation that Porphyro fantasises about, with its intimate physical contact contrasted to the coldness of the moors and the outside of the castle as well as Madeline's strikingly less erotically oriented mindset. Either way, the layering of boulomaic modal worlds in this stanza demonstrates the remoteness of the desired and fantasy worlds from Porphyro's current physical, emotional and sexualised state of being.

5.7 Porphyro and desire as enablement in stanza XVI

XVI
Sudden a thought came like a full-blown rose,
Flushing his brow, and in his pained heart

Made purple riot: then doth he propose
A stratagem, that makes the beldame start:
"A cruel man and impious thou art: 140
"Sweet lady, let her pray, and sleep, and dream
"Alone with her good angels, far apart
"From wicked men like thee. Go, go!—I deem
"Thou canst not surely be the same that thou didst seem.

In stanza XVI, Keats presents Porphyro's acts of desire in a more explicitly forceful manner, and contrasts the effectiveness of the modalised desires of Porphyro and the dreams of Madeline. In stanzas X–XV, Keats outlines how Porphyro has just entered the castle and heard of Madeline's belief in the superstition and of her purpose from Angela. On hearing these, 'his eyes grew brilliant' (stanza XV, 132) and he then suddenly has a 'thought' (136).

This thought represents an important and powerful type of force in the poem since it acts to set up a boulomaic modal desire world. Seen in the context of the poem's narrative structure, it represents a key turning point with an emphasis on Porphyro's desire as a potent determiner of meaning and action (he then goes on to propose a 'stratagem' (139)), responsible for the remainder of the poem's narrative drive. In fact, it could be argued that the desire world changes the poem's landscape insofar as any action that takes place across the remainder of the stanzas is initiated by this very act of desire. As shown in Figure 5.5, the construction of a boulomaic modal desire world in this stanza therefore has a wider facilitating function, and can be viewed as the linguistic-literary realisation

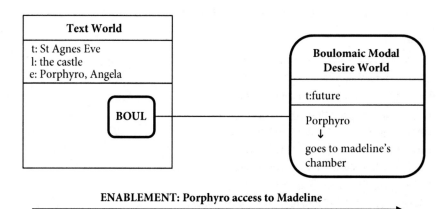

Figure 5.5 Boulomaic modal desire world as ENABLEMENT image-schema in stanza XVI of *The Eve of St Agnes*

of an ENABLEMENT schema, serving as it does for both Porphyro's own desires
and Keats' wider narrative.

5.8 Madeline and Porphyro (1): Boulomaic worlds and edgework in stanzas XXIV–XXXIII

XXIV

A casement high and triple-arch'd there was,
All garlanded with carven imag'ries
Of fruits, and flowers, and bunches of knot-grass,   210
And diamonded with panes of quaint device,
Innumerable of stains and splendid dyes,
As are the tiger-moth's deep-damask'd wings;
And in the midst, 'mong thousand heraldries,
And twilight saints, and dim emblazonings,   215
A shielded scutcheon blush'd with blood of queens and kings.

XXV

Full on this casement shone the wintry moon,
And threw warm gules on Madeline's fair breast,
As down she knelt for heaven's grace and boon;
Rose-bloom fell on her hands, together prest,   220
And on her silver cross soft amethyst,
And on her hair a glory, like a saint:
She seem'd a splendid angel, newly drest,
Save wings, for heaven:—Porphyro grew faint:
She knelt, so pure a thing, so free from mortal taint.   225

XXVI

Anon his heart revives: her vespers done,
Of all its wreathed pearls her hair she frees;
Unclasps her warmed jewels one by one;
Loosens her fragrant boddice; by degrees
Her rich attire creeps rustling to her knees: 230
Half-hidden, like a mermaid in sea-weed,
Pensive awhile she dreams awake, and sees,
In fancy, fair St. Agnes in her bed,
But dares not look behind, or all the charm is fled.

XXVII

Soon, trembling in her soft and chilly nest,   235
In sort of wakeful swoon, perplex'd she lay,
Until the poppied warmth of sleep oppress'd
Her soothed limbs, and soul fatigued away;
Flown, like a thought, until the morrow-day;
Blissfully haven'd both from joy and pain;   240
Clasp'd like a missal where swart Paynims pray;
Blinded alike from sunshine and from rain,
As though a rose should shut, and be a bud again.

XXVIII

Stol'n to this paradise, and so entranced,
Porphyro gazed upon her empty dress,   245
And listen'd to her breathing, if it chanced
To wake into a slumberous tenderness;
Which when he heard, that minute did he bless,
And breath'd himself: then from the closet crept,
Noiseless as fear in a wide wilderness,   250
And over the hush'd carpet, silent, stept,
And 'tween the curtains peep'd, where, lo!—how fast she slept.

XXIX

Then by the bed-side, where the faded moon
Made a dim, silver twilight, soft he set
A table, and, half anguish'd, threw thereon   255
A cloth of woven crimson, gold, and jet:—
O for some drowsy Morphean amulet!
The boisterous, midnight, festive clarion,
The kettle-drum, and far-heard clarionet,
Affray his ears, though but in dying tone:—   260
The hall door shuts again, and all the noise is gone.

XXX

And still she slept an azure-lidded sleep,
In blanched linen, smooth, and lavender'd,
While he from forth the closet brought a heap
Of candied apple, quince, and plum, and gourd;   265
With jellies soother than the creamy curd,
And lucent syrops, tinct with cinnamon;

Manna and dates, in argosy transferr'd
From Fez; and spiced dainties, every one,
From silken Samarcand to cedar'd Lebanon.   270

XXXI

These delicates he heap'd with glowing hand
On golden dishes and in baskets bright
Of wreathed silver: sumptuous they stand
In the retired quiet of the night,
Filling the chilly room with perfume light.—   275
"And now, my love, my seraph fair, awake!
"Thou art my heaven, and I thine eremite:
"Open thine eyes, for meek St. Agnes' sake,
"Or I shall drowse beside thee, so my soul doth ache."

XXXII

Thus whispering, his warm, unnerved arm   280
Sank in her pillow. Shaded was her dream
By the dusk curtains:—'twas a midnight charm
Impossible to melt as iced stream:
The lustrous salvers in the moonlight gleam;
Broad golden fringe upon the carpet lies: 285
It seem'd he never, never could redeem
From such a stedfast spell his lady's eyes;
So mus'd awhile, entoil'd in woofed phantasies.

XXXIII

Awakening up, he took her hollow lute,—
Tumultuous,—and, in chords that tenderest be,   290
He play'd an ancient ditty, long since mute,
In Provence call'd, "La belle dame sans mercy:"
Close to her ear touching the melody;—
Wherewith disturb'd, she utter'd a soft moan:
He ceased—she panted quick—and suddenly   295
Her blue affrayed eyes wide open shone:
Upon his knees he sank, pale as smooth-sculptured stone.

Stanzas XXIV–XXXIII represents the coming together of the contrasting desires of Porphyro and Madeline in what Stillinger (2009: 67) has termed opposing physical and spiritual quests for union. In these stanzas, Porphyro, who at this point is hidden in a closet in Madeline's bedchamber, watches her get undressed and fall asleep, before going to her bedside, arranging a selection of foods at her bed and playing her music. Watching her dreaming, he then engages in his own fantasies. The conceptual organisation of these stanzas is complex and is the consequence of the reader being asked to track a number of different remote conceptual spaces across the ten stanzas. In short, the textual effect achieved by Keats in these lines is a consequence of demands placed on the reader's *edgework*.

As I explained in Chapter 2, edgework was originally used by Young (1987) to describe the textual indicators of boundary edges. Segal (1995b) uses the same term to describe the process of reading in accounting for the kinds of movement readers necessarily make in tracking edges across deictic fields as they move into new deictic spaces and across deictic centres. McIntyre (2006) draws attention to these two different interpretations and meanings, suggesting that there are consequently 'potential pitfalls' (2006: 106) in using the term without explaining specifically which definition is being used. However, it seems to me that the felt impact of moving across or between deictic fields is also a consequence of recognising the distinctive textual indicators that mark their boundaries. In the following analysis, I focus therefore on reader movement while ensuring that I concentrate explicitly on 'describing the actual nature of the edge boundary in textural terms' (Stockwell (2009: 131)). Consequently, I use the term edgework to refer to the process a reader undertakes in moving between different modal worlds, which necessarily means recognising the explicit boundary edges that are distinguished as part of their textural quality.

Stanza XXIV begins in the text world conceptualisation of Madeline's bedchamber, with basic world-building elements 'a casement high and triple-arched there was' (208). Descriptive function-advancing propositions in the form of relational processes add textual detail through a series of minute details about the 'carven imag'ries' (209) on the casement. Further additional function-advancing detail which makes up Keats' visual landscape is in the form of the shining 'wintry moon' (217), and Madeline kneeling down to pray, 'like a saint' (222). At this point in the poem, Keats demands that his reader be aware of two distinct conceptual structures: first, the action of Madeline praying, which forms the main focus of the matrix text world; and secondly, the actions of Porphyro who, from his position in the closet, grows 'faint' (225) before his 'heart revives' (226). As these second actions occur within a different set of deictic parameters – the enclosed nature of the closed closet as opposed to the open bedchamber – the movement between them can be understood as a spatial world-switch. In fact, the rapid succession of clauses, shifting from Madeline to Porphyro demands that the reader cross these world edges a number of times. These edges can therefore be felt as a shifting vision which both supports and gives rise to the rapid cinematic movement within the poem. The effect here is similar to that of the cinematic split screen, allowing a reader/listener/viewer to 'toggle' between alternative perceptual and spatial worlds (Werth 1999: 224–5).

This kind of reader toggling continues in stanza XXVI, where Madeline's undressing is seen from Porphyro's perspective. In this case, the reader is invited to view the scene from Porphyro's deictic centre anchoring the narrative point of view in the closet, since the function-advancing propositions, although filtered through an additional narrative voice, originate from Porphyro's viewpoint: it is he who sees the pearls as 'wreathed' (227), the jewels as 'warmed' (228), the bodice as 'fragrant' (229), her attire as 'rich' (230) and Madeline herself as a 'mermaid in sea-weed' (231). This colouring of focalisation, which is also spatially situated away from the matrix text world (Porphyro is still in the closet looking out at this point in the poem), encourages the reader to share the same deictic space as Porphyro. In essence, we are being invited to share his view of Madeline.

This heavily modalised world, carrying the content of Madeline's undressing and demanding that the reader move across the edge of the matrix world into the focalised modal construction of Porphyro's viewpoint, can be further explained using Stockwell's (2009: 109) notion of the *viewpoint as vector*, a text world approach to viewpoint and empathy which accounts for the degree and ease of access with which a reader is able to identify with a character. Stockwell identifies four properties that govern and affect a reader-character relationship: distance (engagement is easier when there is a sense of physical closeness); direction (a closer connection is established through the direct rather than the indirect viewpoint of a character); pace (narrative techniques that mimic speed, for example, stream of consciousness causes faster connections) and quality (kinds of edges needing to be crossed will alter the kinds of relationships possible).

In the case of stanza XXVI, the movement required towards Porphyro's focalised world by the reader is physically close (the use of the present tense, proximity suggested by the use of third-person pronouns to refer to Madeline), direct (we read from Porphyro's perceptual centre), fast (there is little intervening

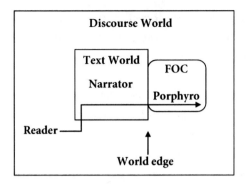

Figure 5.6 Character viewpoint in stanza XXVI of *The Eve of St Agnes*

narrative action) and qualitatively rich (the world is highly modalised). This can be shown in Figure 5.6.

The edge properties (third-person pronouns to refer to Madeline, perceptual viewpoint outwards from the closet, and highly modalised constructions) work to create two particular effects: first, they position the reader as close to and therefore having some degree of empathy with Porphyro as he views Madeline; secondly (and consequently), they provide a subtle blurring of viewpoint where reader, narrator and character seem to merge into one, a kind of composite spectator. Indeed, this kind of conceptual trick is at the heart of Levinson's comments on the poem as a kind of voyeuristic fantasy:

> Voyeurs ourselves, we watch another voyeur (Keats), watching another (Porphyro), watching a woman who broods voluptuously upon herself.
>
> (Levinson 1988: 122)

This rapid edgework required of the reader is a feature of the remainder of the stanza. Madeline's dreams of St Agnes can be seen as initiating a boulomaic modal dream world, in which half awake, she imagines St Agnes appearing at the bottom of her bed, together with a deontic negative modal world in which the necessity for her not to look behind is highlighted through a negative construction of obligation. These modalised constructions create further rich structures that the reader has to conceptualise and again involve movement across world edges, this time from the desire world of Porphyro to the dream state that Madeline is in.

Porphyro is presented as creeping out from the closet once he believes Madeline to be sleeping. Again, the cinematic quality of the backdrop is emphasised through the rich descriptive function-advancing propositions that detail the range of exotic fruits and foods that Porphyro brings to Madeline's bed. Keats' use of direct speech initiates a further remote world, specifically this time one that can be viewed as an example of a boulomaic modal desire world since Porphyro seeks to awaken Madeline in the hope that his desire for physical union will be fulfilled. In fact, Madeline's dream is so deep that he is unable to despite the use of imperative constructions such as 'awake' (276) and 'open thy eyes' (278). The physical nature of his desire is also foregrounded by 'his warm unnerved arm/Sank in her pillow' (280–1). In short, he does everything he can to effect the process of physical union and, when he is unable to do so in the reality world, constructs a fantasy space of his own in which his thoughts are on physical union with Madeline.

At this stage in the poem, we are asked to conceptualise four very different worlds: the matrix world reality of Porphyro's actions and Madeline's state; the desire world conceptualised by Porphyro's explicit lust for Madeline and embedded within that a further dream world containing the 'woofed fantasies' (288) that Porphyro has; and the dream world within which Madeline dreams of her husband-to-be. For each character there is an expectation that their modal world will merge into the matrix world to form a kind of *realis*, as opposed to their current *irrealis* status. In stanza 33, a rapid succession of clauses, 'she uttered', 'he ceased', 'she panted', 'her . . . eyes wide open shone', '. . . . he sank' (294–7), marks the end of these dream and desire states, which rapidly occlude or become marked as one in the physical union suggested by 'into her dream he melted' (321) in stanza XXXVI.

Further investigation of these world types yields a series of patterns that match common readings of the poem. Seen as a poem concerned with 'varying kinds of wish-fulfilment' (Sperry 1973: 375), the modal worlds constructed by the two characters provide a way of comparing the kinds of modal force each holds as they push for their respective physical and spiritual unions. The initial world-switch stands as *realis* since it represents conceived reality (Langacker 2008), as do the subsequent spatial and focalised world-switches with Porphyro at their perceptual deictic centre. The remaining four conceptual spaces, two generated by Madeline and two by Porphyro, stand as forms of *irrealis* as they represent either potential or projected reality states. The key difference lies in their modal force, which is responsible for the grounding of their world propositions.

Table 5.1 World types in stanzas XXIV–XXXIII of *The Eve of St Agnes*

World	Type	Perceptual Centre	Reality status	Type of modal force
1	Text world		Realis	
2	spatial shift	Porphyro	Realis	
3	focalised world	Porphyro	Realis	enablement
4	boulomaic modal dream world	Madeline	Irrealis	attraction
5	negative modal world	Madeline	Irrealis	compulsion
6	boulomaic desire world	Porphyro	Irrealis	enablement
7	boulomaic desire world	Porphyro	Irrealis	enablement

Table 5.1 summarises these world types. The two boulomaic modal dream worlds of Madeline (worlds 4 and 5) can be seen force-dynamically as ATTRACTION and COMPULSION image schemas, respectively. In the first instance, the agonist Madeline's dream fantasy moves unopposed towards its fulfilment, while in the second, the negative modal world embedded within a deontic construction presents the kind of compelling force that precludes certain types of other behaviour, in this instance, looking back. In both cases, although Madeline's imaginative force is strong, her modalised worlds remain less so. In fact, as the types of modal force they represent suggest, they remain relatively weak, the onus on effecting remains solely with Porphyro. Consequently, the two boulomaic desire worlds of Porphyro have a kind of modal force that can be best represented by an ENABLEMENT image schema since they more explicitly act to allow the grounding of their propositional content. This is evident in the fact that it is Porphyro who remains the most active in the poem; his desire worlds must be fully operational in order for him to achieve his goals. His desire, representing a different kind of imaginative modal force to Madeline's, what Hall (1991: 126) terms the 'rival fantasies' of Porphyro's 'activism' and Madeline's 'ritualism', necessarily acts to drive the poem and characters towards wish-fulfilment. The overall conceptualisation of these stanzas is represented in Figure 5.7.

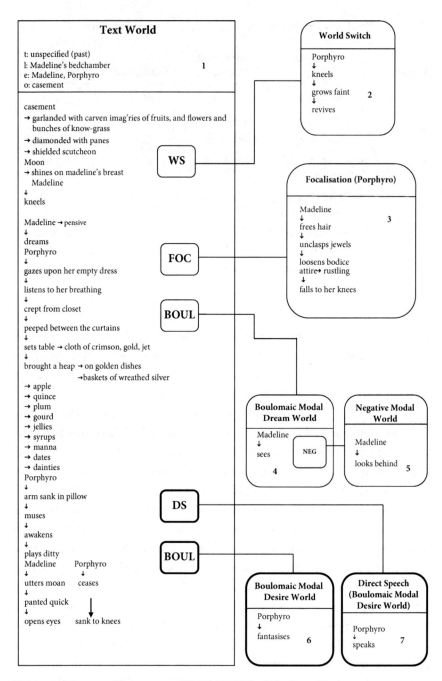

Figure 5.7 Text worlds in stanzas XXIV–XXXIII of *The Eve of St Agnes*

5.9 Madeline and Porphyro (2): Composite characterisation in stanzas XXXIV–XXXVI

XXXIV

Her eyes were open, but she still beheld,
Now wide awake, the vision of her sleep:
There was a painful change, that nigh expell'd   300
The blisses of her dream so pure and deep
At which fair Madeline began to weep,
And moan forth witless words with many a sigh;
While still her gaze on Porphyro would keep;
Who knelt, with joined hands and piteous eye,   305
Fearing to move or speak, she look'd so dreamingly.

XXXV

"Ah, Porphyro!" said she, "but even now
"Thy voice was at sweet tremble in mine ear,
"Made tuneable with every sweetest vow;
"And those sad eyes were spiritual and clear: 310
"How chang'd thou art! how pallid, chill, and drear!
"Give me that voice again, my Porphyro,
"Those looks immortal, those complainings dear!
"Oh leave me not in this eternal woe,
"For if thou diest, my Love, I know not where to go."   315

XXXVI

Beyond a mortal man impassion'd far
At these voluptuous accents, he arose,
Ethereal, flush'd, and like a throbbing star
Seen mid the sapphire heaven's deep repose;
Into her dream he melted, as the rose   320
Blendeth its odour with the violet,—
Solution sweet: meantime the frost-wind blows
Like Love's alarum pattering the sharp sleet
Against the window-panes; St. Agnes' moon hath set.

In this final analytical section, I focus on the three stanzas detailing the awakening of Madeline, her reaction to seeing Porphyro and the sexual union that takes place between the two. Furthermore, I explore how the poem demands that its reader monitor and keep track of a number of different enactors of the two characters as a way of understanding the composition of each of their modalised expressions.

As I explained in Chapter 2, enactors are different versions of a character across any kind of world-switch. So, for example, in stanzas XXXIV–XXXVI there are a number of different enactors of Porphyro and Madeline across the series of modalised worlds that are set up. In the matrix world, in which Porphyro waits at Madeline's bedside, there are two enactors, which we can call P1 and M1. Since these hold a primary position in the discourse conceptualisation – the other modalised constructions branch off from this world – we can call these *primary enactors* to reflect their status. Subsequently, *secondary enactors* of Porphyro and Madeline are also conceptualised and constructed through the two modalised worlds that arise from this matrix world. In the first instance, Madeline's *boulomaic dream world* in which M1 dreams of M2 with P2 (the secondary enactors) is first conceptualised in XXVII. Although we are not told explicitly who or what Madeline dreams of, the fact that she recognises Porphyro on waking is suggestive of his being the 'concrete filling' of her dream (Jones 1969: 240). Secondly, Porphyro's *boulomaic desire world* contains Porphyro's 'woofed fantasies' (288) and the secondary enactors P3 and M3.

Although these worlds have been first primed and then unprimed (Emmott 1997: 123) through reference back to the matrix world, in both of these cases the secondary enactors are bound (Emmott 1997: 123) to their respective worlds. The stage at which Madeline wakes up is therefore a significant one, since it marks a repriming of the dream frame 'the blisses of her dream' at the same time as the waking M1 enactor of Madeline in the matrix world. In other worlds, the reader is asked to simultaneously conceptualise both M1 and M2 as the edges of text worlds become less defined. I suggest that this can be explained in two ways. First, this represents what Emmott (1997: 177) calls 'enactor updating' since our understanding of the primary enactor M1 is modified on the basis of M2 being part of a reprimed world. Consequently, we understand more about the waking Madeline as a result of being told that she has both had and woken from a dream. Secondly, I suggest that the term *composite enactor* can be used to account for the fact that although in Werth's original model character updating is dealt with as reference updating under the more general topic of incrementation (Werth 1999: 310), the model itself pays little real attention to how the phenomenon of multiple enactors as a result of complex world-switching is monitored by a reader and is responsible for a significant literary effect.[6]

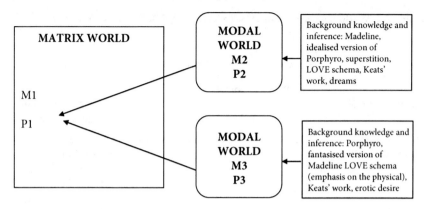

Figure 5.8 'Feed back' to primary enactors in the matrix world in stanza XXXIV of *The Eve of St Agnes*

There remain two more processes that require explanation. First, we can only account for the secondary-enactor updating that allows feedback to the primary level by also acknowledging the role of inference in the modalised worlds inhabited by M2, P2, M3 and P3. So, the limited deictic worlds offered to us by Keats are built up through our background knowledge and inferencing. In the case of Madeline's boulomaic dream world, our knowledge of Madeline as 'full of this whim' (55) and the superstition itself are incremented into the common ground in addition to our general knowledge of the kinds of fantastical worlds represented in dreams and the varying representations of the LOVE schema and knowledge of Keats' work to give rise to a rich sense of the secondary enactors M2/P2. In Porphyro's boulomaic desire world, similar knowledge of Porphyro and the understanding of a more powerful set of ground-effecting desires help support and account for the feeding back from M3/P3 to the primary enactors M1/P1. These are shown in Figure 5.8.

In stanza XXXIV, the matrix world containing the enactors of the sleeping Madeline M1 and waiting Porphyro P1 is updated by the world containing the dreaming Madeline M2 and idealised version of Porphyro P2 to create the composite enactors (E_C), M_C and P_C. This represents the reader's updated primary enactor. In addition, within the narrative world of the poem, M_C's disappointment on waking can be fully understood as the contrast between P1 and P2 where the disappointment itself becomes textually realised through the composite enactor P_C who causes Madeline 'to weep/And moan forth witless words with many a sigh' (302–3).

Table 5.2 World concerns in stanzas XXXIV–XXXV of *The Eve of St Agnes*

World	Prominent Enactors	Concern	Reading
2 boulomaic dream world (M)	M/P 2	spiritual union	The celebration of human love and of imaginative force
3 boulomaic desire world (P)	M/P 3	physical/sexual fantasy	The focus on male desire, Porpyhro as voyeur, Madeline as victim, the power of the imagination in effecting male fantasy
4 direct speech/ epistemic perception (M)	M/P 4	disappointment with matrix world enactor of Porphyro	The disappointing nature of the imagination, the harshness of reality
5 boulomaic desire world (M)	M/P 5	desire for idealised version of lover/enactor	Imagination as powerful yet deceiving/illusory
6 negative modal world (M)	M/P 6	desire for maintenance of desire/dream	

The remaining sections of these stanzas can be read in a similar way. In stanza XXXV, Madeline's direct speech, initiating a modalised world of epistemic perception, binds another enactor of Porphyro P4, who has the unattractive qualities of being 'pallid, chill, and drear!' (312) to Madeline's perception frame. The priming of a further boulomaic desire world, where a new Porphyro P5 has a 'tuneable' (309) voice, 'spiritual and clear' (310) eyes and 'looks immortal' (313), adds another conceptual layer in addition to the unimagined P2 in Madeline's previous dream world, since not only are we asked to conceptualise a brand new space, but also the modal force of Madeline's utterance is clearly here part of a boulomaic desire world rather than a dream one. In addition, a further negative modal world with an additional enactor P6 who leaves Madeline, is conceptualised as a part of a deontic modal world, in which the act of leaving itself is imagined in order to then deny its existence. We can therefore track six different enactors of each of Madeline and Porphyro across these three stanzas. At each point, the reader is asked to conceptualise P/M 1 along with P/M 2–6, and track these later enactors as enriching their primary versions. This complex structure culminates in stanza XXXVI, which iconically marks the physical union of the two lovers.

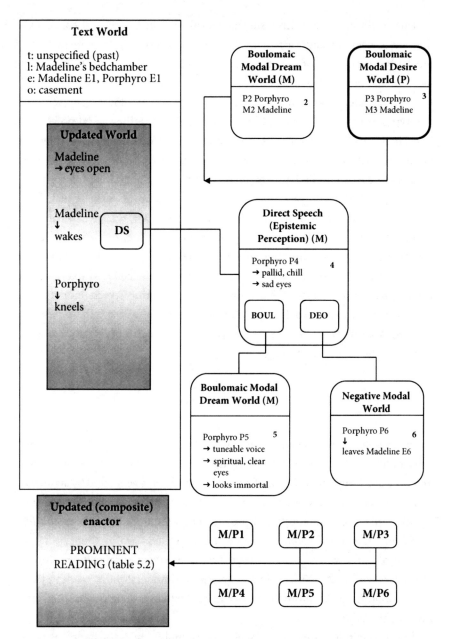

Figure 5.9 Conceptual organisation of stanzas XXXIV–XXXVI of *The Eve of St Agnes*

This reading of these three stanzas reveals one of the central concerns of the poem. Leaving aside the worlds generated through the use of metaphor, the mid-point climax of the stanza is represented in the line 'into her dream he melted' (320), widely acknowledged as an important symbolic moment. In this explicit merging of the spiritual and physical, the union represents the two types of imaginative force in the poem, evident in the modal power held in each enactor in each modalised remote world. Those readers who view the poem as a triumph of the imagination, whether that be of the male-centred sexual fantasy embodied in Porphyro as an emblem of Keats' *imaginative truth* (e.g. Waldoff 1985) or the inherent actualising of male sexual desire through the suppression of the female (Wolfson 1990), will necessarily tend to view the climax with additional prominence given to, or closeness felt to, P3. Alternatively, a reading that interprets the imaginative force in the poem as a negative, disappointing construct (e.g. Rosenfeld 2000) is likely to give prominence or feel closest to P4. In essence, deciding which modal world should retain *prominence* determines what the poem means.[7] These potential readings are summarised in Table 5.2. The complete conceptualisation of these stanzas is shown in Figure 5.9.

5.10 Review

In this chapter, I provided an in-depth analysis of *The Eve of St Agnes*, where I explored the effects generated by Keats' layering of desire and dream worlds and suggested ways of understanding the literary effects generated by significant textual patterns and the ways in which readers are asked to monitor and track the discourse event. In addition, I proposed that the notions of *the establishing world* and the *world zoom* might be useful for text world theory analyses and suggested a way to account for the ways in which composite enactors of characters within the text world are tracked and understood according to the degree of prominence afforded to a particular textual or thematic concern by an individual reader.

This chapter has therefore sought to exemplify in a sustained way my suggestions and revisions to text world theory, in particular, with regard to accounting for the notions of desire and dream. As the first sustained analytical section of this study, this chapter has sought to exemplify the merits and insights that text world theory can offer.

In Chapter 6, I develop my ideas on how dreams can be understood within text world theory by focusing on the literary representation of the nightmare, a particular type of dream that I have so far not considered, and by propose a further addition to the text world theory model, the *nightmare dream world*. Consequently, Chapter 6 builds on my work so far in this study and anticipates a further three analytical chapters in which I aim to apply my theoretical framework to Keats' poetry.

6

Nightmare Worlds

6.1 Introduction

In Chapter 4, I proposed a modification of the existing text world theory treatment of modality to account for desire and dreams. In this chapter, I anticipate Chapters 7, 8 and 9 where I explore the literary representation of the nightmare in three of Keats' poems, proposing that these may be understood as extreme types of dream worlds that I term *nightmare worlds*. In Sections 6.1 and 6.2, I review an eclectic range of work from sleep medicine, psychology and neuroscience on unpleasant dreams and nightmares, highlighting findings which define the nightmare as an intense kind of dream with a clearly defined set of dominant negative emotional concerns. In Section 6.3, I summarise ideas on the nightmare in the later eighteenth and early nineteenth centuries, drawing on theories and uses of the nightmare by contemporary writers with particular emphases on Coleridge and Keats. In Section 6.5, the idea of the nightmare as a negatively oriented world is developed through reviewing work on negation in the fields of semantics, psychology, discourse pragmatics, and cognitive grammar, and in Werth's own text world theory. In these sections, I propose both a modification to an understanding of negation in text world theory and an adaptation of my previous work on dream states to account for the *inherent negativity* in the nightmare world. In Section 6.5.5, I suggest that one way to account stylistically for the kind of inherent intensity of the nightmare world is by using Stockwell's (2009) attention-resonance model. Finally, in Section 6.6, I suggest a model for the nightmare world to be incorporated into the text world theory framework and consequently anticipate subsequent chapters where I provide detailed analyses of *Isabella; or, The Pot of Basil*, 'La belle dame sans merci' and 'This living hand, now warm and capable'.

6.2 Unpleasant dreams

In Chapter 4, I argued that a dream world, whether real or that represented in literary fiction, should be considered on a continuum of mentation states, consistent with Hartmann's continuum of mental functioning and other research that see a continuity between waking and dream cognitive states.[1] I argued that these are best considered as types of modalised expressions since they are attitudinal, guided by the emotional concerns of the conceptualiser, and represent different degrees of closeness to reality. In line with Hartmann's contemporary theory of dreaming, I suggested that dreaming states, ranging from reverie and daydreaming to nocturnal sleep, differ from desire states in that they have increased degrees of non-volition, epistemic rather than deontic modal force and are characterised as thin boundary, 'merging' states due to their use of auto-associative networks, and more broadly and loosely defined connections. I differentiated between type A dream worlds such as reverie and daydreaming, which reflecting a speaker's desire can be viewed to some extent as part of the boulomaic domain, and type B dream worlds, typically (but not always) nocturnal sleep, which although still part of the same mentation continuum should be considered purely epistemic in nature.

The argument for not including all dream worlds within the boulomaic domain becomes apparent when the focus is on those dreams that are unpleasant and cause distress to the dreamer. Clearly, in these cases, it is difficult to understand unpleasant dreams as representing any kind of volition on the part of the dreamer despite the attempts of psychoanalytic practice to explain these as a kind of repressed wish-fulfilment.[2]

As Barrett (1996: 2) points out, limited attention was paid to dreams emanating from traumatic events for the major part of the twentieth century. She suggests that the phenomenon only began to be taken seriously in the latter half of the century, coinciding with high incidences of Vietnam veterans suffering from post-traumatic stress disorder (e.g. Wilmer 1982; Hartmann 1984; Van de Kolk et al. 1984) and the feminist movement's highlighting of the psychological trauma suffered by women in cases of domestic violence (Kemp et al. 1991; Roberts et al. 1998; Thompson et al. 1999). Studies have shown that extreme literal trauma such as that experienced by holocaust survivors (Lavie and Kaminer 1996) and victims of rape and other sexual attacks (King and Sheehan 1996; Muller 1996) can be directly associated with, and held responsible for, the experiencing of traumatic dreams. Nader (1996) finds that many children incorporated intervention fantasies into dreams following traumatic events, expressing a strong desire for revenge, escape, rescue or simply an alternative happy ending to the experience (see also Nader and Pynoos 1991; Pynoos and Nader 1989).

Important to the understanding of both the traumatic dream and unpleasant dreams in general is the centrality of a dominant emotion or set of emotions, which represent the unresolved preoccupations of the dreamer (Domhoff 1993: 297). The importance of emotion in dreaming has been identified through evidence of its activation during dreaming of the amygdala, a structure in the limbic system responsible for acting on external emotion-producing stimuli to trigger emotional responses in emotion-producing areas of the brain (Damasio 1994; Maquet et al. 1996; LeDoux 1996, 2000). Maquet et al. (1996: 166) suggest that this activation, specifically of the negative emotions of fear and aggression and the fight or flight response, can 'account for the perceptual components of dreaming'. In addition, research has shown that traumatic dreams can be caused by an overreactive amygdala, a consequence of stress, sleep deprivation or some other literal trauma (McNamara 2008: 73). In a series of investigations into the nature of traumatic dreams, Kramer (1991: 278) suggests that an emotional surge which exceeds the integrative capacity of the dream experience is responsible for the phenomenon of the bad dream. Powerful emotional responses to literal trauma can therefore be viewed as underlying and being responsible for traumatic dreams, giving them a far greater intensity than non-traumatic dreams. A number of studies have shown that non-traumatic dreams are remembered less vividly and seen as less intense than those of a traumatic nature (Barrett 1996; Hartmann et al. 2001; Hartmann and Brezler 2008).

6.3 The nightmare

6.3.1 A definition of the nightmare

The general sleep medicine definition of a nightmare is a specific kind of unpleasant dream that is very disturbing to the dreamer and causes awakening as a result of imagery and/or emotions (Hartmann 1984; Zadra and Donderi 2000; Blagrove et al. 2004). Thus, a nightmare is distinguished from those dreams that are disturbing or have negative emotional content and/or rating but do not cause the dreamer to wake up. These have been variously defined as *night terrors* (Hartmann 1984), *bad dreams* (Halliday 1987; Zadra and Donderi 2000), *sleep terrors* (Belicki 1992a) and *anxiety dreams* (Hartmann 1999).[3] Blagrove and

Haywood (2006) differentiate between *waking criterion nightmares* that awaken the dreamer and *inclusive definition nightmares* that include both waking criterion nightmares and other traumatic dreams (2006: 117).

There is a strong argument for including 'waking' as a key criterion in defining the nightmare. Zadra and Donderi (2000), for example, propose that the nightmare is in effect an extremely severe version of an unpleasant dream where the severity is marked by the awakening of the dreamer as a result of the strength or intensity of negative emotions experienced.[4]

Since the general consensus in dream research is to distinguish between nightmares and other forms of disturbing dreams, it would be sensible for any text world approach to the representation of the nightmare to adopt the waking-criterion definition and accept the nightmare as an extreme kind of type B dream world, or as Hartmann (1999: 199) suggests, existing at the extreme end of a 'continuum of frightening dreams'.[5] A waking-criterion definition of the nightmare therefore gives it a particular quality in contrast to normal sleep dreams or traumatic or anxiety dreams: its inherent responsibility for triggering deictic movement from one state of consciousness state to another. In text world theory terms, it is responsible for initiating world-switches and therefore can be said to have world-building properties. Although I return to this idea in more detail later in this chapter, as a brief example, we can consider the following nightmare account from stanzas X and XI of 'La belle dame sans merci'. The poem begins with an unidentified speaker, questioning the morose state of a knight he sees in an unidentified natural landscape. The knight proceeds to tell him of his encounter with (another) unidentified 'lady' who leads him to 'her elfin grot' before sending him to sleep. At this point in the poem, the narrator-knight gives details of the ensuing nightmare experience.

X

I saw pale kings, and princes too,
Pale warriors, death-pale were they all;
They cried---" La Belle Dame sans Merci
Thee hath in thrall!"   40

XI

I saw their starved lips in the gloom,
With horrid warning gaped wide,
And I awoke and found me here,
On the cold hill's side.

Dream worlds relayed by enactors will always be enactor-accessible, and in this instance the dream world is triggered by predications setting up a world-switch: 'there she lullèd me asleep/And there I dreamed' (IX, 33–4). Here, the deictic parameters of the originating world have been altered to present a time anterior to the recount time and new enactors in kings, princes and warriors. Although the location is not specified, it is revealed as dark and haunting, 'in the gloam' (41). The switched world is fleshed out through function-advancing propositions, consisting of mental perception processes that detail what the narrator sees in his nightmare vision, and relational processes that describe the characteristics of the enactors in the dream as 'death pale' (38) with 'starved lips' (41) and 'horrid warning gapèd wide' (42). These negative lexical choices act as cohesive devices and can be responsible for triggering a strong emotional reaction. Finally, 'I awoke' (43) acts as a world-switch trigger, an inherent part of the nightmare that transfers the focus of the waking-knight to an alternative deictic space, where the narrator finds himself 'on the cold hillside' (44).

As in text world theory, the conceptualisation of a world is part of a dynamic and changing discourse event, the updating of a text world occurs to match these changing circumstances. In Chapter 2, I explained how Werth accounts for this as part of a process called *incrementation* (Werth 1999: 289). As well as the deictic updating that takes place (there is a time gap between the departure from the originating matrix world and the return following the nightmare and subsequent waking world-switch), the psychological make-up of the knight as understood by the reader is also dramatically altered since we now understand the reasons for his physical countenance at the beginning of the poem. It is the updating of discourse-participant knowledge about the knight in relation to his counterpart in the nightmare world, and the counterpart deictic spaces marked by 'here' that results in a radical kind of change in our understanding of the knight and his relationship to the landscape presented in the poem. Indeed, we could say that the updating of our understanding of the barren originating world is rendered possible by the nightmare itself. Since the nightmare represents a kind of extreme discontinuity that Werth proposes as being essential for world-updating, we can consider the matrix world to which we return following the nightmare as being sufficiently changed to warrant explanation in terms of world updating. This is shown in Figure 6.1.

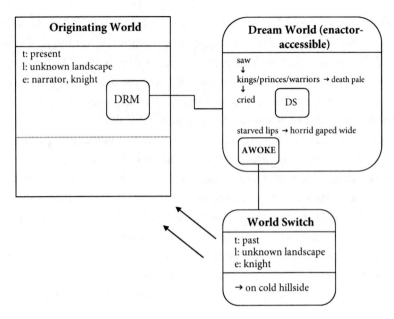

Figure 6.1 Conceptual organisation of stanzas XX–XI of 'La belle dame sans merci'

6.3.2 Nightmare phenomenology

In addition to the waking-criterion that I have already discussed, McNamara (2008: 85–8) suggests a set of formal characteristics of the nightmare that distinguish them from ordinary dreams. First, nightmares are defined by their heightened sense of vividness in foregrounded entities. They are also defined by a sense of total automaticity in that the experiencer has no control over the nightmare content and clearly no desire for the nightmare to exist.[6] In addition, McNamara suggests that one of the defining features of the nightmare rests in the fact that there is a heightened sense of the self as under threat, and in turn a greater degree of self-reflection, which generates the need to both think about and act on nightmares.[7] According to McNamara, nightmares also involve a 'distorted' form of attributing beliefs, desires, intentions and motivation to other people (or characters) to account for their behaviour. This assumption that others have a consciousness, is in what in developmental psychology is known as *theory of the mind* (Premack and Woodruff 1978), becomes in the nightmare, a more narrowed process of attaching malevolent intentionality to characters. Finally, the nightmare phenomenon is characterised by an adherence to general properties of ordinary dreams in that they provide well-formed narratives, and are creative in their merging of imagery and hyper and auto-associative networks.[8]

Table 6.1 Formal features of nightmares, from McNamara (2008:88)

Features of the Nightmare (as compared to ordinary dreams)	Comments
Vivid imagery but darkened menacing background	The visual foreground is vivid, while background settings are dark, unfamiliar, scary and menacing
Increased automaticity	Hard to voluntarily terminate a nightmare
Not confabulatory	Narrative driven by cognitive content, not rationalisations of emotional content
Triggered by retrieval of negative memory	This is an inference from an examination of formal properties
Enhanced creativity	Nightmares have more complex narratives than ordinary dreams
Hyperassociative	Only with respect to negative memories and emotions
Increased focus on 'self' under threat	The dreamer has intense consciousness of self
Problematic narratives	Nightmares are well-formed narratives but may never end with a resolution of conflict
Compellingness	Must be shared with others after awakening
Sharer of nightmare held in awe by others	When nightmares are shared after awakening, the person who shared the nightmare is considered as supremely burdened
Failure of mind reading	Characters in nightmares are not considered to have ordinary minds

6.3.3 Models of nightmare production

According to Nielsen and Levin (2007), it is possible to classify models that have accounted for the functions of dreaming as one of the following: psychoanalytical models, personality and evolutionary models and neurobiological models. In the following sections, I briefly summarise some of the key findings in each.

6.3.3.1 Psychoanalytical models

Freud's (1976) proposal that nightmares represent disguised wish-fulfilments as part of the processes of censorship and distortion is consistent with his general theory that dreams provide a means of maintaining sleep. Later work in psychoanalysis focuses on the nightmare as the result of the failure of the body to cope with traumatic experiences and emotions (Kramer 1991; Greenberg and Pearlman 1993; Lansky and Bley 1995).

6.3.3.2 *Personality and evolutionary models*

The main research using personality models is that of Hartmann's boundary types (1984, 1991, 1998; Levin et al. 1998; Hartmann and Kunzendorf 2005, 2006). Similarly, Cowen and Levin (1995), Blagrove and Akehurst (2000) and Miró and Martinez (2005) all explore and find a relationship between an individual's personality and nightmare frequency. Evolutionary models on the other hand, stress the functional design of nightmares in the light of their consistent form and structure and consequently their adaptive and transformational qualities. These models focus on how the retelling of nightmares, in primitive communities, may have created social identities (Jedrej and Shaw 1992) and developed language skills and a sense of individual prestige (McNamara 2008). Other evolutionary accounts of the function of nightmares stress their therapeutic design in weaving trauma into consciousness so that it becomes less distressing and ultimately accepted (Hartmann 1999), and consider how nightmares serve as mechanisms to rehearse responses to threats to the self in a kind of simulation (Revonsuo 2000). Antrobus (1993: 552) claims that nightmares and dreams in general must have an adaptive purpose since 'a class of information processing must serve some function for the human organism otherwise the process will be discontinued'.

6.3.3.3 *Neurobiological models*

Neurobiological models of dream functionality are proposed by Fisher et al. (1970) and Kramer (1991) as part of the wider conception of dreaming as a mood-regulating mechanism. In each case, nightmares arise as a result of the breakdown of a 'desomatisation' programme (Fisher et al. 1970: 770) that normally regulates the activation of heart rate, respiratory rate and eye movement during sleep. Similarly, Kramer suggests that dreaming functions as an 'emotional thermostat' (1991: 279) and that nightmares occur as a result of an emotional overload. This failure in integration is due in part to the nightmare sufferer's increased sensitivity to a negative emotional state.

6.3.4 Nightmares and emotional content

6.3.4.1 Emotion and feeling

Oatley and Jenkins offer the following working definition:

1. an emotion is usually caused by a person consciously or unconsciously evaluating an event as relevant to a concern (goal) that is important; the emotion is felt as positive when a concern is advanced and negative when a concern is impeded
2. the core of an emotion is readiness to act and the prompting of plans; an emotion gives priority for one or a few kinds of action to which it gives a sense of urgency – so it can interrupt, or compete with, alternative mental processes or actions. Different types of readiness create different outline relationships with others
3. an emotion is usually experienced as a distinctive type of mental state, sometimes accompanied or followed by bodily changes, expressions, actions.

Oatley and Jenkins (1996: 96)

From this, it becomes possible to view the nightmare as a 'distinctive type of mental state' in which the experiencing of the emotion (the idea of its being *felt* in Oatley and Jenkins' terms) can occur. Damasio (2001) differentiates the concepts of *emotion* and *feeling* by defining emotions as patterned collections of brain-produced chemical and neural responses to a perceived object or situation that act as a kind of stimulus (2001: 781). This emotion is responsible for activating a bodily experience in the form of an emotional state and a shift in attention towards the stimulus responsible. As these responses are geared towards self-preservation and protection, emotions therefore can be said to have an adaptive function (2001: 781). In contrast, feelings are 'the mental representation of the physiological changes that characterise emotions' (Damasio 2001: 781). The fact that feelings arise from emotions makes the feeling an internally initiated phenomenon in contrast to the emotion, which is produced as a consequence of the impact of some external input. Feelings therefore can be seen as arising from emotions, as products of the mind and as processes that integrate, address and represent the body-emotion (Damasio 2004: 30).

Damasio's distinction allows us to see the cognitive process of dreaming as a type of feeling and the dream process in general as a *process* of feeling (Pagel 2008: 96). This is consistent with dream theories that see the nightmare like other forms of dreaming, as being a process that both is guided by and builds the emotional concerns of the dreamer (Domhoff 1993, 2001; Hartmann 1998). Since feeling is also concerned with the perception of thinking itself (Damasio 2004: 86), both the experienced and the recalled nightmare can be viewed in this way, the latter as a type of 'conscious experience' (Berkowitz 2000: 11).

6.3.4.2 *The emotional content of nightmares*

In Hartmann's (1998) contemporary theory of dreaming, a *contextualising image*, later the *central image* (Hartmann and Kunzendorf 2005; Hartmann 2008), acts as a picture-context for emotional concerns, providing them with an overall sense of symbolic coherence within the dream narrative. As Hartmann et al. explain:

> thus dreams such as "I was overwhelmed by a huge tidal wave" or "I was swept away in a whirlwind" were found frequently in persons who had undergone a wide variety of trauma (fires, rapes, attacks). Such dream images are clearly not picturing the actual experienced event but rather appear to be finding a picture-context for ("contextualising") the dominant emotion.
>
> (Hartmann et al. 2001: 97)

It is possible to view Hartmann's process of contextualisation as similar to Damasio's notion of feeling. The immediate nature of the process places it in contrast to psychoanalytical theories by suggesting that it is 'upfront' emotional concerns, and not unconscious impulses and repressed memories that provide a context and a meaning for visual dream imagery (Kunzendorf et al. 2000). Hartmann suggests that it is possible to measure the emotional intensity of any given dream by identifying its central image and then rating its intensity on a seven-point scale, together with a dominant emotion that is considered to be contextualised by the central image. The emotion list incorporates both basic (Ekman 1992) and higher cognitive (Griffiths 1997) emotions, which are considered either powerfully negative, other negatively toned or positively toned.

The intensity of the central image is therefore 'a measure of the power of the underlying emotion' (Hartmann 2008: 44), responsible for the explicit conceptualisation and recall of the central image itself. Unsurprisingly, nightmares have been found to contain higher central image scores, demonstrating greater degrees of emotional intensity than do normal and bad dreams (Hartmann et al. 2001; Hartmann and Kunzendorf 2006; Hartmann and Brezler 2008). They have also been found to contain a range of negative

Table 6.2 Emotion list for scoring dream central images, adapted from Hartmann et al. (2001: 36)

Powerful Negative Emotions	Other Negatively Toned Emotions	Positively Toned Emotions
fear, terror, helplessness, vulnerability, being trapped, being immobilised	anxiety, vigilance, guilt grief, loss, sadness, abandonment, disappointment, despair, hopelessness, anger, frustration, disturbing, shame, inadequacy, disgust, repulsion	power, mastery, supremacy, awe, wonder, mystery, happiness, joy, excitement, hope, peace, restfulness, longing, relief, safety, love

emotions (Zadra et al. 1995, 2006; Hartmann et al. 1999; Zadra and Donderi 2000; Hartmann et al. 2001; Domhoff 2010). The effects of emotional intensity in nightmares have been measured by using the concept of *nightmare distress* (Wood and Bootzin 1990; Belicki 1992a, 1992b), to consider the impact that a nightmare has on the experiencer's waking state in terms of subsequent fear and anxiety, on day-to-day living, and on the need to seek therapeutic treatment following nightmare experiences.

6.4 Nightmares in the nineteenth century

Andrew Baxter's belief that nightmares are afflictions with clear physical symptoms and are caused by external forces entering the body is typical of early nineteenth-century views on the nightmare. Baxter sees these spirits as solely responsible for the onset of the nightmare, and makes a claim for the nightmare as a form of possession, with the dreamer lacking any control over the content or direction of the dream. The possessor is a malevolent spirit, an *incubus*, which pushes down on the afflicted individual with such force so as to produce an experience of very real physical pain. This pain is so strong that, according to John Bond (1753) in his *An Essay on the Incubus or Nightmare*, sufferers will

> sigh, groan, utter indistinct sounds, and remain in the jaws of death, till by the utmost efforts of nature, or some external assistance, they escape out of that dreadful torpid state.
>
> (Bond 1753: 2)

Jones (1931: 20), in a wide-ranging survey of eighteenth- and nineteenth-century views of the nightmare, highlights this typical emphasis on the physical in each of his 'three cardinal features of the malady . . . (1) agonizing dread . . . (2) sense of oppression or weight at the chest . . . (3) conviction of helpless paralysis'. He also draws attention to this emphasis in the etymology of the term nightmare.[9]

> The word Nightmare itself comes from the Anglo-Saxon *neaht* or *nicht* (= night) and *mara* (= incubus or succubus). The Anglo-Saxon suffix *a* denotes an agent, so that *mara* from the verb *merran*, literally means 'a crusher' and the connotation of a crushing weight on the breast.
>
> (Jones 1931: 243)

Physical pressure and possession can clearly be seen in Figure 6.2, the artist Henry Fuseli's 'The Nightmare', which was first exhibited in 1782. In this painting, a clearly passive and overpowered sleeping female has an incubus or *mara* pressing on her chest.[10]

A later variation on 'The Nightmare' is found in Erasmus Darwin's *The Botanic Garden* (1789). Darwin, whose work greatly influenced Coleridge,

Figure 6.2 Henry Fuseli's 'The Nightmare' (1782)

sees dreaming in general as a kind of deception, based on two beliefs. First, the absence of feelings caused by objects outside of the dream means that the dream content cannot be compared to real waking sensations (Darwin uses this to explain why surprise is never experienced in a dream); secondly, the loss of volition achieved during dreaming means that the dreamer cannot compare dream content to any knowledge of reality. Thus, the nightmare represents a dream experience of the most severe and extreme kind where an absence of outer sense and an utter lack of volition strive to create the terrifying experience. Indeed, in the third canto of 'The Loves of Plants', the second poem from *The Botanic Garden*, Darwin presents a striking image of the cause and effect of the nightmare, linking together the two images of incubus and horse from Fuseli's poem. Later lines echo contemporary views on the passive nature of the dreamer, held in the uncontrollable force of the nightmare agent.

> On his Night-Mare, through the evening fog,
> Fits the squab fiend o'er fen, and lake, and bog,
> Seeks some love-wilder'd Maid with sleep oppress'd
> Alights, and grinning sits upon her breast.
> Such as of late amid the murky sky
> Was mark'd by *Fuseli's* poetic eye (51–5)

> In vain to scream with quivering lips she tries,
> And strains in palsy'd lids her tremulous eyes;
> In vain she *wills* to run, fly, swim, walk creep;
> The *Will* presides not in the bower of *Sleep*! (71–4)

(Darwin 1789)

Fuseli's painting is also representative of an interest shown in artistic (including literary) representations of the nightmare that can be credited to late- eighteenth-early nineteenth-century interest in the *Gothic* (Frayling 2006: 20). Although a term used to describe a wide range of textual conventions and thematic, cultural and sociopolitical concerns, representations of the *Gothic* focus on the supernatural, fantasy worlds, barren landscapes and deserted castles and stock heroic and villainous characters. Hopkins (2005), writing on the gothic in film, draws on Freud's notion of the 'uncanny', the unfamiliar and frightening as the repressed familiar, in discussing how these exaggerations or extremes, developed beyond simple stereotypes by nineteenth-century artists, explore the ideas of polarities and doubleness.

The nightmare represents the *Gothic* shadow, the darker half of the human imagination and experience:

> the classic genre marker of the *Gothic* in film is doubleness, for it is the dualities typically created by the *Gothic* that invest it with its uncanny ability to hold its darkly shadowed mirror up to its own age.
>
> Hopkins (2005: 12)

The emotions of fear and terror were also understood as powerful psychological entities. The influence of Edmund Burke's notion of them as the source of *the sublime*, the 'strongest emotion which the mind is capable of feeling' (Burke 1958: 39), is evident in the work of late-eighteenth and early nineteenth-century poets, many of whom showed a profound interest in the nightmare. Shelley was a frequent sufferer of somnambulism, nightmares and extreme fear on waking (Holmes 1974: 6, 13) and kept an account of all of his dreams, where he developed a fascination for exploring his darker and more disturbing visions. His essay *Speculations on Metaphysics* contains a brief account of a disturbing dream containing a series of recurring and hauntingly familiar images, so much so that they cause him to abandon his recount of it, the essay remaining unfinished with only the following explanation: '[Footnote: Here I was obliged to leave off, overcome by thrilling horror]' (Shelley 1909: 72). In Book X of *The Prelude*, Wordsworth uses the effect of a nightmare to represent his pain at the fallen ideals of revolutionary France when he finds that the horrors witnessed manifest themselves in terrifying dreams:

> My nights were miserable;
> Through months, through years, long after the last beat
> Of those atrocities, the hour of sleep
> To me came rarely charged with natural gifts,
> Such ghastly visions had I of despair
> And tyranny, and implements of death. (398–403)
>
> (Wordsworth 1936)

For others, the nightmare was a powerfully potent symbol of distorted ideals. Blake, like Wordsworth, uses the nightmare to explore his horror at, and dissatisfaction with, the revolution in France in 'The French Revolution' (Blake 2004), while in *Frankenstein*, Mary Shelley represents Frankenstein's 'breathless horror and disgust' (Shelley 1998: 62) immediately following his creation in Chapter 5 through the detailing of his subsequent nightmare experience. In addition, her preface to the 1831 edition makes dramatic use of a nightmare-state to describe how the initial ideas for the story came to her as she tried to sleep 'with a vividness far beyond the usual bounds of reverie' (Shelley 1998: 11). Nightmares were also associated with hallucinatory states of mind following experimentation with drugs. De Quincey describes how his opium addiction was responsible for experiences in which 'a theatre seemed suddenly opened and lighted up within my brain' and yet at the same time were marked by powerful and incontrollable feelings of terror and helplessness.

> This and all other changes in my dreams were accompanied by deep-seated anxiety and funereal melancholy, such as are wholly incommunicable by words. I seemed every night to descend – into chasms and sunless abysses, depths below depths, from which it seemed hopeless that I would ever re-ascend.
>
> (De Quincey 1993: 185)

Samuel Taylor Coleridge was a frequent sufferer of nightmares and his ideas provide the most developed attempt to link the psychological and physical nature of the *nighmair*.[11] Coleridge explores the nightmare through his concept of *touch*, which he defines as the felt experience of a sensation passed from body to brain. He distinguishes between *single touch*, the sensation felt when being touched, and *double touch*, the sensation felt when simultaneously touching and being touched (Coleridge likens double touch to the feeling gained when one's own hand touches its own side). While single touch is experienced through general sensory input, for example, in seeing or hearing, Coleridge views double touch as a multi-sensory experience, making various connections at physical and psychological levels. It is in this multi-sensory experience of the physical and the psychological that Coleridge recognises the heightened power and terror of the nightmare. In the following account, Coleridge emphasises how the physical aspect of the nightmare is developed as part of a wider imaginative force acting on that primary sensation. The physical presence and bodily sensation become a distorted kind of psychological haunting, manifesting itself as double touch; the subsequent effect is the powerful and frightening vision.

> As if the finger which I saw with eyes Had, as it were, another finger invisible – Touching me with a ghostly touch, even while I feared the real Touch from it.
>
> (Coleridge 1962: e. 3215)

Coleridge (1973: e.4046) also classifies the nightmare as a particular 'species of Reverie' and as a distinct kind of mentation state, which he defines as 'a *twinkling* as it were, of sleeping and waking' (Coleridge 1987: 136). In this state, the content of the nightmare, unlike in normal dreams, is experienced in a way that appears very real. However, the difference remains that in a waking state, volition exists; in the nightmare it does not. As a consequence of both the nightmare sufferer's lack of control and the power and intensity of the dream content, the nightmare becomes the ultimate terrifying experience.

Generally, there is little evidence of any interest shown by Keats in the nightmare.[12] However, in his poetry, Keats was moving away from an understanding of the dream as a benign imaginative force. In the verse letter 'To J. H. Reynolds, Esq.' composed in March 1818, Keats remarks on a much darker aspect of dreaming:

> O that our dreamings all, of sleep or wake,
> Would all their colours from the sunset take,
> From something of material sublime,
> Rather than shadow our own soul's daytime
> In the dark void of night. (67–71)

These preoccupations with the darker side of the imagination and elements of dream content are far removed from the naïve idealism of early poems such as *Endymion* and 'Sleep and Poetry', and become important thematic concerns and focuses in Keats' later work. It would therefore be reasonable to see the seeds of such thinking here even at an early stage (the epistle was composed just after books III and IV of *Endymion* and before the entire poem's publication). Indeed, in an explanation that ties philosophic and poetical concerns to biographical ones, Motion suggests that Keats was

> heavily oppressed by his own experience, too troubled by Tom's condition and too uncertain about the future his brothers faced in America.
>
> (Motion 1997: 246)

6.5 Nightmares in the text world theory model

So far I have suggested that a dream world consisting of a nightmare can be viewed as an extreme version of a type B dream state which has decreased volition (and consequently increased automaticity) and a sense of the self under threat. The waking-criterion definition of the nightmare means that a nightmare world has inherent world-switching potential: the end of the nightmare immediately triggers a world-switch across the mentation continuum to a waking state, which may or may not correspond with the originating matrix world. The nightmare effect is consequently felt in the updating of the matrix world to account for the shift in emotional state for which the nightmare is responsible. Furthermore, the emotional intensity that exists in nightmares also marks them as vividly comparable to that experienced in waking states (in line with Coleridge's view of the nightmare as a type of in-between state, what he refers to as the 'twinkling' between sleeping and waking). This emotional intensity as a consequence of the felt expression of negative emotion manifests itself in an extreme type of dream world: *the nightmare world*.

Despite these points, there is little that allows us to explain the linguistic representation of negative states and emotional intensity in nightmares. The following sections therefore draw on two further areas that I feel need to be addressed. First, since accounts of nightmares, both real and fictional, make extensive use of lexical and syntactic negation (see, for example, Belicki and Cuddy 1996; Garfield 1996), Section 6.6 focuses on negation. Secondly, I use Stockwell's (2009) work on attention and resonance as a way of accounting for the kinds of emotional intensity realised or felt in the act of experiencing, writing about or conceptualising the nightmare.

6.6 Negation

6.6.1 Logical and pragmatic approaches to negation

From a logical semantic perspective, negation can be viewed as a way of constructing from any proposition, p, its negative ~p. As Lyons (1977a) explains, this provides a system from which we can assign truth values to utterances as in the following:

> Anthony loved Cleopatra = p
> It is not the case that Anthony loved Cleopatra = ~p
> If p is true, then ~p is false
> If p is false, then ~p is true.
>
> Lyons (1977a: 143)

This treatment of negation is unsatisfactory from pragmatic and cognitive perspectives since it pays little attention to the real contexts in which negative utterances typically appear and which provide rich meaning beyond that of a simple propositional value (Givón 1989, Jordan 1998). As Givón (1993:188) indicates, an explanation of negation in logical terms can only account for a superficial understanding of how negation *functions* in language. In contrast, pragmatic attempts to explain negation have arisen from the premises that negative constructions are harder to process than their positive counterparts (Wason 1961), evident in the fact that children find negative words harder to acquire than positive ones (Clark and Clark 1977) and that negation is a phenomenon that emphasises the defeating of a certain expectation arising from the text that a reader/listener understands as part of a presupposed background (Wason 1965; Givón 1993). Leech (1983), for example, explains the use of negation through Grice's (1975) conversational maxims and the notion of implicature. In the first instance, Leech proposes negation to be the flouting of the Gricean maxim of quantity since negative expressions tend to be less informative than positive ones. He uses his sub-maxim of 'negative uninformativeness' (Leech 1983: 101) to explain how since positive versions carry greater informativity, the choice of a negative construction must signal a particular exception to the rule and draw attention to the specific informativity of the negative construction. He uses the following examples to illustrate his case.

> [39] Abraham Lincoln was not shot by Ivan Mazeppa
> [40] Abraham Lincoln was shot by John Wilkes Booth.
> (Leech 1983: 100, original numbering)

Leech argues that there is clearly a greater number of people apart from Ivan Mazeppa who could fulfil the adverbial role in sentence [39], as opposed to those who could accurately fulfil the role in sentence [40]; consequently then, [40] is sufficiently focused enough to be inherently more informative. In other cases, the violation of the maxim of manner can be used to explain those negative constructions that are just as informative as positive ones. So, in an example such as 'our cat is not male', Leech suggests that the preference of the marked over an unmarked construction, such as 'our cat is female', is a deliberate violation of the maxim of manner. Consequently, the utterance can be seen as one of denial (Leech 1983: 101).

Jordan (1998) criticises Leech's 'Abraham Lincoln' examples by arguing that these insufficiently deal with context since they do not take account of the wider situation of each utterance nor 'why it was uttered as part of a broader passage or exchange of views' (Jordan 1998: 708). Jordan's point here is that there are clearly a number of possible contexts in which sentence [39] is inherently more informative and meaningful than [40], for example (although admittedly far-fetched), a student erroneously thinking that Ivan Mazeppa was responsible for the death of Abraham Lincoln.[13]

Jordan instead proposes a contextual view of negation on the basis of an understanding that the denial of expectation does not always have to occur as a result of the reader's presupposition being created earlier in the text. He cites the example of a 'NO ENTRY' sign, where there is no previous text to create an expectation in a reader's mind. In a similar way, he draws attention to extra-textual cultural knowledge that could create an expectation that negation then denies (see also Givón 1993: 188; Pagano 1994: 258). In this way, Jordan stresses the role that background encyclopaedic knowledge plays in understanding a need

> for the consideration of the *wider context of situation* (the 'contextual' considerations) in many instances of negation – not just textual matters of connection and cohesion.
>
> (Jordan 1998: 711), added emphasis)

Givón (2005) also holds a more discourse-based concept of context in relation to negation. He identifies three context types, each corresponding to a neuro-cognitive representation and retrieval system.

Context	Representation system
The shared generic network	Permanent semantic memory
The shared speech situation	Working memory/attention focus
The shared current text	Early episodic memory

(Givón 2005: 101)

In this model, the shared generic network refers to those shared knowledge items and understood conventions that are essentially generic (although they may of course be culturally specific). Givón gives the following examples:

a. There was once a man who **didn't** have a head
b. There was once a man who had a head
c. There was once a man who **didn't** look like a frog
d. There was once a man who looked like a frog.

(Givón (1993: 189, original emphasis)

Examples (a) and (d) are understood to be unusual and accepted as pragmatically felicitous since they defeat expectations set up from the shared knowledge that (a) men have heads and (b) men don't (usually) look like frogs. In this respect, the shared generic network can be compared to Werth's notion of *general knowledge*

(1999: 94). In contrast, the notion of the shared speech situation refers to the spatial and temporal deictic parameters that define a current discourse event, and which can be referred to by participants largely through deictic referencing. The shared notion of text allows for the understanding that recently transacted discourse is still accessible to both discourse participants and is referenced through the use of anaphora (Givón 2005: 103). These last two contexts can therefore be considered as similar to Werth's notion of *mutual knowledge* (1999: 94), and overall, Givón's notion of context can be seen as similar to Werth's building up of the discourse *common ground* (1999: 95).

6.6.2 Negation in cognitive linguistics

6.6.2.1 *Negation, schemas and frames*

A similar emphasis on a wider context of situation is inherent in a schema-frame semantics treatment of negation (Fillmore 1985; Pagano 1994). As schemas are responsible for determining sets of expectations, negation can be viewed as a process that either seeks to deny an understood part of that particular schema or, in more extreme cases, is part of a larger process of discourse deviance leading to schema disruption and refreshment (Cook 1994). Pagano provides a clear example of the first kind of process.

> If somebody comments after a picnic *The picnic was nice but* **nobody took any food**, it is because they expected the people going picnicking to take food. 'Food' is a defining element in the schema of a picnic. If, on the other hand, somebody commented *The picnic was nice but* **nobody watered the grass**, this would sound an odd comment on a picnic: when you go on a picnic, you do not normally water the grass of the place where you stay. This seems to indicate that the things we can plausibly deny concerning a schema have to be considered as likely to be part of that schema.
>
> (Pagano 1994: 257, original emphasis)

Fillmore draws attention to the difference between *context sensitive* and *context free* negation using the following examples:

> a. Her father doesn't have any teeth
> b. Her father doesn't have any walnut shells.
>
> (Fillmore 1985: 241)

Example (a) is context-free in Fillmore's terms since there is no need for participants to make use of any contextual knowledge from a previous part of the discourse. Instead, the general frames of FATHERS and THE HUMAN FACE are used and the negative construction modifies this general frame knowledge for this instance to provide a specific understanding of the physical characteristics of this particular individual (Fillmore 1985: 242). This type of negation again relies on a similar principle to Werth's notion of general knowledge as part of the common discourse ground. In comparison, example (b) needs to be supported by a specific context since the proposition lacks an interpretative structure on its own (Fillmore 1985: 242). Indeed since the general frame of FATHER does not contain the property of WALNUTS, there can be no inherent understanding in the same way as in example (a). Consequently, a meaningful expression can only occur through some additional context. This context could, of course, be any one of Givón's context types.

In a study that combines the stylistic treatment of literary discourse with schema theory, Cook (1994: 190) identifies three types of experience: direct sensory experience, experience mediated through language but representing a state of reality and experience mediated through language, with no corresponding reality state but promoting an illusory or imaginative one. Cook argues that typically literary discourse is of the last type and allows for a relatively safe re-organisation of schematic knowledge since reading is essentially (although not always of course) a private experience (1994: 191). Consequently, Cook classifies discourse as either schema reinforcing, preserving or disrupting (which in turn leads to schema refreshment).[14] In Cook's model, schema refreshment arises as a result of deviation at more than one of the interrelated hierarchical levels of world schemata, text schemata and language schemata, corresponding to world knowledge, text structure and linguistic form (1994: 197). Consequently, patterns of normality and deviation at these three levels will result in either schema preservation or refreshment (1994: 200). Finally, Cook suggests that the quality of schema refreshment relies on a comparison between existing knowledge or expectation and text structure and language.

> A reader's feeling that the text structure or linguistic choices of a given discourse are normal or deviant derives from a comparison of its text structure (T) and its language (L) with the reader's pre-existing text schemata S(T) and language schemata S(L). The interaction of these interactions creates the illusion of a 'world' in the discourse (W), which can then be compared with the world schemata of the reader, yielding a judgement as to the normality or deviance of the illusory world.
>
> (Cook 1994: 201)

Although Cook does not treat negation directly, it is clear that any perceived deviance at (T) and (L) levels could be as a result of negative constructions, resulting in a particular kind of discourse (W) which is compared to existing world schemata. At this level, Cook's approach is completely consistent with a view of negation that explores its impact as both the defeating of expectations and more radical re-organisation of existing knowledge.

Hwang (1992) provides a detailed exploration of the function of negation in narrative discourse, drawing attention to the use of negation at both a micro and macro level. Hwang asserts that in narratives which might usually be expected to report sequences of events rather than non-events, negatives are used to draw attention to some kind of break from an expectation or normally expected pattern based on previous narrative detail or cultural expectation, what Givón (1979: 139) refers to as the *presuppositional nature of negation*. To illustrate his point, Hwang uses the following examples from *The Three Little Pigs*.

> (2) **But** the house of bricks did **not** fall down
> (3) The wolf was very angry, **but** he pretended **not** to be
> (4) The little pig was very frightened, **but** he pretended **not** to be
> (5) The little pig was very frightened, **but** he said **nothing**.
>
> (Hwang 1992: 325, original emphasis)

In example 2, the expectation from the previous narrative events is that the third pig's house will be blown down by the wolf, since this has happened to the houses of the first and second little pigs. The negative construction therefore marks this as a break in the script set up as part of a 'textual expectation' (1992: 325). On the other hand, examples 3–5 are breaks as a result of generic cultural knowledge about feelings of anger and fear and normal human (or at least those of pigs being given human characteristics) reactions to them. In both cases, the updating text knowledge is at a localised level. Alternatively, negation may be seen as acting at a more global level. So for example, Hwang suggests that turning and high tension points in a narrative that lead to plot changes are often realised by negative constructions acting under the control of 'the macrostructure, the germinal idea of the whole discourse' (1992: 321).

6.6.2.2 *The ontology of negation*

Givón (1979, 1993) discusses the ontology of negative properties and events from a cognitive perspective by using the notions of *figure* and *ground*. He discusses an imaginary universe where one type of property and two individual entities, one possessing that property and one not possessing that property, exist. Since it would be impossible to decide which entity was marked by the presence of the property and which by the absence, either could be foreground as the prominent figure against the ground (background). In contrast, in a universe where there was a perceived difference between a set of 24 individuals and one lone individual, it would be easy to see the single individual as standing out from the rest, given its perceptual saliency against the ground of 24. Givón explains that in this instance, assigning the value 'having the property' to the 24 individuals would be uneconomical since there would be a further need to differentiate between these. However, assigning the value of 'having the property' to the single individual is a cognitively economical enterprise and marks the positive, informative item as the figure against the ground (Givón 1979: 132–3).

In a similar way, event processes that represent changes are necessarily more infrequent than non-events or stasis (Givón 1993: 93). These can then be generally understood as cognitively salient figures against the ground of non-events. Negation necessarily inverts this figure-ground relationship by presenting the lack of change as a more informative counter-norm against the corresponding affirmative event which remains in the background. Givón provides the following example.

a. When John comes, I'll leave
b. When John **doesn't** come, I'll leave.

(Givón 1993: 193)

Clearly, (a) appears felicitous since the change (John coming) is much more infrequent and thus stands as figure to the non-event (John not coming), which must, by definition, occur more frequently.[15]

6.6.2.3 *Negation as conceptual comparison*

The positioning of a negative construction as the perceptual figure against the understood background of its affirmative counterpart is in line with a more broadly cognitive linguistic view of negation as primarily an act of comparison between a real situation that lacks some element and an imaginary situation that contains it (Lawler 2010). Thus, Langacker (1991: 134) compares two mental spaces, 'M', which contains a given entity and the negative version of that space in which the entity does not appear but which is made textually explicit through either clausal or nominal grounding. The cognitive explanation for negation is therefore a process of conceptual comparison, where 'negation evokes as background the positive conception of what is being denied' (Langacker

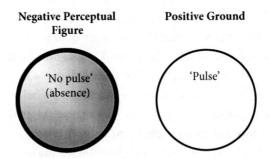

Figure 6.3 Negation as conceptual contrast

2008: 59).[16] For example, in the penultimate line of Keats' *Lamia*, the description of the dead Lycius as found by his friends 'no pulse, or breath they found' (310) is given structure and realised in its linguistic manifestation through nominal grounding, which allows conceptual comparison with its positive counterpart. The space in which 'no pulse' exists receives attention as a figure against the ground of its positive counterpart. This can be seen in Figure 6.3.

6.6.3 Types of negation

Givón (1993) differentiates between three types of negation. The first two involve some modification to a pre-existing affirmative structure: *syntactic negation* or *VP-negation* by using a negating operator, with a further sub-type of *contracted syntactic negation*; and *morphological negation* by using a prefix, also known as *affixal negation* (Givón 1984: 346). Givón refers to the third type, where lexical items, usually adjectives or verbs, hold inherently negative value by incorporating a negative operator into their structure as *lexical* or *incorporated negation* (1984: 345) and later as *inherent negation* (1993: 202).[17] Examples of the three types of negation, all taken from Lamia, are as follows:

> *Syntactic*
> Thou **didst not hear**/The soft, lute fingered Muses chanting clear (72–3);
> *Morphological/affixal*
> Were strewn rich gifts, **unknown** to any Muse (19);
> *Inherent/lexical/incorporated*
> The ever-smitten Hermes **empty** left. (7)

Inherent negation (I shall adopt Givón's (1993) term) has received relatively little interest and coverage than either syntactic or morphological negation (again I adopt Givón's (1993) term). For example, Nørgaard (2007), despite a detailed examination of negative polarity as a stylistic marker of characterisation and viewpoint in James Joyce's 'Two Gallants', suggests that inherent negation, although interesting in its own right within literary linguistics, remains a less concrete and more of a 'fuzzy area of semantically determined categorisation' (2007: 37) to suggest warranting further discussion.

A relative lack of focus on inherent negation in other examples of stylistic practice (e.g. Hidalgo Downing 2000b, 2003) could well be explained by the less obviously marked nature of the inherent form as well as by the fact that syntactic and morphological negation tend to represent stronger acts of denial and the defeating of expectations (Givón 1984: 346). However, in the following example, taken from Keats' 'What can I do to drive away', it becomes clear that inherent negation can produce striking stylistic effects that are worthy of consideration:

> Where shall I learn to get my peace again?
> To banish thoughts of that most hateful land,
> Dungeoner of my friends, that wicked strand
> Where they were wrecked and live a wreckèd life;
> That monstrous region, whose dull rivers pour,
> Ever from their sordid urns into the shore. (30–5)

In this part of the poem, the speaker creates a boulomaic desire world as a way of escaping and alternative to the more heavily fleshed-out and negatively charged text world, evident in the choice of the positive lexical item 'peace' (30) and a series of inherently negative terms: 'hateful' (31), 'dungeoner' (32), 'wicked' (32), wrecked' (33), 'wreckèd' (33), 'monstrous' (34) 'dull' (34) and 'sordid' (35). This seems to me to have two effects. First, it creates a rich series of negative constructions which may be seen as one unified world in comparison with the less richly formed desire space. In fact, the introduction of these inherently negative lexical items draws cognitive attention to their positive counterparts, which implicitly (since we might assume that they are wished for) form part of the desire world but which the use of inherent negation simultaneously denies. This dual mechanism of introducing and denying is an example of what Werth calls *negative accommodation* (see Chapter 2), albeit this time using inherent rather than syntactic or morphological forms. Secondly, since the weighting is heavily in favour of negative polarity, the modal force of the desire world is relatively weak: the 'stacking up' of a negative deictic space means that the speaker's desire to free himself from the woes of life is seen as increasingly difficult to the point of being impossible. In fact, at the end of the poem, the speaker resorts to puerile

and erotic fantasy as a means of escapism in the construction of a modally
weaker dream world:

> 'Enough! Enough! It is enough for me
> To dream of thee! (56–7)

This would clearly seem to support this very reading of a desire world negated
by a stronger opposing force.

6.6.4 Text world theory and negation

As I discussed in Chapter 2, Werth proposes that there are two kinds of
negation. In *prototypical negation*, a negative construction acting as a negative
sub-world with a different set of deictic parameters from that of the matrix
world denies or defeats an expectation held in the participants' common ground
and subsequently identified in the text world. Since the denial or defeating of
expectations permanently alters the deictic make-up of the matrix world, the
negative construction can be understood as updating through the process of
incrementation. The second type, *negative accommodation*, occurs when a
negative construction both introduces an entity or process and simultaneously
denies it. Again since in this instance, the notion of accessibility is taken to an
extreme, negative accommodation is best viewed as an example of incrementation
or world updating.

In Chapter 2, I also discussed Werth's dissatisfaction with the notion of sub-
world machinery to account for negation since the act of negating, as noted
above, appears to act outside of Werth's own sub-world functioning (1999:
255). In this case and given that recent developments in text world theory have
dispensed with the term sub-world altogether (Gavins 2005a), we might consider
negation simply as a type of world-switch. In this case, the world-switch allows
for the type of conceptual contrast to take place that was explained in Section
6.5.2.3. In this instance, a text world containing positive entities or propositions
is contrasted with its negative counterpart, and it is the negated entity or state
of affairs that assumes attention as figure in the conceptual contrast. This can be
demonstrated by returning to the example we previously looked at from *Lamia*:
'No pulse or breath they found'.

In this example, the negative construction, triggered by the negator 'no',
has influential scope over both nouns 'pulse' and 'breath'. This demands a
conceptualisation of a text world in the form of a world-switch in which Lycius
has a pulse and is breathing but where attention is returned to the matrix world

where this is not the case. The matrix world is updated through this conceptual contrast, since in this case it is responsible for the defeating of expectations: we expect bodies to have pulses and breathe and we know that Lycius has been alive up until this point in the poem.

6.6.5 Measuring negative intensity: Attention and resonance

In Section 6.2.2, I described how one of the defining features of the nightmare in experienced and represented forms is the intensity both of emotion and of a particular striking, central image or set of images. Since research in sleep medicine has shown that both recounts of nightmares in general, and specific episodes or images from nightmare events are more vividly remembered, it can be argued that they have greater resonance than other types of dreams. In this section, I consider how these manifestations of intensity are shown stylistically by using Stockwell's (2009) attention-resonance model as a way of capturing the intensity inherent in the nightmare world. As text world theory has generally been more concerned with exploring movement across worlds, in world edges or boundaries and in the perceived difference in texture between types of world,[18] the following aims to look more closely at the deictic make-up of world-building elements within the text world itself.

Stockwell (2009: 18) defines resonance as a 'measurement of intensity' and proposes a model that develops work in cognitive psychology (e.g. Styles 2006) to account for how perceptual elements are configured to generate a coherent form in keeping with the basic cognitive configuration of figure-ground. Attractors, which form the basis of perceptual attention, are given prominence and 'figure-ness' in literary discourse through being *newly introduced* or through the *maintenance* of existing attractor elements. The deictic space they invoke is maintained either by *sustaining* a focus or by the absence of any explicit movement towards a competing element or alternative deictic centre.[19] Those elements not selected for attention consequently become *neglected*. In addition, a reader may *disengage* with a previous attractor, through either the conscious *lifting* of the element out of the attentional field or a more subtle movement away from it in perceptual saliency as a form of *drag*. A more direct removal of attention through another element taking over perceptual prominence occurs through *occlusion*, either instantaneous (e.g. the mentioning of the removal of an element) or more gradual (e.g. the gradual fading away of an element through its not being textually maintained). The model is completed with the understanding that the movement from attraction to occlusion is mirrored by a *cline of prominence* that identifies degrees of figured elements against their background and a *cline of resonance* ranging from strong intensity at one end to echo and resonance at the other.

Stockwell also identifies a list of the characteristics of typically good textual attractors. I refer to these in my discussion of world zooms in *The Eve of St Agnes* in Chapter 5. For ease of reference, these are also reproduced below.

- *newness*
- *agency*
- *topicality*
- *empathetic responsibility*
- *definiteness*
- *activeness*
- *brightness*
- *fullness*
- *largeness*
- *height*
- *noisiness*
- *aesthetic distance from the norm*

Stockwell (2009: 25)

Since I am arguing that absence is best understood as a figure against the background of the affirmative counterpart proposition, it is clearly possible to describe syntactic and morphological negation as prototypical attractors. In this way, these forms of negation could be exemplified in any of the above ways. So, returning to the line 'no pulse or breath they found' from *Lamia*, it is the absence rather than the presence of these attributes that become understood as the focus of attention. Perceived in contrast to their affirmative counterparts, they are conceptualised as felt absences, *negative blobs* (Carstensen 2007) or *lacunae* (Stockwell 2009: 32) and as examples of instant occlusion (the occluded element here is Lycius's life) through the two uses of the negating particle 'no'. This in conjunction with the unconventional complement-subject-verb syntax, which places the absence of life as a conceptual figure, provides the heavily resonant final image of death to the poem and leads to the updated text world that starkly presents Lycius's death.

Stockwell's model is perhaps more useful for accounting for inherent negation. In my discussion of lines 30–5 from 'What can I do to drive away' in Section 6.5.3, I demonstrate some of the effects generated by clusters of inherently negative lexical items, suggesting that the rich negative deictic space set up by their use could be seen as an example of Werth's negative accommodation. These lines are reproduced below with inherently negative lexical items in italics.

> Where shall I learn to get my peace again?
> To *banish* thoughts of that most *hateful* land,
> *Dungeoner* of my friends, that *wicked* strand
> Where they were *wrecked* and live a *wreckèd* life;
> That *monstrous* region, whose *dull* rivers pour,
> Ever from their *sordid* urns into the shore. (30–5)

In these lines, negatively oriented lexical items are attentionally prominent and figure strongly in the violent verb 'banish' (31) and the noun 'dungeoner', which is in turn given structural prominence at the head of line 32. The adjectives 'hateful' (31), 'wicked' (32), 'wreckèd' (33), 'monstrous', 'dull' (34) and 'sordid' (35) acting as pre-modifiers in noun phrases are all marked as denoting a considerable distance from an expected norm and are intensely evaluative. Equally, the use of a complement adjective 'wrecked' (33) is suggestive of an absoluteness. The intensity of description is evident in the superlative construction 'most hateful' (31) and the emphasis on dark colouring 'dull' and 'sordid', which prevents any strong competing attractor from emerging as a figure. In short, the tight negative deictic space creates a strong negatively oriented landscape that resonates in its darkness. As I suggest, this resonance makes it impossible for any modal desire world to be realised.

As a final example of how inherently negative lexical items are responsible for providing a sense of intensity, I return to my discussion of 'La belle dame sans merci' in Section 6.2.1. The knight's dream world is reproduced as Figure 6.4, with the inherently negative lexical items underlined.

Figure 6.4 Dream world in 'La belle dame sans merci'

As I have discussed earlier in this chapter, the world-switch into the dream at this point in the poem is responsible for allowing the reader to understand the knight's psychological constitution and his relationship to the physical landscape as part of a process of incrementation. In this instance, the deictic parameters are set up by the description of firstly the kings, and then the princes and warriors as 'pale' and then 'death-pale'. Thus, the focus is maintained through both the repetition of 'pale' and the reference-chaining lexis 'too' and 'all'. The intensity of the experience is heightened by the use of the compound 'death-pale' and by the agency afforded to them in their ability to speak. In stanza XI, the placing of strong physical descriptions from a FACE frame provides maintenance through metonymic association. These descriptions formed from exaggerated dissonance, 'starved lips', and the extended noun phrase denoting quantity of size, 'horrid warning gaped wide', are perceived as attractors and given prominence against the dimness of the background of the locative prepositional phrase 'in the gloam'. The darkening down of the background allows for the positioning of the horrific images as strong perceptual figures and is understood as part of the conventional use of lexical items to represent negative events.[20] The waking moment instigates a world-switch to an alternative deictic space, where the occlusion of the kings, princes and warriors is gradual rather than instant – they are simply not mentioned again. The attractors, marked by their intensity and inherently negative content, retain a resonance that is felt back in the text world, in contrast to the barren landscape inhabited by the narrator and knight in the poem.

The use of this model provides a framework for accounting for the intensity of a recounted nightmare experience that is in line with accounts of the phenomenon in sleep medicine. It provides a way of systematically accounting for a particular type of dream world, which I term the *nightmare world*.

6.7 The Nightmare world model

My discussion of nightmares and negation in previous sections suggests that for the purposes of text world theory, a nightmare world can be defined and understood in the following ways:

1. The nightmare world is any representation (including that for literary effect) of a nightmare, understood as an unpleasant dream that causes the dreamer to awaken. This means that the nightmare world is understood as a world that inherently holds its return potential to the matrix world, which in turn

is updated as a result of the nightmare experience. The decomposition of the nightmare world, triggered either explicitly or implicitly, further updates the originating world since its impact is felt as an integral part of the reading experience, manifesting itself in a type of resonance.

2. The nightmare is an extreme kind of type B dream world. Its automaticity means that it is purely epistemic, yet it retains the intensity and vividness of waking thought. This manifests itself in the understanding of the immediate waking moment as captured in the moment of transition from dreaming to waking.

3. The nightmare world as a relayed representation of experience is characterised by its lexical, semantic and emotional intensity. This may be in the form of a central image (or set of images), or a marked sense of negative colouring through any one of the three types of negation: syntactic, morphological and inherent. These act as clusters of stylistic attractors that are responsible for representing the types of felt resonance of the nightmare experience. This intensity can be measured stylistically by using the attention-resonance model proposed by Stockwell (2009).

4. Negation relies on a reversal of figure and ground so that an affirmative proposition becomes the expected background against which the negative construction is more perceptually salient. Consequently, the nightmare world may be seen as mirroring this structure so that its deviant nature, both structurally and in contrast to a desired set of affairs, becomes more salient in the discourse event. This allows the nightmare world to be seen as a key and meaningful structure in its own right.

5. A nightmare world is therefore responsible for the denying and defeating of expectations, including those elements that would normally be part of an assumed desire world. At a local level, these may work to negate with textual or culturally specific expectations. At a more global level, these may represent key turning points in comparison with alternative discourse levels, including being responsible for schema disruption and subsequent refreshment.

6. The movement in literary texts between waking states and nightmare worlds can be analysed stylistically to draw attention to salient patterns and their potential effects on interpretation. Equally, the nightmare world can also be seen as a discrete discourse unit that is more complex and cognitively challenging than both worlds at a higher ontological level and dreams worlds at the same level. It thus lends itself to being analysed using a text world theory approach.

6.8 Review

In this chapter, I have set out a proposal for a nightmare world to be incorporated into text world theory. In Sections 6.1 and 6.2, I discussed the phenomenology of the nightmare and explained the importance of using the waking-criterion in a definition of the nightmare. This was used to show how an emerging view of the nightmare world includes its inherent world-switching abilities from one mentation state to another. In these sections, I used McNamara's taxonomy of the formal features of the nightmare to anticipate my definition of the nightmare world later in the chapter. These sections also included a discussion of nightmare function and drew attention to research that noted the marked emotional content of nightmares. In Section 6.3, I provided an overview of nineteenth-century views of the nightmare and, in particular, looked at Coleridge's treatment of nightmares and disturbing dreams as well as illustrated examples of how the nightmare became used in a literary context among Keats' contemporaries. In Section 6.4, I proposed a need for the *nightmare world* to account for its own negative lexical and semantic values. This led to a detailed discussion in Section 6.5, of negation as a form of conceptual contrast. Finally, I adopted Stockwell's (2009) attention-resonance model to account for the intensity and resonance of negatively oriented lexis as part of the nightmare experience. This chapter therefore has anticipated my detailed analyses of three of Keats' poems in the following chapters, by proposing a plausible model for the nightmare world to be incorporated into text world theory.

Isabella; or, The Pot of Basil

7.1 Introduction

In Chapter 6, I suggested that a nightmare world should be considered an extreme type B dream world that captured some of the typical characteristics of the nightmare both stylistically and iconically. These were, namely, a striking intensity in imagery, often around a central contextualising image or set of images, and a reliance on negation as a salient matter of style. In this chapter, I explore Keats' use of the nightmare world in his narrative poem *Isabella; or The Pot of Basil*, focusing on the representation of Isabella's nightmare experience as a central and defining moment.

In Sections 7.2 and 7.3, I provide an overview of the poem's origins, conception and central ideas, drawing attention to a range of existing critical opinion relevant to my discussion. In Section 7.4, I use text world theory to draw attention to the conceptual structure of the opening stanzas of the poem, arguing that the setting up of remote and unrealised dream worlds is important in anticipating their demise later in the poem in contrast to the more powerful desire worlds of Isabella's capitalist brothers. I continue with this emphasis on function in Section 7.5 by focusing on the two nightmare experiences that sit at the heart of the poem. Despite acknowledging the importance of Isabella's vision of her dead lover Lorenzo as a turning point in the poem, few if any critical accounts have focused explicitly on either the language of the vision or subsequent sections of the poem as a direct consequence of the nightmare itself. In this section, I provide an account of this phenomenon that highlights the nightmare both as a significant textual event and reading experience, and considers its resonance throughout and impact on the remainder of the poem. I also draw attention to how Keats' construction of a nightmare world acts as an important contrast to the desire and dream worlds that form the focus of the opening half of the poem. Finally, in Section 7.6, I argue that Keats utilises the nightmare experience and the conceptualisation of a nightmare world as a type of *information route* for the reader into Isabella's psyche. I also suggest a way that in the context of Keats' own changing ideas on the role and validity of the imagination, the use of an explicitly unpleasant dream can be seen as an educative experience for Isabella.

7.2 Origins and conception

Isabella was the second poem in Keats' 1820 volume *Lamia, Isabella, The Eve of St Agnes and Other Poems* and is thought to have been written in the early months of 1818 and before the publication of *Endymion* The poem, based on a narrative in Boccaccio's 'Decameron', was initially part of a collaboration between Keats and Reynolds, who had planned a volume of English verse inspired and influenced by the Italian poet, with Reynolds eventually publishing two of his own poems in 1821 (Cox 2009).[1]

Stillinger (2009) argues that Keats' reading of Wordsworth had a profound influence on the poem and, in particular, on Keats' decision to foreground certain aspects not present in the original, such as the extended focus on the lovers at the beginning and a stronger emphasis on the strange, the macabre and 'the gruesome' (Stillinger 2009: 29). He draws attention to shared thematic concerns between *Isabella* and 'Michael' and 'The Ruined Cottage' from Book I of *The Excursion* and echoes of language from Wordsworth's characterisation of Martha Ray in 'The Thorn'. Lagory (1995: 332) also emphasises the influence of Keats' reading of Wordsworth at this stage of his career by drawing attention to a similar focus on Isabella's psychological development to that of the heroine in Wordsworth's 'Immortality' ode. Equally, the omnipresent echoes of Shakespeare's *Romeo and Juliet*, developed in different ways in the later poems *The Eve of St Agnes* and *Lamia*, can be found in Keats' treatment of his young lovers, doomed to an early death and tragic fate. Goellnicht (1984), Richardson (2001) and Turley (2004) all argue that Keats made extensive use of his medical training and employed a distinct scientific lexicon to provide realistic descriptions of both the murder and later decapitation of Lorenzo.

The poem has one of the more complex revision histories. Affected by the negative reviews of *Endymion*, Keats had for some time suggested that the poem was unfit for publication (*Letters* II, 174, n.194),[2] and it was finally published nearly two years after Keats' initial draft. In the process of producing a final transcript, Woodhouse made substantial changes to the early version, mostly focusing on aspects of punctuation and vocabulary choices (Stillinger 1974: 182–6). Leader (1996: 294) suggests that Woodhouse's central concern was that the poem would be a commercial success; ensuring that it did not attract the kind of criticism of style that was levelled at *Endymion* was therefore at the heart of the corrections that he made.

7.3 Thematic concerns and critical response

The poem's narrative centres on Isabella and her two merchant brothers, who wish her to be married into nobility to protect their own pecuniary interests. Isabella however has fallen in love with Lorenzo, an employee of the brothers, and of the opening sections of the poem detail the intensely secretive, yet ultimately unfulfilling imaginative world that the lovers inhabit. This intimacy is destroyed by the brothers who on discovering the romance, murder Lorenzo. Lorenzo's ghost appears to Isabella and directs her to the place where his body is buried. In an attempt to reanimate their relationship, she severs the head and buries it in a pot of basil, feeding it with her tears. This second relationship is again destroyed by the brothers who steal the basil pot before fleeing into exile, leaving Isabella to once more mourn her lost love, and descend into madness and ultimately death. The poem ends with its narrator mourning the loss of Isabella, but stressing how sympathy for her will survive through the subsequent retellings of her story.

Keats' feelings on the poem are well documented. In a letter to Woodhouse on the 21–22 September 1819, he voiced his fears that the poem would be open to criticism because of its sentimentality, claiming that the poem was too 'smokeable', that there was 'too much inexperience of live [sic] and simplicity of knowledge in it' and that 'Isabella is what I should call were I a reviewer "A weak-sided Poem with an amusing sober-sadness about it"' (*Letters* II, 174, n.194). However, as Everest (1995: 110) suggests, the savage reviews of 'Endymion' were more likely to have been responsible for Keats' wariness over 'Isabella' than any strong feeling on his own part that the poem was a poetic failure. Heinzelman (1988: 186) takes a similar view of Keats' judgement of the likely reception of the poem by placing this letter in the context of Keats' clear concerns about the 'politics of the literary marketplace', and his own economic welfare and stability. Early reviews of the 1820 volume were mixed. The reviewer for the *Monthly Review* called the poem 'the worst part of the volume' (Schwartz 1973: 204), while a review in the *St James's Chronicle* criticised the poem's style as similar to *Endymion* by commenting on its 'effected peculiarity of expression' (Schwartz 1973: 206). More favourable reviews as expected came from Leigh Hunt in *The Indicator* and Charles Lamb in the *New Times*, who called it 'the finest thing in the volume' (Schwartz 1973: 211). Many early reviewers drew comparisons between Keats' poem and Barry Cornwall's earlier version of the same tale *A Sicilian Story*, which presents incestuous jealousy rather than economic concern as the motivating force for the sole brother's murder of Lorenzo (Schwartz 1973: 221, 233, 261).

Despite its prominent position in the 1820 volume, the poem was omitted from many of the dominant critical studies of Keats in the early and mid-twentieth century. Stillinger (1971: 37) captures the feeling of many mid-twentieth century critics by suggesting that there is an overriding sense of 'puzzlement' towards the poem and its intended meaning. Later developments in historicism, materialism and feminism have led to a renewed focus on the poem, and fresh interpretations. Both Heinzelman (1988) and Watkins (1989) read the poem as situated firmly in the political and economic climate of 1818–1819, and emphasise the impact such a climate had on Keats' views of himself as a working writer. Everest (1995: 110), on the other hand, argues that a reading of the poem founded on a crude distinction between 'Romantic enchantment' and 'colder actuality' (see also, for example, Sharrock 1961; Sandy 2000) is too simplistic and instead stresses the increased irony with which the lovers' self-marginalisation is presented, which 'questions the viability of their idealism' (Everest 1995: 113).

Other readings of the poem have focused on its position as a clear marker of a development in Keats' poetic and narrative style and his awareness of the roles of both author and reader in the (re)writing of history (Bennett 1994) and as a powerful example of negative capability in the poet's characterisation of Isabella (Jones 1969). Lagory (1995) draws attention to the nurturing of Lorenzo's head in the pot of basil as a type of maternal action that emphasises the regenerative aspect of Isabella's actions in the later part of the poem. Smith (1974) argues that ultimately, images of regeneration balance out those of death, and Heinzelman (1988) suggests that this regeneration is mirrored in the replacing of an older economic social order by one that is founded on human sympathy and sustained by art, evident in the grief shared by the citizens of Florence, the sharing of the 'sad ditty' throughout the country and its resonant echo as a result of subsequent readings of the poem.

7.4 The representation of love (1): Desire in stanzas I–IX

I

Fair Isabel, poor simple Isabel!
   Lorenzo, a young palmer in Love's eye!
They could not in the self-same mansion dwell
   Without some stir of heart, some malady;
They could not sit at meals but feel how well   5
   It soothed each to be the other by;
They could not, sure, beneath the same roof sleep
But to each other dream, and nightly weep.

II

With every morn their love grew tenderer,
   With every eve deeper and tenderer still;   10
He might not in house, field, or garden stir,
   But her full shape would all his seeing fill;
And his continual voice was pleasanter
   To her, than noise of trees or hidden rill;
Her lute-string gave an echo of his name,   15
She spoilt her half-done broidery with the same.

III

He knew whose gentle hand was at the latch,
   Before the door had given her to his eyes;
And from her chamber-window he would catch
   Her beauty farther than the falcon spies;   20
And constant as her vespers would he watch,
   Because her face was turn'd to the same skies;
And with sick longing all the night outwear,
To hear her morning-step upon the stair.

IV

A whole long month of May in this sad plight   25
   Made their cheeks paler by the break of June:

'To morrow will I bow to my delight,
    To-morrow will I ask my lady's boon.'
'O may I never see another night,
    Lorenzo, if thy lips breathe not love's tune.'   30
So spake they to their pillows; but, alas,
Honeyless days and days did he let pass -

V

Until sweet Isabella's untouch'd cheek
    Fell sick within the rose's just domain,
Fell thin as a young mother's, who doth seek   35
    By every lull to cool her infant's pain:
'How ill she is,' said he, 'I may not speak,
    And yet I will, and tell my love all plain:
If looks speak love-laws, I will drink her tears,
And at the least 'twill startle off her cares.'   40

VI

So said he one fair morning, and all day
    His heart beat awfully against his side;
And to his heart he inwardly did pray
    For power to speak; but still the ruddy tide
Stifled his voice, and puls'd resolve away—   45
    Fever'd his high conceit of such a bride,
Yet brought him to the meekness of a child:
Alas! when passion is both meek and wild!

VII

So once more he had waked and anguished
    A dreary night of love and misery,   50
If Isabel's quick eye had not been wed
    To every symbol on his forehead high;
She saw it waxing very pale and dead,
    And straight all flush'd; so, lisped tenderly,
'Lorenzo!"—here she ceas'd her timid quest,   55
But in her tone and look he read the rest.

VIII

'O Isabella, I can half perceive
    That I may speak my grief into thine ear;
If thou didst ever any thing believe,
    Believe how I love thee, believe how near   60

My soul is to its doom: I would not grieve
    Thy hand by unwelcome pressing, would not fear
Thine eyes by gazing; but I cannot live
Another night, and not my passion shrive.

IX

Love! thou art leading me from wintry cold,   65
    Lady! thou leadest me to summer clime,
And I must taste the blossoms that unfold
    In its ripe warmth this gracious morning time.'
So said, his erewhile timid lips grew bold,
    And poesied with hers in dewy rhyme: 70
Great bliss was with them, and great happiness
Grew, like a lusty flower in June's caress.

The narrative voice establishes a text world in these opening lines in which enactors of Isabella and Lorenzo are presented through a further series of desire worlds that mark the intense, secret and self-absorbed nature of their love. In stanza I, the initial representations of Isabella and Lorenzo are quickly replaced by counterparts of them in a state of desire, made possible by the metaphorical reference to Lorenzo as a 'young palmer' (2). Since text world theory treats metaphor as a kind of conceptual *double vision* (Werth 1994; Gavins 2007a), which allows for a reader to toggle between two sets of representations, the metaphorical structure acts as a kind of macro-structure (Werth 1994), identifying an enactor of Lorenzo worshipping an enactor of Isabella in an intensely private and isolated space. The metaphor, a clear allusion to Shakespeare's *Romeo and Juliet*, defines the lovers in the roles of *desirer* and *desired*, representing in particular, Isabella's sense of self as being dependent on Lorenzo's objectification. The defining of Isabella as little more than 'property value' (Heinzelman 1988: 179) here provides an avenue for the later exploitation of Isabella by her brothers.

    With this in mind, it is now possible to schematise the development of the opening four stanzas. Keats presents the self-absorbing nature of their love through a series of expressions which deny the lovers the option of being in control of their own feelings and emotions, 'they could not' (3, 5, 7).[3] These function by carrying significant degrees of obligatory modal force, and in image-schematic terms represent a combination of BLOCKAGE (Isabella and Lorenzo are prevented from acting in a certain way) and COMPULSION (they are required to demonstrate certain attributes as part of a sequence of causality) gestalt forms (Johnson 1987). These constructions are therefore best considered as functioning in the same way as deontic ones while also representing some degree of volition. I would suggest therefore that these are best viewed as type A dream worlds. The intensity of these worlds is further realised by the fact that the syntactic patterning in stanza I makes use of negation as a way of foregrounding the opposite of what might be deemed expected behaviour. So, the line 'they could not in the self same mansion dwell' demands that we conceptualise both the negative proposition and its affirmative counterpart, and the resulting clauses further clarify what the lovers can and cannot do. Together this combination of modal force and negation provides a global coherence to the opening stanza and marks the lovers as paralysed by their own fantasies. The updated dream world is made possible by both the initial metaphor blend and those following the negated constructions. These are responsible for the process of incrementation, leading to a fuller understanding of the conditions of the lovers' world. The conceptualisation of this stanza is shown in Figure 7.1.

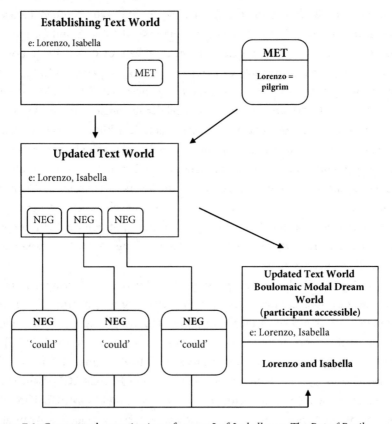

Figure 7.1 Conceptual organisation of stanza I of *Isabella; or, The Pot of Basil*

This degree of self-paralysis continues across the next two stanzas, as the lovers remain trapped in a series of dream worlds that have degrees of volition but are limited in terms of how much that desire can be realised. This is marked in stanzas II–III by a succession of references to perception verbs and noun phrases relating to sight ('seeing' (12) 'given her to his eyes' (18), 'catch her beauty' (19–20), 'watch' (21)) and to hearing ('continual voice' (13), 'gave an echo of his name' (15), 'hear her morning step' (24)). These emphases on perception and the imagined are presented above those indicating a more physical relationship, and determine the capacity of the lovers to exist simply within the constraints of their own fantasy world.

The self-limiting nature of the dream worlds that Isabella and Lorenzo inhabit remains sharply defined in stanzas IV–VII. Here, Keats utilises direct speech to show Lorenzo's intentions in a future temporal world. These form unrealised boulomaic modal desire worlds as the lovers are unable to carry out their intentions, speaking instead only 'to their pillows' (31). Consequently, since they are not fully grounded, they simply decompose. The remaining opening stanzas present a similar pattern. Lorenzo is unable to speak to Isabella since the 'ruddy tide/Stifled his voice, and pushed resolve away' (44–5). The inability to vocalise intentions and the way in which those stronger desire worlds are negated are indicative of the self-limiting aspect of the lovers in the opening section of the poem. Even when the two are finally brought together, there is a clear element of temporality to their existence, evident in the references to the seasons in stanza IX (65–72). The 'summer clime' (66) and 'June's caress' (72) are suggestive of a love that will not endure. In the opening section to the poem, the prominence given by Keats to unfulfilled dream worlds and desire spaces becomes significant when read against the later function of the nightmare world set up by the visit of Lorenzo's ghost, which does focus on physicality and voice, and retains an intensity not evident in the dream worlds within which the opening of the poem operates.

The impotence of the lovers' desire can also be measured against the stronger force of the brothers in stanzas XXI and XXII. This is shown in Figure 7.2.

Here, the brothers' intentions are more directly intimated through two boulomaic modal desire worlds: 'twas their plan to coax her by degrees/To some high noble and his olive-trees' (168) and 'For they resolvèd in some forest dim/ To kill Lorenzo, and there bury him' (176). Significantly, unlike those Keats uses to characterise Lorenzo and Isabella earlier, these have considerable modal force, given the brothers' dominant status. The first desire world, fuelled by the brothers' concern for their own well-being, allows the realisation of the second,

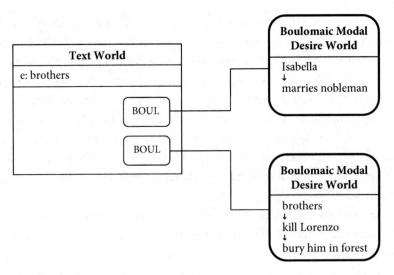

Figure 7.2 Boulomaic modal desire worlds in stanzas XXI and XXII of *Isabella; or, The Pot of Basil*

the murder of Lorenzo, which marks the turning point in the poem. These then become functionally significant as representative of the dominant economic forces at work, in contrast to the self-absorbed and ultimately powerless dream worlds of Isabella and Lorenzo.[4]

7.5 The representation of love (2): The nightmare world of stanzas XXXIII–XLI

XXXIII

Because Lorenzo came not. Oftentimes
   She asked her brothers, with an eye all pale,
Striving to be itself, what dungeon climes
   Could keep him off so long? They spake a tale   260
Time after time, to quiet her. Their crimes
   Came on them, like a smoke from Hinnom's vale;
And every night in dreams they groaned aloud,
To see their sister in her snowy shroud.

XXXIV

And she had died in drowsy ignorance,   265
   But for a thing more deadly dark than all;

It came like a fierce potion, drunk by chance,
    Which saves a sick man from the feathered pall
For some few gasping moments; like a lance,
    Waking an Indian from his cloudy hall   270
With cruel pierce, and bringing him again
Sense of the gnawing fire at heart and brain.

XXXV

It was a vision.—In the drowsy gloom,
    The dull of midnight, at her couch's foot
Lorenzo stood, and wept: the forest tomb   275
    Had marr'd his glossy hair which once could shoot
Lustre into the sun, and put cold doom
    Upon his lips, and taken the soft lute
From his lorn voice, and past his loamed ears
Had made a miry channel for his tears.   280

XXXVI

Strange sound it was, when the pale shadow spake;
    For there was striving, in its piteous tongue,
To speak as when on earth it was awake,
    And Isabella on its music hung:
Languor there was in it, and tremulous shake,   285
    As in a palsied Druid's harp unstrung;
And through it moaned a ghostly under-song,
Like hoarse night-gusts sepulchral briars among.

XXXVII

Its eyes, though wild, were still all dewy bright
    With love, and kept all phantom fear aloof   290
From the poor girl by magic of their light,
    The while it did unthread the horrid woof
Of the late darkened time,—the murderous spite
    Of pride and avarice,—the dark pine roof
In the forest, and the sodden turfed dell,   295
Where, without any word, from stabs he fell.

XXXVIII

Saying moreover, 'Isabel, my sweet!
    Red whortle-berries droop above my head,
And a large flint-stone weighs upon my feet;
    Around me beeches and high chestnuts shed   300

Their leaves and prickly nuts; a sheep-fold bleat
    Comes from beyond the river to my bed:
Go, shed one tear upon my heather-bloom,
And it shall comfort me within the tomb.

XXXIX

'I am a shadow now, alas! alas!   305
    Upon the skirts of human-nature dwelling
Alone: I chant alone the holy mass,
    While little sounds of life are round me knelling,
And glossy bees at noon do fieldward pass,
    And many a chapel bell the hour is telling,   310
Paining me through: those sounds grow strange to me,
And thou art distant in humanity.

XL

'I know what was, I feel full well what is,
    And I should rage, if spirits could go mad;
Though I forget the taste of earthly bliss,   315
    That paleness warms my grave, as though I had
A Seraph chosen from the bright abyss
    To be my spouse: thy paleness makes me glad;
Thy beauty grows upon me, and I feel
A greater love through all my essence steal.'   320

XLI

The Spirit mourn'd 'Adieu!'—dissolv'd, and left
    The atom darkness in a slow turmoil;
As when of healthful midnight sleep bereft,
    Thinking on rugged hours and fruitless toil,
We put our eyes into a pillowy cleft,   325
    And see the spangly gloom froth up and boil:
It made sad Isabella's eyelids ache,
And in the dawn she started up awake -

Stanzas IX–XXXIII provide further descriptions of the brothers and explicit attacks on their capitalist enterprise. The brothers, having planned to kill Lorenzo, carry out their action and inform Isabella that Lorenzo 'had ta'en ship for foreign lands/Because of some great urgency and need/In their affairs' (226–8). When Lorenzo does not return, they maintain a series of lies to conceal the truth of their actions.

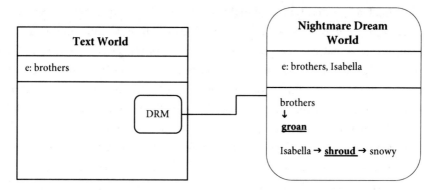

Figure 7.3 Nightmare dream world in stanza XXXIII of *Isabella; or, The Pot of Basil*

Stanzas XXXIII–XLI, shown in Figure 7.3, consist of two nightmare experiences that explain the psychological profile of their dreamers: the guilt of the murderous brothers and Isabella's grief.

Although the middle section of the poem is dominated by Isabella's vision of Lorenzo, stanza XXXIII provides a less prototypical and developed example of a nightmare world experienced by the brothers. Here, a distinct conceptual structure is triggered through the prepositional phrase 'in dreams' (263), which shifts the deictic content from one mentation state to another. Since the recounting of the nightmare experience exists in a world created by the narrator acting as an accepted discourse participant, this is a participant-accessible world, understood as unpleasant through the use of the inherently negative speech verb 'they groaned' (263), and characterised by the striking intensity of Isabella dressed in a 'snowy shroud' (264). This phrase is a strong example of an attractor through its attention to brightness, its alliterative qualities and its position both at the end of the verse line and stanza. In the absence of any other world-building elements or function-advancing propositions, it maintains a resonant, haunting quality that both stands in contrast to the image of the naive Isabella earlier and anticipates her demise at the poem's end. However, unlike a prototypical nightmare world, there is no world-switching proposition to mark the dreamer's waking and therefore no return to the matrix text world.[5]

Isabella's nightmare, occupying the central stanzas of the poem, has an important functional role.[6] In stanza XXXV, a nightmare world is triggered by the world-building clause 'it was a vision' (273). This is situated in the prominent intimate surrounding of Isabella's bed chamber 'at her couch's foot' (274), yet is dampened by the strong sense of dimming-down to provide the kind of dark menacing background typical of nightmares (see McNamara 2008 and Section 7.2.2) with inherently negative lexis: 'dull' (274), 'drowsy' and 'gloom' (273). Against this backdrop, the ghost of Lorenzo appears, given prominence as an active figure and clause subject but represented by the inherently negative verb 'wept' (275). The remainder of this stanza fleshes out the text world to amplify this initial feeling of menace and gloom. So, Lorenzo's hair, marked by a world-switch to a contrasting and strikingly intense description of him pre-death with the positively-oriented lexis 'glossy' (276), 'lustre' (277) and 'sun' (277), is now described as 'marred' (276), and similar effects are assigned to his lips, voice, ears and eyes, again represented through the inherent negation of 'cold doom' (277), 'lorn' (279), and in this context, 'loamèd' (279) and 'miry' (280). The maintained focus on these aspects of physical appearance in the current nightmare world not only presents the dreaming Isabella in an intimacy with Lorenzo that was not afforded to the enactors of the lovers in the early stages of the poem, but also acts as a strong contrast to the previously cued-up enactor of Lorenzo. In this instance, the dimming-down of the nightmare world allows for the striking intensity offered by the subordinate world-switch, which is figured against this ground. This initial conceptualisation can be seen in Figure 7.4. Again, inherently negative lexical items have been underlined.

The fact that the nightmare world is intensely defined, has subordinate world structures and is sustained across another six stanzas is enough to suggest that it temporarily replaces the previous text world as the default matrix world in the process of reading the poem. In stanza XXXVI, the world triggered and built up in stanza XXXV is maintained through reference to the enactor of Lorenzo as a 'pale shadow' (281), a description which heightens the sense of menace, yet retains the type of bright focus evident in the previous stanza. This is supported by the further descriptions that emphasise the sound of the ghost's speech and consequently maintain that sound as an element that attracts our attention. Furthermore, the shift in referencing from 'his' (276) to 'its' (282) suggests the enactor/ghost's movement away from being closely related to the living Lorenzo to a more distant and ominous supernatural figure. However, the conceptualisation of these descriptions remains complex. Again, Keats relies on diverting the reader's attention away from the matrix world to an alternative deictic space, here characterised by its attention to the qualities of the living Lorenzo in a similar way to the contrasting use of the world switch in stanza XXXV. The focus initially here, of course, is on a flashback to the Lorenzo of stanzas VIII and IX rather than on the earlier Lorenzo in the poem who finds

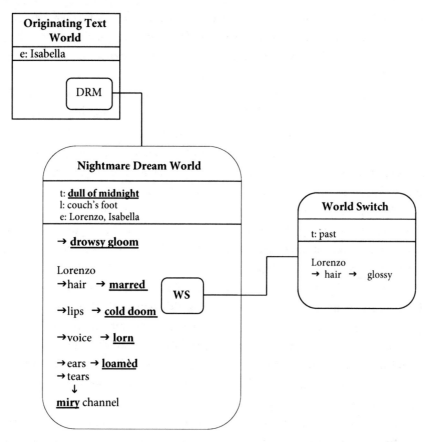

Figure 7.4 Nightmare dream world in stanza XXXV of *Isabella; or, The Pot of Basil*

himself unable to speak; yet the inability of the 'pale shade' to move beyond 'langour . . . and tremulous shake' (285) equally draws attention to that previous impotence. The metaphorical structures realised through 'As in a palsied Druid's harp unstrung' (286) provide temporary conceptual spaces in which the matrix world is updated to incorporate the reader's understanding of the similes. These metaphor worlds are rich with inherently negative lexis and consequently play an important role in updating and enriching the matrix space and maintaining the consistency of the nightmare.

This maintenance of the nightmare world continues in stanza XXXVII. Again, the emphasis on Lorenzo's physical characteristics is sharply defined in terms of brightness against the dark background of the dream and the abundance of inherently negative lexical items. So, a continued richness and prominence is afforded to Lorenzo's ghost by 'wild' and 'dewy bright' (289) and by the elaborated noun phrase 'magic of their light' (291). A further temporal world-switch, marked by the reporting of the ghost's speech act in the telling of his murder, in keeping with previous subordinate structures, is ominous: 'darkened time' (293), 'dark pine roof' (294) and 'sodden turfèd dell' (295), and contains a stark sole function-advancing proposition 'from stabs he fell' (296). A further three stanzas XXXVIII–XL offer more alternative subordinate structures since they represent examples of direct speech. Again, these provide a further sustained focus on Lorenzo's ghost and afford a vibrancy and vitality to Lorenzo's voice that was not given to the living enactor at the beginning of the poem. In stanza XLI, which marks the end of the nightmare experience and the departure from the nightmare world, Lorenzo's ghost, on whom the nightmare world had predominantly focused, appears to be instantly occluded through the verb phrases 'dissolved' and 'left' (321). However, crucially, the intensity of previous descriptions of him, as well as the adverbial 'in a slow turmoil' (322), suggests that this occlusion will be a more gradual one. Then, following two incidental analogies, the world-switching trigger 'started up awake' (328) marks the end of the nightmare world and transports Isabella and the reader back to the originating matrix world from which the nightmare world was formed. The nightmare experience and world have now faded from explicit conceptualisation, but as I suggest in Section 7.6, their resonance is felt across the remainder of the poem.

Across the space of six stanzas then, the literary representation of the nightmare as experienced by Isabella and conceptualised and tracked by the reader is triggered as a movement into an alternative state of consciousness that exists beyond that of normal waking thought. This is characterised by world-building elements that provide a sense of darkness and menace, and which are realised stylistically through negatively oriented lexis. Function-advancing propositions maintain this background through extensive use of inherent negation that mark an experience that is typical of the nightmare, while the intensity of the experience is captured in a series of striking images, formed from elements acting as attractors to maintain an intensity and a resonance beyond the experience itself. The nightmare is also both complex and creative in its movement out into alternative conceptual spaces that represent contrasting temporal states and present alternative enactors of Lorenzo. The importance and prominence of this nightmare is such that it assumes the role of default matrix world in being maintained for a significant number of stanzas. It represents a prototypical nightmare through its waking criterion clause, which marks a return to its own matrix world. The nightmare

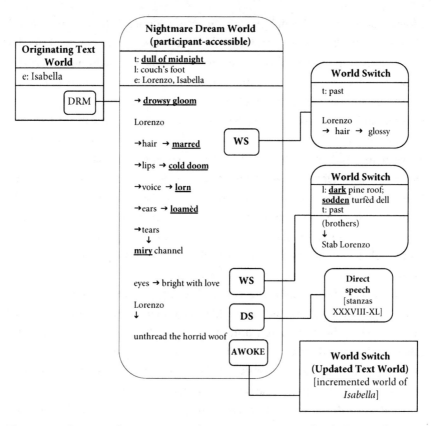

Figure 7.5 Conceptual organisation of stanzas XXXV–XLI of *Isabella; or, The Pot of Basil*

world is therefore the vehicle for experiencing the horror of Lorenzo's visit and its impact in a vibrant way, and an information route for understanding the development of Isabella's character in so far as the experience is incremented into the parent text world and updates our tracking of both narrative and character. A final, complete diagrammatic conceptualisation of these seven stanzas is shown in Figure 7.5.

7.6 The nightmare world at a global level: The function of the experience

The nightmare world in which Lorenzo's ghost appears is clearly a prominent and meaningful episode, sitting as it does at the heart of the poem. Its lexical intensity, reminiscent of an actual nightmare experience, is such that it represents a force that resonates through the remainder of the poem. The visit of Lorenzo's ghost not only affects the character of Isabella but also has a key role in shaping and maintaining the global coherence of the poem. The nightmare inevitably causes Isabella a significant amount of *nightmare distress*, evident in her reaction on waking and her later descent into madness. Furthermore, its *central image* is undoubtedly the vision of Lorenzo, who represents the lost world of idealised love and the naive belief in the power of the imagination of earlier stanzas. Standing between this earlier idealism and the later descent of Isabella into madness and death, the nightmare world therefore provides a distinct conceptual space from which to value and judge the deficiencies of the alternative realities in the poem as well as anticipating those to follow. In this way, the nightmare world can be seen as functioning in two distinct ways. First, its premonitory nature is responsible for triggering the remainder of the poem, anticipating the discovery of Lorenzo's body, further pain and Isabella's madness and demise. In this way, it provides a type of *information route* into Isabella's psyche in the movement across world edges from originating text world to nightmare, and back to the updated matrix world.[7] The nightmare world can therefore be viewed as a perceptually salient and inverted form of the earlier worlds of the opening stanzas, yet one in which ultimately, like in the earlier dream worlds, real intimacy is denied. This inverted or negatively charged conceptual space leads to the regeneration initiated through the planting of Lorenzo's head in the pot of basil, which sets up a replicated form of love, complete with its secretive nature and ultimate destruction by the brothers. On this occasion, although the parallel state of affairs ends in the restorative story that marks the end of the poem, the telling of Isabella's story and its echoing through history, like the telling of Lorenzo's fate in the nightmare, represents the kind of immortalisation through storytelling ascribed to the poem (Smith 1974).[8]

Secondly and alternatively, as Lagory (1995: 338) notes, the intrusion of Lorenzo into Isabella's thought through her nightmare acts as a way of drawing attention in a more abstract way to the illusory nature of her early naivety and as an antidote to Keats' earlier thinking on the power of the imagination (*Letters* I, 184–5, n. 43). The nightmare world in this instance can be viewed and acts as a symbolic conceptualisation of Keats' changing philosophy on the imagination and the realities of life. This second interpretation also allows for a reading of the poem that acknowledges the metaphorical journey that Isabella undertakes. Since research in sleep medicine has shown that nightmares are the most powerful of dream experiences (Hartmann 1999), and have an adaptive function resulting in a heightened sense of the self and a subsequent self-reflectiveness (McNamara

2008), the nightmare world in the poem may be considered in conjunction with Keats' own ideas on human maturation made explicit, in his letter to Reynolds on the 3 May 1818, written shortly after he had finished *Isabella*.

> I compare human life to a large mansion of Many Apartments, two of which I can only describe, the doors of the rest being as yet shut upon me – The first we step into we call the infant or thoughtless Chamber, in which we remain as long as we do not think – We remain there a long while, and not withstanding the doors of the second Chamber remain wide open, showing a bright appearance, we care not to hasten to it; but are at length imperceptibly impelled by the awakening of the thinking principle within us – we no sooner get into the second Chamber, which I shall call the Chamber of Maiden-Thought, than we become intoxicated with the light and the atmosphere, we see nothing but pleasant wonders, and think of delaying there for ever in delight: However among the effects this breathing is father of is that tremendous one of sharpening one's vision into the heart and nature of Man – of convincing ones nerves that the World is full of Misery and Heartbreak, Pain, Sickness and oppression – whereby This Chamber of Maiden thought becomes gradually darken'd and at the same time on all sides of it many doors are set open – but all dark – all leading to dark passages – We see not the balance of good and evil. We are in a Mist – We are now in that state – We feel the "burden of the Mystery".
>
> (*Letters* I, 280–1, n. 80)

Although Lagory (1995: 338) suggests that the poem sets out to educate and that Isabella's learning experience comes about as a result of her crossing into 'reality's dark dream', he offers no account of just how the construction of the nightmare may be read as an integral part of this. It now becomes possible to see Isabella's movement between mentation states, from waking thought to nightmare/dream and back to waking thought as a mirror image of Keats' own philosophical movement through the various apartments of the 'large mansion'.[9] Keats' nightmare world in the poem can be likened to the intoxicating light and atmosphere of the chamber of maiden thought, as an intensely bright and resonant conceptual space, evident in the early world-building elements and Isabella's initial viewing of Lorenzo. Equally, the experience, defined by the clusters of inherently negative lexical items, the retelling of the murder and the increasingly isolated figure of Lorenzo in the direct speech world switches, marks it as a space full of 'Misery and Heartbreak, Pain, Sickness and oppression'. Isabella's journey through the seven stanzas of the nightmare world can be read as a way of both demonstrating her feeling of 'the burden of the Mystery' and initiating the kind of self-knowledge that was missing in the early naivety of the opening dream worlds.

In a letter-journal to the George Keatses written on 21 April 1819, some 12 months after completing the poem, Keats proposed that human identity could only be truly found and developed through experiencing a series of difficulties and crises that formed part of the educating process of life.

> I will call the *world* a School instituted for the purpose of teaching little children to read – I will call the *human heart* the *horn Book* used in that School – and I will call the *Child able to read, the Soul* made from that school and its hornbook. Do you not see how necessary a World of Pains and troubles is to school an Intelligence and make it a soul? A Place where the heart must feel and suffer in a thousand diverse ways!
>
> (*Letters* II, 102, n.159)

From a functional perspective then, the nightmare world of *Isabella* clearly has an adaptive role in the poem's global design that can be read in conjunction with this late philosophical position. The ripple effect of this particular traumatic experience consequently becomes a felt experience for character and reader throughout the remainder of the poem.

7.7 Review

In this chapter, I have provided a text world theory analysis of *Isabella; or, The Pot of Basil* that explores Isabella's nightmare experience as a central event in the poem. I used my concept of the nightmare world to explain how the striking intensity and resonance of Isabella's experience acts a strong contrastive conceptual space, drawing attention to the poem's central concerns and holding an important functional role. I suggested that the nightmare world is functionally significant in drawing attention to more idealised forms of love in the poem, which are denied and defeated through both the stronger boulomaic modal desire worlds of Isabella's brothers and the negatively formed space that marks the central nightmare experience of the poem. This nightmare world in turn is responsible for both guiding and explaining the remainder of the poem's narrative. Consequently, my central aims in this chapter have been to exemplify my notion of a prototypical nightmare world as a movement across mentation states in the emulation of a terrifying experience, and to explore how Keats utilises this as an integral and significant aspect of the poem.

As the first of three chapters on nightmare worlds in Keats' poetry, my analysis of *Isabella; or, The Pot of Basil* demonstrates the value of using text world theory as a way of substantiating insights that have been claimed for the poem in literary criticism. Moreover, I have demonstrated that the inherent make-up of the nightmare world is responsible for much of the poem's texture and consequently has both a functional and experiential ripple effect through the remainder of the poem.

In Chapter 8, I develop more extensively an analysis that utilises the concept of the nightmare world as one of a series of remote and inaccessible spaces in 'La belle dame sans merci'. In this way, I further explore the use of the nightmare world both functionally and as part of the reading experience in Keats' poetry.

'La belle dame sans merci'

8.1 Introduction

In this chapter, I explore another prototypical nightmare world, this time in 'La belle dame sans merci'. As in Chapter 7, I develop my ideas on the nightmare world as an extreme and intense representation of a state of consciousness and in this instance explore its central position in the poem with regard to the general world tracking and maintenance that the reader is asked to undertake.

In Sections 8.2 and 8.3, I follow the structure of my previous analytical chapters and provide an overview of the poem's origins, conception and central ideas. In Section 8.4, I explore the conceptual organisation of the opening three stanzas of the poem, drawing attention to how the use of direct speech serves to create an *empty text world* (Lahey 2004), marking the beginning of a series of restrictions in accessibility for the reader. In this section, I also highlight the setting up of a negative conceptual space, in contrast to the conventions of the romance genre that Keats adopts, and suggest that this deictic pattern acts to contextualise the poem's central concerns of separation and desolation. In Section 8.5, I explore the first perceptual shift in the poem that arises as a result of the knight's narrative and argue that this movement into a new deictic space provides a heightened sense of dislocation in the poem, since the movement is as equally inaccessible to the reader as to the first speaking voice. As the nightmare world in this poem, unlike that in *Isabella; or, The Pot of Basil*, is enactor-accessible, the nightmare experience here serves a very different function to that in Keats' earlier poem. Consequently, in Section 8.6, I explore the notion of inaccessibility in more detail and place the nightmare world at the centre of a series of embedded worlds that form the global structure of the poem. Finally, I use this structure to explain some of the ways that the poem has been interpreted and to account for the overall jarring nature of the reader's edgework in moving across text worlds. I use this latter notion to support general readings of the poem that have emphasised the ambiguous nature of the knight's final words and the position of the reader, deictically stranded in a world that fails to shift back to its originating structure.

8.2 Origins and conception

'La belle dame sans merci' first appears in Keats' letter-journal to George and Georgiana Keats in April 1819. This version with some minor changes transcribed by Keats' associate and some-time collaborator Charles Brown remained unpublished until its appearance in volume II of Richard Monckton Milnes's 1848 *Life, Letters and Literary Remains of John Keats*. In 1820, a variation on the original, with substantially more changes than that of the 1848 version, was published in Leigh Hunt's *Indicator* under the pseudonym 'Caviare'.[1] Reading 'La belle dame sans merci' as a literary meta-poem, Bentley (2003) suggests that Keats was responding to Lockhart and Wilson's scathing 'Cockney School of Poetry' articles, in one of which he had been advised that 'It is a better and wiser thing to be a starved apothecary than a starved poet: so back to the shop Mr John, back to the "plasters, pills and ointment boxes"' (Schwartz 1973: 127). In Keats' description of a pale knight trapped by a female who represents literary imagination and tradition, Bentley reads the poem as 'the subtle reworking of Z's terms' (2003: 59) to allow Keats to celebrate aligning himself with Wordsworth, Shakespeare and Coleridge as fellow sufferers of poetic fever and his anonymity as a parody of the Blackwood's reviewers use of the signature 'Z'. The literary sources for the poem include those firmly rooted in the romance genre such as Alain Chartier's fifteenth-century French romance of the same title, Spenser's *The Faerie Queene* and the *Thomas the Rhymer True* ballad, available to Keats in Jamieson's 1806 *Popular Ballads* collection (Strachan 2003) and the recent revivification of the ballad as a literary form by Scott, Burns, Wordsworth and Coleridge (Thayer 1945; Kelley 1987).

8.3 Thematic concerns and critical response

'La belle dame sans merci' details a story told by a knight to an anonymous initial speaker who questions him on his physical and mental situation in the barren landscape that he inhabits at the beginning of the poem. The knight tells how he has been enthralled by a mysterious woman, has a nightmare vision in which he is warned of her dangerous and destructive qualities and wakes to find himself alone in the same landscape. The poem ends with the knight 'answering' the questioner by merely echoing most of his original words.

Waldoff (1985: 82) suggests that twentieth-century readings of the poem have identified two dominant concerns, namely the questioning of the role and validity of the visionary imagination, and the representation of the deceptive nature of the female. The ambiguous nature of the poem and the difficulties in interpreting its climax have led to a series of readings that view the poem as a quest by the poet-knight for an imaginative truth in the sensuous details of his experience with the belle dame, which although denied by the harsher waking realities of the dream-nightmare are still found to be attractive.[2] The resulting uncertainty surrounding the poem's conclusion and its open-endedness have been read as part of the poem's inherent reliance on the symbolic, which consequently can never allow itself to be truly explained or understood (Stillinger 1999). As such, it is often read as a poem both about the flexibility and constraints of the poetic imaginative mind.

Waldoff also acknowledges the poem's position in the context of Keats' development as a poet, mapping its place between *Endymion* and the late odes as a literary realisation of Keats' increasing psychological and intellectual maturation. In particular, he sees the poem as mapping out a landscape and set of characters that in their very being are suggestive of scepticism towards the role of the imagination as a visionary force. The haunting resonance of la belle dame serves to blur the boundaries between the modes of reality and imagination, placing the poem at a distance from Keats' assimilation of the two in *Endymion* and instead generating a kind of psychological anxiety. In this way, Allen (1960), reading the poem as a response to Keats' anxiety over the reliance on idealism in the structuring of *Endymion*, suggests that 'La belle dame sans merci' represents the inner struggle to move away from the idealised but ultimately empty notions of imagination and beauty portrayed in the earlier poem, and as such represents a significant shift from early Keatsian sentimentality towards a more refined outlook and poetic maturity.

Another type of anxiety is suggested in the treatment of and reaction to la belle dame as a female character. Biographical readings have variously identified her in a non-sympathetic light in line with Madeline, Isabella and Lamia, as Fanny Brawne (Murry 1925) and the fictitious Amena Bellefila, the supposed author of faked love letters sent to his brother Tom (Gittings 1954; Ward 1963). Read in the context of some of Keats' later poems to Fanny Brawne expressing his concern over their separation, Waldoff (1985) suggests that the poem represents the kind of anxiety Keats felt generally towards women, evident in letters such as that to Bailey in July 1818 where he writes:

> When among men I have no evil thoughts, no malice, no spleen – I feel free to speak or to be silent – I can listen and from every one I can learn – my hands are in my pockets I am free from all suspicion and comfortable. When I am among Women I have evil thoughts, malice spleen – I cannot speak or be silent – I am full of Suspicions and therefore listen to no thing.
>
> (*Letters* II, 341, n. 99)

Alternatively, feminist readings, for example, Levinson (1988) and Swann (1988), centre on the ways in which the knight is presented as the possessor of la belle dame who for her part is denied any voice or identity other than that suggested through the male perspective. Mellor (2001: 223) echoes Swann's comments by finding that the poem exists simply as a form of 'harassment' in its representation of the female. She adds that the prominence given to the dominant male voices ensures that 'the poem becomes . . . a sexual and verbal assault upon a female whose response is neither listened to nor recorded' (2001: 223).

8.4 Identity, genre, poetic landscape and negative worlds: Stanzas I–III

I
Ah, what can ail thee, knight at arms,
Alone and palely loitering?
The sedge has withered from the lake,
And no birds sing.

II
Ah, what can ail thee, knight at arms,   5
So haggard and so woe-begone
The squirrel's granary is full,
And the harvest's done.

III
I see a lily on thy brow
With anguish moist and fever dew,   10
And on thy cheek a fading rose
Fast withereth too.

The poem begins with a speaker addressing the knight with a question that occupies the opening two stanzas. Since in this instance, the speaker's words constitute an example of *free direct speech* (Leech and Short 2007: 258), in Werth's original text world framework they already represent a departure from an originating text world in the formation of a sub-world, as Werth explains:

> [Direct speech] is not normally thought of as a temporal variation at all, but its main effect is to change the basic time-signature of the text world, for example by injecting some Present Tense utterances into a Past Tense narrative. This takes us, as it were, directly into the character's discourse world: the tenses used are then regrouped around the ST of this discourse world, rather than that of the participants.
>
> (Werth 1999: 221)

In Gavins' (2001, 2005a, 2007a) subsequent work on text world theory, sub-worlds become reconfigured as world-switches. Consequently, the opening stanza of the poem can be deemed an example of a direct speech world-switch from an as yet unspecified establishing matrix text world. In a split discourse world, unlike in prototypical face-to-face discourse, the absence of a discourse participant means that it is usual for a reader to have to accept a narrator as the equivalent of a real discourse co-participant. In this example, however, the initial speaking voice is a textual entity at the same ontological level as the knight who speaks in stanza IV and one stage removed from a narratorial or implied authorial voice. Consequently, the entry point for the reader in the poem is the deictic centre of this speaking voice, and the established parameters of that world are from a perspective to which we as readers have no access. In this instance, the free direct speech therefore initiates an immediate world-switch into an enactor-accessible focalised world of the *initial speaker*.[3]

However, since in the text world theory framework, there must always be a text world (Werth 1999: 87), the originating world must be accounted for. Lahey (2004: 26) suggests that when a reader enters a text at a level below that of the normally expected text world, that skipped conceptual space can be deemed an *empty text world*, a minimal deictic space built from inference and containing only basic knowledge about enactors and their relationships. In this example, since the reader is drawn immediately into an enactor-accessible focalised world, we can only infer that there is an initial speaker and a knight and that the relationally deictic term 'knight-at-arms' (1) is a marker of their relationship. The initial speaker uses the address 'knight-at-arms' rather than the term 'man-at-arms' that would denote a lesser rank and status, and we can therefore assume some degree of formal distance between them.[4] Furthermore, the only function-advancing proposition that we can note is that of a speech verb initiating a world-switch into a world in which the deictic parameters have been altered to account for the immediacy of speech time and the focalised account. The effects of this significant conceptual structure of the opening of the poem are as follows: First, the fact that we enter the poem through skipping the text world level lends itself to those readings of the poem that have emphasised the sense of the ambiguous, mysterious and the feeling of estrangement that accompanies a reading (e.g. Stillinger 1999). Secondly, the perspective of the initial speaking voice impacts on the accessibility afforded by the poem's worlds. Since the initial world is an enactor-accessible direct speech focalised world, according to the principles of text world theory, it remains inaccessible to discourse participants who consequently have no way of verifying its truth or reliability.[5] The questions of accessibility, perspective and reliability are important in this poem and are dealt with throughout the next three sections before I summarise their importance in the poem as a whole in Section 8.6. However, even at this early stage, an explanation of this conceptual structure in text world terms can account for, as Stillinger (1999: 111) notes, why the details of the knight's description and the barren surroundings, originating from the perspective of the initial speaker, are not necessarily a true representation of the knight's condition. Such a reading foregrounds the importance of perspective and the construction of identity in a poem where the reader has to immediately accept a representation of events even though there is no way of verifying them. This conceptual structure at the opening of the poem is shown in Figure 8.1.

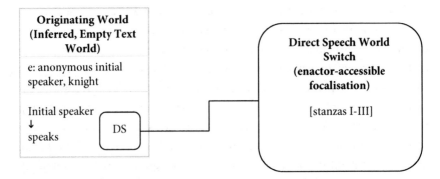

Figure 8.1 Empty text world and direct speech in stanza I of 'La belle dame sans merci'

Since the empty text world is relegated to being less perceptually salient than the world initiated by the direct speech, there is less attention afforded to it and consequently no fleshing out of its own deictic parameters. In the course of reading the poem, it may be said to decompose. Equally, the implied narrator, given no textual prominence in comparison to the initial speaking voice, is denied the opportunity to become an authoritative presence in the poem.

Viewed from the deictic centre of the initial speaker, the world-switch develops into a default platform for establishing the main parameters of the poem's text world in the first three stanzas. The knight is described through a series of inherently negative lexis that serve as function advancers: 'alone', 'palely loitering' (2) and 'haggard', 'woe-begone' (6). These are afforded prominence and thus attention in their emphasised position at the beginning or end of each of their respective lines. Additionally, in stanza three, the newness and immediacy of the knight's situation, described through the use of present simple and present progressive tense clauses ('see' (9) and 'withereth' (12)), maintain the reader's attention on the continual nature of the knight's physical condition. Equally, his lack of vibrancy and languid movement, suggested in the use of the present participle 'loitering', position him as a more global figure, placed in opposition to the agricultural industry evident in the finite clauses 'granary is full' (7) and 'the harvest's done' (8).

The initial speaker's presentation of the knight's physical countenance is in line with that of his comments on the physical landscape where the use of both inherent 'has withered' (3) and syntactic negation 'no birds sing' (4) serves to create a richly intense, yet bleak natural world. In Chapter 6, I explained that syntactic negation is best served in the text world model by considering it as a kind of conceptual contrast between a negative construction and its positive counterpart, realised in a figure-ground relationship. In turn, this negated construction updates the originating world and has a marked effect and impact. In this example, the conceptual prominence given to 'no birds sing' defeats the kind of schematic expectations bound up in a reading of a poem that explicitly draws attention to itself as an example of the romance genre. Both the poem's title and the extended use of the definite article, where the knight as addressee and the reader are invited to share a common deictic space, point towards a landscape typically and conventionally associated with the genre that is then defeated through the two negative constructions. This jarring of generic expectations is, as Sandy (2000: 1) suggests, the mark of a poem that redesigns the romance genre and instead presents a space that represents a nightmare-esque altered state of consciousness.[6] Both the world presented at

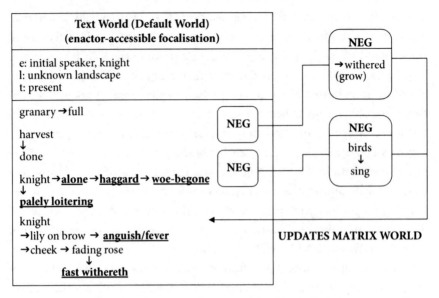

Figure 8.2 Conceptual organisation of stanzas I–III of 'La belle dame sans merci'

the beginning of the poem and the focalising initial speaker's perspective are not dissimilar to the typical characteristics of a nightmare experience in the intensity of represented experience, a menacing background and the extended use of negatively oriented lexis and syntax to provide a central contextualising image of decay, desolation and nothingness as perceived from the perspective of the initial focalising speaker. This conceptualisation of the opening three stanzas is shown in Figure 8.2. The initial empty text world of Figure 8.1 has been omitted.

8.5 The nightmare voice (1): Perspective and accessibility in stanzas IV–IX

IV
I met a lady in the meads,
Full beautiful, a faery's child:
Her hair was long, her foot was light,   15
And her eyes were wild.

V
I set her on my pacing steed,
And nothing else saw all day long;

For sideways would she lean, and sing
A faery's song.   20

VI

I made a garland for her head,
And bracelets too, and fragrant zone;
She looked at me as she did love,
And made sweet moan.

VII

She found me roots of relish sweet,   25
And honey wild, and manna dew,
And sure in language strange she said,
"I love thee true!"

VIII

She took me to her elfin grot,
And there she gazed and sighed full sore,   30
And there I shut her wild, wild eyes–
With kisses four.

IX

And there she lulled me asleep,
And there I dreamed – Ah! woe betide! –
The latest dream I ever dreamed   35
On the cold hill side.

Analysed from a text world perspective, the complex conceptual structures of the opening three stanzas give rise to the particular sense of dislocation that a reader experiences through the immediate inaccessibility and estrangement of the focalised world and the intense negative world that they present. The remainder of the poem continues to develop in a way that draws further attention to the notions of perspective and accessibility, and anticipates the centrality of the nightmare experience, which is triggered in stanza IX.

The shift in perception to an alternative deictic centre in stanza IV is generally accepted as being a shift from the initial speaker to the knight who now speaks of his meeting with the 'lady in the meads' (13). Textually, this is marked by the shift to a simple past reporting tense, in contrast to the reliance on present tense forms in the first three stanzas; the 'I' of the speaking voice is now projected from the deictic centre of the knight and all world-building and function-advancing material is from the perspective of a new focaliser. This shift in attitudinal position and perspective means that a new enactor-accessible focalised modal world, originating from the empty text world, is activated. This new focalised world becomes the default platform for the relaying of events over the course of the next few stanzas and since the representation of la belle dame is filtered through the knight's tale, readers continue to have no direct access to its contents or are able to verify them as reliable. As before, this fixed focalisation has the effect of providing a narrow interpretation of events from a perspective that is removed from the reader's initial position as discourse participant.

The new focalised world is built up from the spatial locative 'in the meads' (13), as well as the 'lady' (13) and a new past enactor of the speaking knight. Function-advancing propositions centre on the physical description of the lady filtered through the speaking knight's perspective: 'full beautiful, a faery's child' (14); 'her hair was long, her foot was light' (15) and 'eyes were wild' (16). In stanzas V and VI, the world is enriched through function-advancing propositions that mark the actions that the knight carries out, such as setting her on his stead and making a garland and bracelet for her. The strong focus on the knight throughout is maintained through the sustained use of the anti-shifting first-person pronoun 'I', the negated perception world that draws attention to the exclusive nature of the knight's attention, the maintenance of the perceptual deictic centre despite the spatial shift to the 'elfin grot' (29) and the filtering of all the lady's actions through the knight's interpretative systems through the use of third-person referencing, 'she looked at me' (23) and 'she found' (25). It is precisely this sustained focalisation and filtering that can account for the feminist readings of Swann (1988) and Mellor (2001) since it is the maintenance of the deictic centre of the knight and the consequent denial of any female perspective that emphasise the appropriation of the female voice.

In addition, further filtering and control of representation occurs on the four occasions where the knight reports la belle dame's speech. Three of these, 'would she lean and sing' (19), 'And made sweet moan' (24) and 'sighed full sore' (30), are examples of the *narrative reporting of speech* acts (NRSA) (Leech and Short 2007: 259). Since NRSA places the speech act itself entirely under the control of the narrator (here the knight), these accounts remain heavily focalised and consequently, in text world terms, inaccessible. On one occasion, the knight does report what la belle dame says verbatim, generating a prototypical direct speech world-switch which changes the temporal parameters through inserting present tense speech into the past tense narrative. However, even this world-switch is

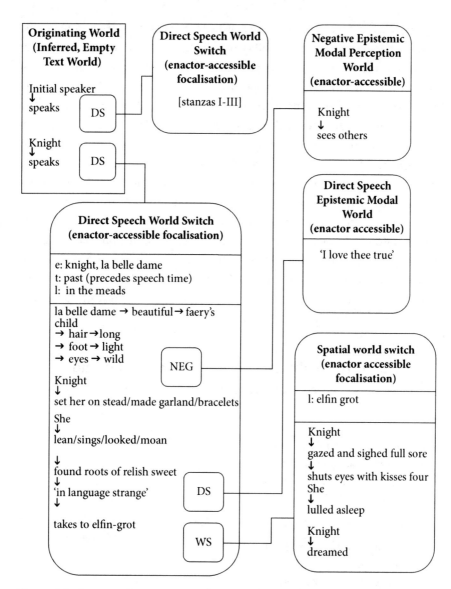

Figure 8.3 Conceptual organisation of stanzas IV–VIII of 'La belle dame sans merci'

coloured by the knight's own pre-modifying prepositional phrase 'in language strange' (27), which adds epistemic uncertainty to the contents of that world. Consequently, the validity of the knight's representation remains questionable since the use of direct speech as a marker of reliability is made redundant. The words cannot be a direct representation of what was said if the knight himself highlights his own potential for misunderstanding them.

Overall, the conceptual structure of these stanzas provides a double kind of dislocating force. Since the ability to validate the knight's version of events does not exist, the reader, having previously been compelled to accept a similar enactor-accessible world and perspective, has to do so again in the process of moving across world boundaries from the originating and rendered empty world to the second of two focalised spaces. Equally, the knight himself as a textual enactor within the world that temporarily becomes the default platform for the poem, although finding beauty in la belle dame and her actions, is troubled by his inability to fully interpret and understand her words. The direct speech world-switch remains for him as remote, inaccessible and prone to misunderstanding as his own perspective is to the reader. In presenting an interpretation, the text world notion of restricted accessibility in this section of the poem can account not only for those readings that stress the knight's subjugation of the la belle dame and the suppression of her voice but also for those that explicitly question the authority of the knight's narrative.[7] The conceptual structure of stanzas IV–VIII is shown in Figure 8.3.

8.6 The nightmare voice (2): Accessibility and world structure in stanzas X–XII

X
I saw pale kings, and princes too,
Pale warriors, death-pale were they all;
They cried –'La Belle Dame sans Merci
Thee hath in thrall!'   40

XI
I saw their starved lips in the gloam,
With horrid warning gaped wide,
And I awoke and found me here,
On the cold hill's side.

XII
And that is why I sojourn here,   45
Alone and palely loitering,
Though the sedge is withered from the lake,
And no birds sing.

In Chapter 6, I explained the conceptual structure of this nightmare world by drawing attention to the rich intensity of images that populate the nightmare

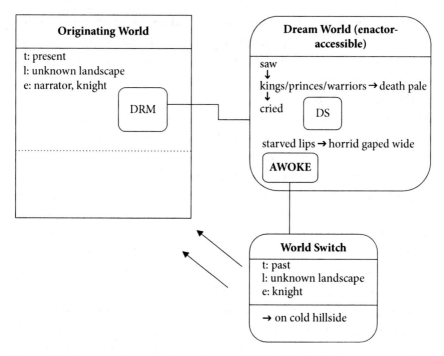

Figure 8.4 Conceptual organisation of stanzas X–XI of 'La belle dame sans merci'

space, formed from a range of elements that act as attractors against the
dimmed out background. These are maintained for the entire representation of
the nightmare experience and are responsible for a resonant texture that feeds
back into the previous conceptual space as part of the text world process of
incrementation. In this way, I suggested that the nightmare experience itself is felt
across world edges and that inferences made – in this case an explanation of the
knight's physiological make-up – update the originating text world. Figure 8.4
reproduces the original conceptual structure from that chapter.

Within the nightmare experience, the direct speech world initiated by the
trigger 'they cried' (39) again provides present tense material into the past
tense narrativised account. In this instance, the switch is to an even more
remote space embedded inside the nightmare world that the knight recounts
and is projected from the perceptual deictic centre of those speaking entities in
the nightmare, the 'pale kings', 'princes' (37) and 'pale warriors' (38).

Since direct speech is always under the control of the speaking voice and
remains an example of an enactor-accessible world, the content of the speech
itself yet again remains inaccessible for the reader tracking this movement
into a further space. Consequently, the representation of the knight being 'in
thrall' (40) is told from a perspective that neither the knight experiencing then

recounting the nightmare nor the reader can take as being genuinely reliable. The adding of another layer of inaccessibility to our notions of what is real and unreal in the poem through the embedded direct speech world thus compounds the dislocating effect generated by previous world-switches.

This initial conceptualisation, which I used in Chapter 6 primarily to demonstrate the inherent properties of a nightmare world, does need to be reviewed in the context of the poem's overall structure. The waking trigger 'I awoke' (43) remains within the same general parameters as the knight's story and overall nightmare experience, although it clearly shifts to a different spatial location and refers to a later time period. The world-switch initiated by this trigger therefore places an enactor of the knight in a landscape, only identified by the locative 'on the cold hillside' (44), but crucially this space, unlike the preceding two, must also be inhabited by the initial speaker since the knight refers to a shared understanding of location through the use of the proximal deictic term 'here' (44). Furthermore, in this instance, the waking from the nightmare world does not result in the usual expected movement back into the parent world but instead into an altogether new one as 'here' clearly refers to the landscape in which the initial speaker and the knight converse and not to the world of the 'elfin grot' or even the world of the meads that formed the location of the knight's main recount.[8] The effect of this unusual nightmare experience positions a reader tracking the movement between conceptual structures in a further state of disorientation since the movement back across world edges is not what is expected. The jarring uneasiness that emerges from Keats' manipulation of and the constraints generated by the poem's world-switches is clearly in line with the uneasiness felt by nightmare sufferers on waking as the felt experience of the nightmare permeates through the remainder of the poem.

This emphasis on shared deictic space is maintained in the final stanza of the poem. Spatial proximity is matched by a movement into the present time zone to provide a sense of immediacy to the knight's words. In this instance, the time zone is now the same as that of the present tense first enactor-accessible focalised world of the initial speaker since speech time is now equivalent to the time in which events occur in the poem, which is marked by the use of the present simple tense. The final space is therefore an additional enactor-accessible focalised world, this time from the deictic centre of the knight, whose account of the landscape he inhabits provides the poem's final voice. Temporally and spatially, this provides a neat symmetry to the entire poem, shown in the summary of world structure in Figure 8.5.

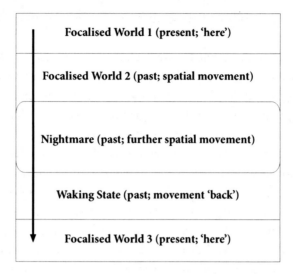

Figure 8.5 Temporal and spatial world structure in 'La belle dame sans merci'

The effect of this structure can be seen in the ways in which the poem can be and has been read and understood. The lack of a perceptual shift back to the originating text world, the shared deictic area evident in the use of the spatial deictic terms and the almost verbatim echoing of the initial speaker's words all suggest a merging of the voices of the initial speaker and knight. This has been read as the voices of the knight and la belle dame as dream, visionary and imaginative forces being defeated and consumed by that of the initial questioning speaker into a gritty realistic and objective working out of the limits of dream and fantasy (Stillinger 1999). This particular reading is supported by understanding the poem as one that professes Keats' scepticism towards the visionary imagination (see, for example, the reading by Waldoff (1985), see Section 8.3).[9] A more extreme reading of this position and one that would call for a more radical re-conceptualisation of the world structure in the poem would be to fully equate the speaking voices of the initial speaker and the knight into a single yet conflicting perspective. In this case, both focalised worlds 1 and 3 would be a more upfront state of consciousness from the perceptual centre of the initial speaker, while the embedded structures (focalised world 2, the nightmare and the waking state) would all be seen as representations of a more internal self in a process of dramatising its internal conflicts and concerns, a reading suggested by Motion (1997). At a higher level of course, both the initial speaker and knight have their discourses appropriated by the implicit narrative voice that reports the first of the focalised worlds and above that still by Keats as ultimate discourse participant.

Alternatively, some explicit textual differences can account for different readings that are possible, given the text world structure of the poem. Levinson (1988: 70–1) suggests that the initial speaker (she terms this voice the 'minstrel') and the knight are not so much a merging of voices but in sharing narrative and representational concerns become 'repetitions in finer and coarser tone: or again, facing page translations'. She points out the crucial difference between the class resonances attached to 'loiter' evoking 'urban unemployment' and 'sojourn' evoking 'civilized leisure' (1997: 69) as indicative of this difference. Furthermore, the initial speaker's use of 'loitering' and its later mitigation by the knight into 'that is why I sojourn here' acts as his response to the challenge of idleness, since 'sojourn' is seen in more positive terms as a kind of purposeful poetic indulgence. The knight's imaginative projections are therefore representative of the type of resistant answering-back Bentley suggests in his reading of the poem as a literary response to the challenge of wastefulness and the indulgence of *Endymion* by Blackwood's 'Z'. In this way, the voice of the knight neatly answers his critics simply by not answering them, and the echoing of the initial speaker's lines with a few carefully chosen changes is seen to be simply an ironic challenge to any attack on poetic form or ambition.

8.7 The nightmare effect: Interpretative function and readerly cognitive constraints

Figure 8.5 demonstrates the central position of the nightmare world in the movement across world edges that the reader is asked to undertake when reading 'La belle dame sans merci'. This means that as in *Isabella; or, The Pot of Basil*, the nightmare experience has an important functional role in the poem. Its representation as a striking set of images, its textual resonance and its placing of vivid, negative images against a dark background all serve to mirror the kind of negative experience of the knight, and can support readings that variously highlight unpleasant aspects of imagination and poetic composition, the effects of less than complimentary critical response and the pain associated with both being with and being separated from females. Furthermore, the influence of the nightmare experience spreads across the remaining examples of world-switches in the poem, creating the kind of ripple effect through the blurring of boundary edges that Sandy (2000: 1) has termed Keats' creation of a 'negative poetic fiction' and 'a literary terrain rich with potential that permits a reorientation to an aesthetic which embraces tragedy through a series of negating images'. The intense, problematic and ambiguous nature of this world and the complex connections between deictic spaces remain consistent with the hyperassociative nature of dreams and nightmares, and the resonant effect of the nightmare experience on the knight who awakens to merely repeat the initial speaker's words can be read as a type of *nightmare distress* (see Section 6.3.4.2), a measure of the impact of the nightmare experience on subsequent functioning encountered by nightmare sufferers. In this poem, the nightmare experience has a disabling function on the knight, updating the discourse as the poem proceeds, and finally measured in his description of himself as an eternal sufferer in the bleak landscape of the poem. As a functional construct then, the nightmare is clearly important.

Keats' use of the nightmare can also be examined in the light of Coleridge's views on the phenomenon, given that Keats' meeting with the older poet on 11 April 1819 (see Section 3.3.2) is recounted in the letter-journal in which 'La belle dame sans merci' appears. The nightmare experience in the poem, drawing attention to the relationship between psychological/inner torment and physiological/outer state and emphasising the physical countenance of the knight as an inverted form of the chivalric norm, clearly matches Coleridge's own views on the nightmare as a felt experience and the consequences of that experience as manifested in a 'bodily sensation' (Coleridge 1973: e.3322 and see Section 6.3). In this instance, Coleridge's complex notion of double touch, of which Keats indicates that Coleridge had spoken to him, becomes realised in the disarticulating nature of the embedded world structure of the poem and the concentrating of horror into a single moment when the knight finds himself alone in the barren landscape.[10]

Its functional role in the poem aside, this embedded structure also serves to leave the reader deictically stranded, whichever reading is assigned to the agency of voice at the end of the poem. Equally, the nightmare world sits at the heart of a poem where world tracking and maintenance make it problematic for the reader to assign reliability to any of the textual voices, prominent or otherwise, or indeed to that of the narrator, implied author or real author. These cognitive constraints on the reader are felt in the subsequent disarming and dislocating force of movement across world edges. In particular, as I explained in Section 8.5, the movement into the further embedded worlds of the knight's dream and the nightmare experience and direct speech world of the pale warriors, pale kings and princes result in a continual and progressive movement into more remote enactor-accessible focalised worlds that are marked as existing at a significant epistemic distance from the reader's discourse world. As a consequence and guided by the principle of accessibility in text world theory, moving through the world structure identified in Figure 8e, the reader becomes increasingly unable to verify the representation of characters and events in these remote enactor-produced spaces since these characters and events exist only as the products of enactor-activated worlds. This notion of restricted accessibility also helps to define the kind of dislocating effect that a reading of the poem generates. The waking trigger, resulting in a shift back to a world with different spatio-temporal co-ordinates to that of the initiating world of the 'elfin grot', results in the kind of jarring edgework that is indicative of a poem where boundaries appear blurred and world edges seem to disintegrate, leaving it difficult to ascertain concrete deictic centres. As I have discussed, this dislocation of normative movement from world to world in the poem is significant regardless of how a reader chooses to interpret the poem's various symbols and assign a sense of meaning. Keats' positioning of the nightmare world at the heart of the poem and the demands placed on the reader to track and move across world edges provide the experience of reading 'La belle dame sans merci' with a striking and felt resonance. These attributes remain central to reading, understanding and interpreting a poem where the 'answer' to the initial speaker's question is not revealing but rather, as critical response has shown, simply puzzling.

8.8 Review

In Chapter 7, my focus was on exemplifying my notion of a nightmare world in *Isabella; or, the Pot of Basil*, formed from an explicit sleeping trigger and responsible for the building of the remote conceptual space, which held a functionally important role at the heart of the poem. In this chapter, I have provided further exemplification of a prototypical nightmare world but also developed my discussion in significant ways to consider the deictic pattern of worlds and reader tracking in more detail. Here, I have demonstrated the setting up of a negative conceptual space, crucial to the defeating of generic expectations, which colours the poem's opening and emphasises the functional design of the nightmare world as the centre point of an increasingly problematic series of world-switches. Consequently, I have suggested that 'La belle dame sand merci' makes extensive demands and places constraints on the reader's ability to accurately verify the contents of the poem's worlds, a phenomenon that text world theory terms accessibility. Consequently, I have demonstrated how this leads to a series of enactor-accessible spaces centred round the explicit nightmare world which serve to make the reading experience of the poem a disorientating one. I have maintained the focus on reading as an experience by considering how Keats presents the nightmare world as explicitly emulating a nightmare experience. My focus here, unlike in the previous chapter, has been not only on the world-building elements and function-advancing propositions that formulate nightmare worlds but also on the movement across world edges acting as states of consciousness. My analysis, as in other chapters has therefore been able to account for existing conventional criticism in a more rigorous text-centred way. This chapter anticipates my final one on Keats' fragment 'This living hand, now warm and capable', where I explore the nightmare world as the emulation of a nightmare experience that is the act of reading an entire poem.

'This living hand, now warm and capable'

9.1 Introduction

In this chapter, I complete my analyses of nightmare experiences by exploring the fragment 'This living hand, now warm and capable', often considered a candidate for Keats' final poem. Here, I suggest that the poem, and particularly the edgework required in moving across world structures in the process of reading, is an example of extreme iconicity. In Sections 9.2 and 9.3, I follow the structure of my previous analytical chapters and provide an overview of the poem's origins, conception and central ideas. In the remaining sections, I present a text world reading that provides a rigorous and systematic account of the poem's language and the cognitive demands placed on a reader in a series of cross-world movements. In Section 9.4, I draw attention to the different ways in which the opening sequence of the poem may be understood, arguing that the conceptualisation necessarily involves imagining the image of the hand in a striking intensity reminiscent of a typical nightmare. In Section 9.5, I explore the subsequent, more complex series of embedded worlds, beginning with the hypothetical situation presented as a way of suggesting that the poem continues to present itself as an on-going nightmare experience marked by the presence of an increasingly powerful speaker and increasingly passive addressee. In Section 9.6, I develop this idea by examining how the reference to either the living or dead hand in the final two lines is necessarily a conceptual move back to the situation at the beginning of the poem. Consequently, I show how the world-switch initiated in the final lines marks a movement back to the potential for haunting afforded to the hand in the poem's opening. Furthermore, I demonstrate how a text world theory analysis of the poem can account for both the living and dead hand as reference points, an area of discussion in literary criticism. In Section 9.7, I draw together my work from previous sections to suggest that the poem is best considered as a composite nightmare experience and suggest a reconfiguration of the poem's conceptual structure. In this section, in the light of work on addressivity and second person fiction, I also explore how this composite structure might influence the degree of reader self-implication and provide discrete text world-sensitive models of *detachment*, *involvement* and *empathy* to account for the various positions of identification a reader might undertake reading the poem. Finally, I briefly propose that the poem's physicality, its felt resonance as a result of defined edgework, can be viewed in light of Coleridge's notion of touch and its possible influence on Keats, which I discussed in Chapters 3 and 6.

9.2 Origins and conception

At some point in the months of November and December 1819, Keats began work on an ambitious yet ultimately unfinished and unsuccessful satire *The Cap and Bells*. In a space in the manuscript, he wrote the short fragment 'This living hand', which remained unpublished until 1898 when it appeared in H. B. Forman's *Poetical Works of John Keats* (Stillinger 1974). The poem's fragmentary nature, together with the fact that Keats does not make any direct reference to it in any of his correspondence, has resulted in a lack of any uniform agreement as to its origins and intended possible use.[1] It is clear that the lines were written during a time when Keats was affected by some form of psychological suffering. Bate (1963) places the writing of the poem in the context of Keats' increasing illness, his perceived failure in and increasing frustration over his career as a poet and his relationship with Fanny Brawne. Letters from the final months of 1819 demonstrate these very frustrations and show Keats as increasingly prone to states of intense unhappiness. In letters, to Fanny Brawne, dated 11, 13 and 19 October 1819, he writes 'I feel myself at your mercy' (*Letters* II, 222, n.202), 'I should be exquisitely miserable without the hope of seeing you soon. . . . . . I cannot breathe without you' (*Letters* II, 223–4, n.203) and 'my mind is in a tremble' (*Letters* II, 224, n.204). And, in a letter to Joseph Severn on the 10 November, he shows his general state of mind when he speaks of being 'lax, unemployed, unmeridian'd' (*Letters* II, 227, n.207).[2]

9.3 Thematic concerns and critical response

The few studies there are of the poem have largely drawn attention to its potential to be understood as a dramatic speech written to be performed, or as a poem addressed either to a real life person (usually assumed to be Fanny Brawne), or else a potentially infinite number of audiences and readerships (Lipking 1981; Bahti 1986; Su 1994). Culler (1977: 69) considers it as 'Keats' most fascinating work', and Hopkins (1989: 37) stresses the 'complicated' nature of trying to unravel its meaning. Without exception, those commentators who have written on the poem refer to both the power of the writing and its haunting, chilling effect.

Biographical readings have understandably sought to rely on Keats' relationship with Fanny Brawne as a way of providing a referent for the 'you' of the poem and a motivation for the speaking voice. In a study of Keats' late short lyrics, Wolfson (2001: 102) suggests that the poem sits at the centre of a series of several 'inspired, or haunted, by Fanny Brawne', while Gittings (1968) reads it more explicitly in the context and as an extension of Keats' letters to her, arguing that the fragment retains characteristics of the letters' style and tone.

In contrast, a focus on the poem's textual and contextual indeterminacy has sought to explain how its consequent power is lost if a purely biographical approach is taken. Lipking (1981) proposes that the poem's strength is its constitution as 'one of the best examples in literature of a radical ambiguity or "rabbit-duck" – an artifact that can be read in two fully coherent yet mutually exclusive ways' (1981: 181). He argues that the poem can either be treated as more of a dramatic text, in which speaker and listener inhabit the same shared space of communication (or discourse world in text world theory terms) or, more conventionally in a non-face-to-face discourse context, as a poem addressed to and read by a reader removed in time and space from the originating speaking voice or discourse participant. In the first instance, the hand and its imagined dead counterpart both have a physical presence and are clearly visible to the listener; in the second and as a prototypical split discourse world event, they rely instead on a combination of the horror of the projecting speaking voice and the reader's imagination to construct meaningful text worlds around them. In this way, the potential for multiple reading contexts becomes more attractive than simply accepting a more obvious and ready-made one.

Similarly, Waters (2000, 2003) insists that the poem loses its mysterious and haunting power if read simply as a poem of revenge on a specified individual, since such a reading that references the 'you' of the poem to a third person in the past misses out on the immense power of the second person lexical choice to reach out in a more immediate and intimate manner to any individual engaged in a reading of the poem. The configuration of spaces of speaking, listening and interpreting are equally evident in Bruhn (2005), who insists on the poem as a figure of collapsed space in which textual immediacy is mirrored in spatio-temporal terms in the 'here' and 'now' of reading with a clearly defined and shared proximal field providing the platform from which the poem is experienced in its truest sense.

Less language-focused accounts of the poem have suggested readings that are heavily bound up with Keats as a writer, and the poetics and politics of writing in the nineteenth century in general. Yet, these too stress the power of the poem to produce a kind of haunting resonance. Bennett (1994: 178) reads the poem's active, reaching hand as the 'synecdochic dead hand of poetry as a figure for the death of the reader' and the poem as a symbol of posterity for the writing Romantic self at the expense of the reader, whose imagined death in re-animating the speaker's body is inevitable to allow for the 'posthumous life of writing' (1994: 11). In a similar vein, Corcoran (2009: 321) places the poem in the context of Keats' own preoccupation with his impending death and concerns over his status as a poet, by stressing the way in which it is written and consequently interpreted to allow it to 'live through' the poet's own death. Hopkins (1989) devotes a whole article to a Freudian exploration of 'This living hand', suggesting that the regeneration of the hand through the act of reading is prototypically *uncanny* (Freud 1985b) through its immediate and unsettling sense of being experienced.

9.4 The opening experience

This living hand, now warm and capable
Of earnest grasping, (1–2)

The poem consists of a single speaker acting as both a narrating and focalising enactor and through whom all of the textual information is filtered. Consequently, the entry point for the reader, in a similar way to 'La belle dame sans merci', is by the means of the focalised space projected from this deictic centre. Again, since a focalised world automatically represents a departure from an unspecified matrix world, the originating world is effectively left redundant, and as I explained in Chapter 8, in text world theory is defined as an *empty text world* (Lahey 2004). The relationship between the empty text world and the focalised space depends on how the poem is read and conceptualised since a number of ways are possible. First, the lines can be considered as part of a thought process of an individual, unknown speaker to an imagined addressee. In this instance, the poem's opening lines would form a direct thought world, initiated by an inferred thought verb in the matrix text world. Alternatively, the words could form a direct speech world, with the speaking voice addressing an enactor present in the inferred text world. Lastly, the direct speech world could be addressed to an imagined addressee, not present in the matrix world. In fact, any building of a text world, in the absence of any specific world-building information, necessarily comes from any imagined or inferred detail, general knowledge and more specific choices based on biographical knowledge, for example the assigning of the role of addressee to Fanny Brawne. In view of this, it consequently becomes possible to account to some degree using text world terms for the indeterminacy of the poem's initial context, a subject I return to in Section 9.4. For the remainder of this section, I treat this entry point simply as an epistemic modal focalisation world.

In Chapter 8, I also explained that although a focalised world is by its very nature enactor-accessible, the reader as a discourse participant is placed in the position of having to accept its contents as reliable and credible if reading is to take place at all. The combination of an anonymous and remote speaking voice and the absence of any other world-building information mean that the reader is immediately drawn into a space that is without any defined deictic parameters. However, as I demonstrate in the remainder of this section, the clear suggestion of proximity and consequently familiarity throughout the speaker's words appears at odds with the distance suggested by the inaccessibility of the focalised world. It is this synthesis of the detached focalised space with its sudden and anonymous voice and the prominence of lexical items relating to proximity and a sudden shared sense of remembering, that Hopkins (1989) uses as a basis for his Freudian reading of the poem. Clearly, whichever context a reader chooses, the closeness suggested by the proximal deictic term 'this' appears strangely at odds with the anonymous voice and lack of background world-building detail, accounting for what Waters (2003: 147) insists is the poem's 'strange spell'.

There are two distinct ways of conceptualising the opening words beyond their position as part of a focalised space remote from an inferred empty matrix world. First, and aside from any metonymic association of the hand with the domain of writing and poetical craft in general, it is part of a human body. Consequently, a reader utilises general background knowledge that hands are usually attached to bodies and are unable to move on their own, to understand 'this living hand' as a metonym for the speaker's full human existence with an undisclosed body that must function as a world-building enactor. In this instance, the focus on the hand represents a world zoom (see Chapter 5) in which prominence is simply afforded to one part of the body which is given close attention within the focalised world. In this instance, the supernatural element therefore remains the hidden agency behind the hand. Alternatively, to read the image as Wolfson (2001: 116) does as a 'ghoulishly amputated somatic animation' is to give a more shocking supernatural prominence to the hand itself, understood as lacking any attachment with a human body. Conceptualising the opening focalised space in this way allows for a reading where the hand takes on an infinitely more terrifying power as it assumes its own agency, 'capable of earnest grasping' (2).[3]

The significant ways in which attention is drawn to each textual entity provides the opening space with a clear vibrancy. Returning to Stockwell's characteristics of good textual attractors (see Sections 5.5 and 6.6.5), it is possible to identify a whole range of textual entities that provide a rich intensity to the opening words of the poem. So, in these lines attention is afforded through *agency* (the hand as noun phrase is given prominence through its topic position), *definiteness* (the proximal deictic 'this' (1) anchors a specific and focused entity extending from the speaking deictic centre), *newness* (the present verb participle acting as an attributive adjective 'living' (1) and temporal adverb 'now' (1) both denote a sense of immediacy and freshness) and *fullness* (the adjective 'warm' (1) denotes a richness and vitality). In addition to this, a second conceptual space is created through the second adjectival phrase 'capable of earnest grasping'. Strictly speaking, the modal category that deals with capability is dynamic modality (Palmer 2001) but here since the phrase is marked as an example of the speaking voice's attitude towards the possibility of a state of affairs, it should be considered more as an epistemic form. As the ability of the hand to grasp points towards a state of affairs that is possible but as yet to be realised, it stands as somewhere in between what Langacker (2008: 306) terms *projected* and *potential reality* (see Chapter 4), with either the projected or potential grounding force of the expression remaining internal to the conceptualiser, in this case either the ghostly speaking voice or more ominously the hand itself. In either case, this second epistemic modal world shares the vibrancy and intensity of its parent space in its newness and immediacy, with the further verb participle 'grasping' premodified by the attributive adjective 'earnest' suggesting the intentionality of the floating hand, maintaining both the supernatural terror of these opening words and the kind of raw intensity typical of a nightmare experience.

Overall then, these opening ten words create a pair of text worlds that together mirror the kind of experience typical of a more general nightmare

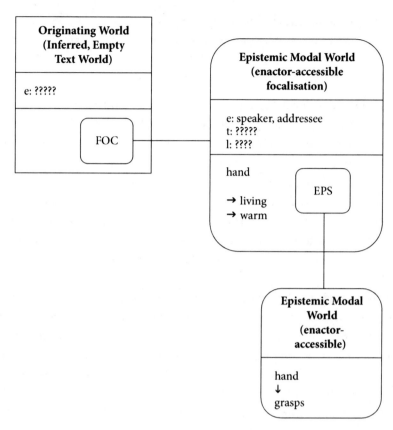

Figure 9.1 Conceptual organisation of 'This living hand, now warm and capable of earnest grasping'

world. This is evident in the conceptualisation of the focalised space that offers the floating terror of the hand in all of its intensity, creating a striking visual foreground. In addition, the indeterminate and ambiguous nature of the hand's origins and its potential ability to reach out towards the reader is in line with the typical enhanced creativity of the nightmare experience (McNamara 2008) and the intensity of a central contextualising image (Hartmann 2008). The conceptualisation of these opening words is shown in Figure 9.1.

9.5 Hypotheticality, embedded worlds and the on-going nightmare experience

. . . would, if it were cold
And in the icy silence of the tomb,

So haunt thy days and chill thy dreaming nights
That thou would wish thine own heart dry of blood,
So in my veins red life might stream again,
And thou be conscience-calm'd. (2–7)

The middle section has been generally read as the most haunting part of the poem, generating a 'chilling effect' (Waters 2003: 146) in its presentation of the 'daunting consequence' (Wolfson 2001: 116) of the imagined altered state of the hand. In text world theory terms, the middle section provides a further series of worlds originating from the initial focalised space that build on the initial conceptualisation and are developed to represent an even more shocking and frightening experience. The first and most complex of these embedded worlds marked by the triggers 'would' and an *if*-clause set up a hypothetical situation in which the proximal, warm and vibrant hand is replaced by a remote, cold and dead one.

In his discussion of conditionality and cognition, Werth (1997) explores the structure of hypotheticals using the traditional grammatical division of *protasis* and *apodosis*. The protasis has two components: a proposition denoting a situation, in this case the position of the cold hand in the tomb; and, a remoteness marker pointing towards the potential existence of this situation, in this case 'if'. Together these set up a 'theoretical situation' (Werth 1997: 252) which is marked as remote from the actual and localised current text world situation. The protasis has world-building properties since it moves beyond the deictic spatio-temporal parameters of the existing world space and forms an alternative state of affairs which is clearly as yet unrealised. Alternatively, the apodosis can be seen as supplying function-advancing material to the newly created world, marking it with 'some degree of probability' (Werth 1997: 252) depending on the modalised expression used. In this instance, the modal 'would' adds a degree of high epistemicity to the following clauses that map out processes completing the conceptual structure of the newly-formed world.[4]

In the middle section of the poem, the protasis consists of the if-clause 'if it were cold/And in the icy silence of the tomb' (2–3). This sets up a remote space with deictic parameters that are different from those of the originating world. Furthermore, strong lexical contrasts exist between the pairs 'living'/'tomb' and 'warm'/'cold'-'icy', drawing attention to a darker more ominous set of world-builders and marking a shift to a more menacing background, more indicative of a prototypical nightmare experience in its cluster of inherently negative lexis. From this initial space, the remaining lines of the middle section form

Table 9.1 Protasis and apodosis in the middle section of 'This living hand, now warm and capable'

Protasis	Apodosis
'if it were cold/And in the icy silence of the tomb'	So haunt thy days and chill thy dreaming nights That thou would wish thine own heart dry of blood, So in my veins red life might stream again, And thou be conscience-calm'd.

the apodosis, providing the consequence of that initial condition and given structure through a series of function advancing propositional clauses. Using this simple distinction, the middle section of the poem can be mapped out as in Table 9.1.

However, this simple distinction between protasis and apodosis remains too crude to account for the rich literary effect generated by Keats' conceptual layering of worlds. Indeed, the poem's power comes from the fact that the apodosis contains a number of discretely realised further embedded text worlds and that it is this interplay between the modes of desire on the part of the increasingly powerful speaking voice and the nightmare spaces imagined as part of the increasingly passive addressee's experience that provide the truly haunting resonance of this middle section. So, the *if*-clause, acting as the protasis initiates a hypothetical epistemic modal world with parameters that are strikingly different from those of its originating space and relying, as I previously discuss, on inherent negation, to create a dark, menacing background. Subsequently, the three parts of the original apodosis can now be viewed as conceptual worlds in their own right. First, the function advancing material evident in 'so haunt thy days' (4) in which an enactor of the addressee is made textually explicit for the first time in the poem through the use of the possessive second person form 'thy', triggers a switch to an imagined world, remote in time and space from the original world of the tomb.[5] Following this, a further remote world in which a further enactor of the addressee dreaming is triggered. In this instance, the addressee is asked to imagine more explicitly, as a consequence of the hypothetical situation of an embedded nightmare experience, an event where the ghostly hand is able to 'chill' the dreamer's dream content. In being asked to conceptualise simultaneously both nightmare worlds, the power of the experience becomes so terrifying that the addressee is asked to imagine a scenario where the compulsion is to 'wish thine own heart dry of blood' (5): in effect, to yearn for death.

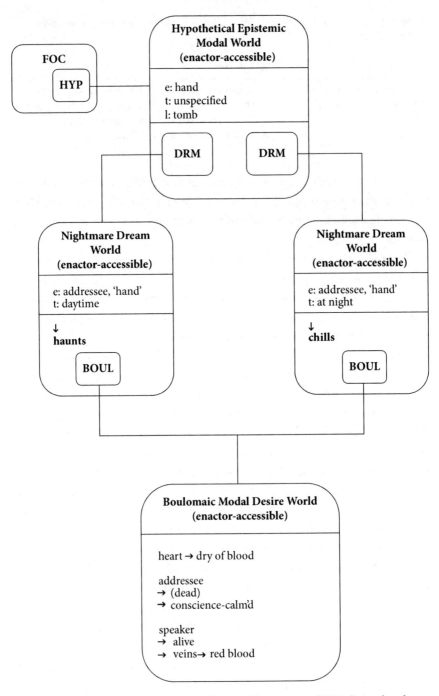

Figure 9.2 Conceptual organisation of the middle section of 'This living hand, now warm and capable'

This would normally be viewed as a boulomaic modal desire world since it sets up a state of affairs through the boulomaic modal lexical verb 'wish'. However, the situation that it points towards would clearly not conventionally be considered one of desire. In fact, the modalised space acts here more as a type of obligatory modal force, the kind represented by Johnson's (1987) COMPULSION image-schema. The strength of this desire world remains dependent on the terror inherent in the nightmare space in which the addressee is haunted both by day and by night by the hand. In this way, the desire space despite the fact that it originates from the deictic centre of the addressee, is understood more as the imagined desire of the speaker. The addressee, by contrast, is afforded no modal power and enactors of that entity in both the nightmare and desire worlds effectively remain subordinate to the fantasy of revenge that the poem maps out. The imagined experience becomes a particularly terrifying one since any agency is afforded to either the speaking voice or to the floating, haunting hand. The overall conceptualisation of the middle section of the poem is shown in Figure 9.2.

9.6 The ending: Cycles of haunting

. . . see, here it is –
I hold it towards you. (7–8)

In his analysis of the poem, Timothy Bahti (1986: 220) asks: 'Is "it" the living hand, or the dead one?' Using text world theory to map out the structure of the final lines can demonstrate that both referents are possible but as I suggest in the following discussion, each involves a different configuration of world structures and generates a distinct literary effect.

In general, the time zone of the final lines remains consistent with the opening of the poem in its use of the present tense, 'see', 'is' (7) and 'hold' (8) and the spatial adverb 'here' (7), which matches the proximal deictic 'this' of the initial world and points towards a return to the same spatio-temporal dimensions. As a result, the final lines of the poem can be understood as triggering a world switch back to the epistemic modal focalised world with which the poem begins. However, since the experience of reading the poem is necessarily a dynamic one, the original space must be updated as part of the process of incrementation, a result of the kind of extreme discontinuity that the radical shifts in time, space and reality of the hypothetical world represent.

In effect, this also means that the strong reaction to the inherently negative content of the nightmare worlds is felt through the movement back across a number of world edges – the process of deictic edgework – into the originating matrix world. The updated world is also afforded a striking intensity, evident in attention afforded to *newness* (the maintenance of the present tense to denote the currency of reading), *topicality* (the imperative mood with the fronted verb 'see') and *activeness* (the movement away from the speaking deictic centre and towards the reader suggested by the preposition 'towards' (8)). Overall, the final lines of the poem maintain the combination of readerly attractiveness, familiarity and proximity that mark its opening.

It is possible to reach a decision on a textual reference for 'it' (7–8) by considering how text world theory deals with anaphors. In his discussion of the phenomenon, Werth proposes that

> anaphors, then, are reference maintainers. This implies that they are specialised forms whose function is to maintain a particular concept in the active register of the discourse. In order to do this, it is essential that they be *traceable* to the concept they are maintaining.
>
> (Werth 1999: 292)

The assigning of a referent for 'it' is dependent on whether the reader accepts its reference as the enactor of the original focalised world or of the hypothetical world. So, nominating 'it' as the living hand understands the anaphoric pronoun 'it' as referring back to the hand of the original focalised space. Given the world-switch back to the matrix world, this would clearly appear to be the most logical and straightforward reading.[6] In this case, the preference for assigning reference to the living hand over the dead one would be the consequence of knowledge about the specific situation in so far as the hand is 'living' in the original world and it is this hand rather than the hand of the remote and hypothetical situation that is still likely to be present as well as more general knowledge about the unlikelihood of a dead hand being animate and able to move.

This first reading then, represents an example of what Werth (1999: 292) terms 'within-world anaphora'. In this case, the return to the initial text world at the end of the poem both repeats the initial focus on the 'living hand' and initiates a further cycle of reading and haunting in its reference to the living hand moving towards the reader as a perceptual figure against the hypothetical dead hand now as background. In doing so, the reader is offered once again the potential for the hypothetical space to be realised since drawing attention to the living hand again serves to trigger a conceptualisation of the imagined dead hand. In this way, the reality space that is the text world only serves to offer an endless cycle of future potential terror, and the poem's power exists in the imagined haunting spaces of the embedded nightmare worlds and suffocating compulsion and desire for death that the reader is asked to conceptualise. The poem haunts then because we always *come back*: as the poem continues to draw attention once more to its intense and central image of the floating hand, it regenerates its power. In this way, as Wolfson (2001: 116) suggests, 'the poem works for ever'.

A second, alternative reading of the poem's final lines is to assign reference to the dead hand of the hypothetical epistemic modal world and subsequent nightmare worlds.[7] Using Werth's notion of anaphor probability, this reading would proceed on the basis that the dead hand has had considerably more recent mention than its living counterpart since the hypothetical space is textually closer to the poem's final lines. Additionally, the attributing of a supernatural feel to the poem means that it is possible to override more general knowledge and accept the possibility of a dead hand being offered, making this reading of the poem arguably even more chilling than the first. Critical to this second reading would appear to be the assigning of Keats to the role of the speaking focaliser-enactor in a way that begins to flesh out the empty text world in more detail than is afforded by the first reading. In this instance, a reader might utilise specific biographical and contextual knowledge about Keats and more general knowledge about human mortality, for as Waters (2003) notes, the situations described in the hypothetical and its subsequent embedded worlds point towards an imminent death that would not have been far from Keats' mind. Subsequently, any reading of the poem after and in the knowledge of the poet's death necessarily means that the protasis of the hypothetical world is now a reality and the initial state of affairs now consigned to history.

This second reading relies of course on treating the poem as a prototypical split discourse world event and placing the *nineteenth century poet John Keats* as a malevolent enactor seeking revenge through death; it simply does not have the same legitimacy under any other circumstances. Whereas the power of the first reading comes in the potential for the experience to be replicated again as a part of an ongoing cycle, the second reading then provokes an equally terrifying experience since in nominating the cross-world counterpart as a referent it inverts the reality statuses of the living and non-living hands. Consequently, the poem logically dictates that as the hypothetical is now the real and is unmarked for modality, the world-building and function advancing material of the embedded nightmare worlds and further desire space will be viewed as part of a conceived reality. In this way, the second reading emphasises the certainty of the fate of the addressee through the cross-world movement of the hand from an imagined to a present space.

9.7 The nightmare experience: The composite nightmare world and addressivity

In previous sections, I have focused on a reading of the poem that draws attention to the ways in which Keats manipulates the reader's movement across a series of text worlds, between an initial state of reality and a subsequent more complex series of hypothetical and subsequent embedded worlds. I have argued that mapping out the movement between worlds and across world edges in the readerly process of edgework allows for an explanation of the effects of terror and helplessness that stem from the interplay of embedded worlds, with an increasingly powerful speaker/agent and submissive addressee. It is clear from my discussion that I consider that the poem's potential cycles of haunting allow for conceptualising the entire reading event as emulating an unpleasant experience. Consequently, the act of reading can be re-imagined as a wider structuring frame, with the result that the initial focalised space simply forms the opening sequence of the nightmare experience, which in turn triggers a series of further embedded text worlds constituting the reader's movement through the poem. This reconfiguration only affects the poem's holding global structure in a minor way: the focalised world and its subsequent worlds are now enclosed in a larger framing nightmare world. The frame becomes a natural way of conceptualising this experience as each discrete world is characterised by the semantic and emotional intensity normally associated with a nightmare world. In addition, the reversal of the typical figure-ground relationship between the boulomaic modal desire world and the world-switch back several layers and worlds have all the hallmarks of a typical nightmare experience, where expectations that would normally be part of a desire space are defeated. The discrete worlds together make up a larger more significant composite nightmare experience, more complex in its associations and movements across space than a smaller more discrete nightmare world, a structure I term a *composite nightmare world*.

Since in the cycle of haunting, there is no explicit waking trigger, the world-switch with which the poem ends can be explained as simply a movement across world edges to the higher order matrix world within the same global structure, which is then re-initiated. Consequently, Wolfson's (2001) suggestion that the poem never seems to end can be explained simply by acknowledging that we never seem to move beyond the composite holding and framing structure. The collapsing of time and space within the composite nightmare world therefore becomes completely natural in the context of a dream experience, where normal laws of space and time do not hold. Reading the poem in this way allows for the justification of universal critical agreement about the poem's haunting resonance simply because having no way of pushing out from the holding structure, the reader becomes stranded within the composite nightmare world. Only a more radical jump back to the discourse world, through disengaging with the reading process, provides an escape from the experience of the poem. The conceptualisation of such an overarching structure to show the composite nightmare world of the poem is represented in Figure 9.3.

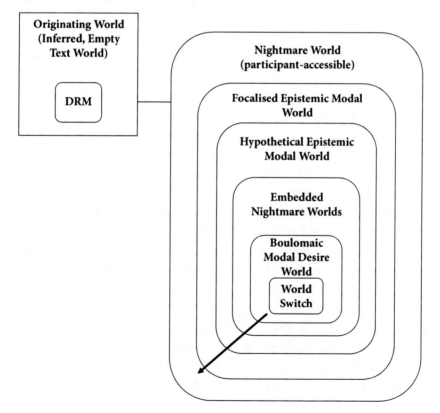

Figure 9.3 The composite nightmare world of 'This living hand, now warm and capable'

In addition to the discussion of the exact referent of 'it', there has been debate about to whom the 'you' of the poem might refer (see in particular Bahti 1986; Waters 2000, 2003). Fludernik (1995) suggests that where texts employ a second person pronoun, they tend to have the following effect:

> one has the curious situation or paradox of *you* forcing the addressee to absolutely invoke self-identity, whereas the interlocutor's *I* merely leads to a kind of empathetic but distanced observation, with an effect of vicarious experience. It is this pronominal or deictic set-up which underlies second person fiction and prepares the way for the special effects of involvement that this form tends to produce. *You,* even if it turns out to refer to a fictional protagonist, initially always seems to involve the actual reader.
>
> (Fludernik 1995: 106)

Waters (2003) examines a wide range of second-person poems, proposing that this kind of general involvement will in reality mean that a reader responds to the use of the second person pronoun in fiction through the positioning of the reading self in one of three participant roles: as overhearer to distinct enactors of the speaker (I) and addressee (you); as addressee of the speaking 'I'; and, assuming the role of speaker and addressing an additional enactor-participant through identifying with the speaking 'I' of the poem. In the first, as overhearer, the 'you' of the poem has an enactor that is not the reader as its referent, possibly unknown to the reader. In the case of 'This living hand', this is most often considered as Fanny Brawne (Wolfson 2001). Assigning the 'you' of the poem in this way means that the reader will tend to flesh out the empty text world of the poem by nominating Keats and Fanny Brawne as enactors in that text world as well as their implied or real life counterparts in the discourse world, with the first spoken lines of the poem initiating either a direct speech or direct thought world as I indicated in Section 9.2. The reader as overhearer therefore becomes an additional enactor in the poem's fictional worlds through the experiencing of the poem but plays no role as a participant in any processes that act as function advancing material.

In the second way of responding to the poem's 'you', the second person pronoun refers to an enactor of the reader so that the reader becomes the nominated addressee of the poem and is consequently invited to self-identify with this text world enactor throughout the subsequent content of the poem. A third and more radical way of responding is to bypass any identification with the 'you' of the poem and instead align oneself with the speaking voice so that the reader is simultaneously speaking and reading but speaking in this instance to an imagined addressee. Text world theory has adopted the concept of *self-implication* (Gerrig 1993) to explain the degrees to which these kinds of identification take place in a fictional event. Gavins (2007a: 86) suggests that any text using a second person pronoun will automatically force the reader to inhabit the speaking deictic centre. She proposes that the degree of implication will depend on the closeness between the life of the text-world enactor and the life of the real-world reader. In this instance, readers' willingness to implicate themselves as referents of the 'you' of a text will depend to what extent their knowledge and belief frames match, as far as they can tell, that of the text-world enactor. However, since in this poem there is no prior information on the text world enactor with which to contrast the reader's own existing knowledge and belief systems, and no further characterisation on which this can be later based, there is a need for an alternative explanation of the potential for self-implication in the poem.

In a wide ranging empirical study, Kuiken et al. (2004: 182–4) identify two distinct ways by which literary discourse resonates particular readers. First, the authors suggest that readers may respond to a literary text by finding similarities between the events and characters of a fictional world and those in their own lives so that they draw explicit comparisons between them. So, for example, one of their respondents in an earlier study (Miall and Kuiken 1994) commented that a description in a short story of houses that looked as though they had been cut out with a pair of steel scissors and pasted into the sky was similar to the respondent's own memories of the street on which she grew up. In this first instance, self-implication occurs through a mapping process based on the model of a simile, 'A is like B', where A is the reader and B the fictional enactor. In the second type of self-implication, a stronger form of self-identification through metaphorical mapping occurs in that readers identify themselves as the same kind of person as an enactor in a fictional world with an ability to place themselves empathetically in that character's situation within the fictional event. In this case, self-implication is understood as the copula metaphorical structure 'A is B'.

Although elaborate and detailed, the authors base their models and observations on the responses of readers to literary texts rather than identifying any structures and features inherent in texts themselves that might be responsible for positioning readers into degrees of self-implication. Given text world theory's insistence on the principle of text-drivenness as the primary driving factor for world construction, it should be possible to suggest ways in which world structure itself might be possible to account for self-implication beyond the use of a second person pronoun. This is addressed in Stockwell (2011), who drawing on the conceptual metaphor of READING IS INVESTMENT, sketches out an 'investment model of reading' to account for the differences between what he terms *sympathy* and *empathy*. Although not focusing on second person fiction, Stockwell draws attention to the ways in which world structure and in particular the perceived movement between and across conceptual spaces may yield patterns, which account for the constraints on the kind of involvement a reader may experience. These are exemplified through the analyses of two poems by the Polish poet Jan Kochanowski. In the first, a reader as discourse world participant is removed from the main processes of the poem through a series of increasingly remote world switches, which being enactor-accessible mean that the reader is left in a deictically remote position relative to the main action. The effect of this is that the reader occupies the role of an observer and is consequently only able to sympathise with the text world enactor of the speaking voice. Alternatively, empathy is possible where there are fewer world switches, fewer problems with inaccessibility and consequently fewer constraints applied to the reader. Stockwell suggests that there is a correlation therefore between reader involvement and accessibility in the process of edgework and that this accounts for the degrees of sympathy and empathy possible.

It would be possible of course for the reader to assume any of the positions of 'overhearer', 'addressee' and 'speaker' in the process of reading 'This living hand, now warm and capable'. In the first, as I suggest earlier in this section, the literary reader as a discourse participant will more than likely nominate text world enactors of Keats and Fanny Brawne based on general knowledge about Keats, his state of mind at the supposed time of composition and details of his relationship with Fanny Brawne, possibly gained through reading his letters and other biographical accounts. As Semino (1995: 147) notes, in poems where there is considerable extra-textual detail to support identifying the poet and speaking voice of the poem, readers often make this type of nomination. The reader in this instance as overhearer would not undertake the explicit role of a text world enactor and therefore becomes detached from the subsequent world switches that make up the remainder of the poem. In this case, we might say that the reader's role in the poem and degree of investment is similar to Stockwell's notion of sympathy. For the purposes of this discussion, I term this particular effect *detachment.*

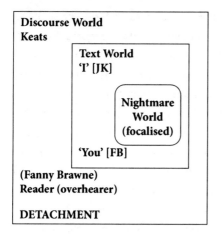
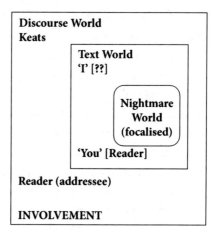
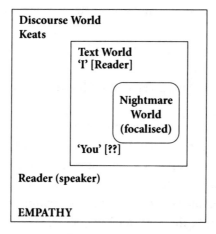

Figure 9.4 Reader identification in 'This living hand, now warm and capable'

Alternatively, for a reader to self-implicate and assume the role of addressee in the poem would be to reconfigure the original world-building elements so that the reader now becomes a prominent enactor, with another speaking enactor who may or may not be conceptualised as the voice of the poet. Finally, the more radical approach of reader-as-speaker allows for an even greater degree of identification as the reader assumes the role of the deictic centre speaking voice. The final two ways generate a movement of a more intensely felt kind across text worlds, allowing for a greater intensity of feeling, and in Stockwell's terms a greater degree of empathy. However, I distinguish between them through the term *involvement* when a reader self-implicates with the second person addressee and *empathy* when a reader identifies with the poem's speaking voice. These two will necessarily be the positions that yield the greatest return on an emotional investment since the reader is forced to undergo the sequence of deictic shifts inwards that mark the composite nightmare world. Since the difference between experiencing the poem as speaker and as addressee is that of positioning oneself as increasingly powerful or increasingly submissive and under varying degrees of compulsion, it can be said that the latter provides the most shocking reading. Since in Fludernik's terms the default position when faced with a literary text that addresses a 'you' is to self-implicate, the poem's world structure can be seen to build on this to situate its reader as an intensely involved but incarcerated participant in the nightmare experience, drawn into an increasingly terrifying series of world-switches.[8] These three types of potential reader identification structures are shown in Figure 9.4. In each case, the layering of embedded worlds identifies how the potential referents for the 'I' and 'you' of the poem form a pattern of movement into the central nightmare world.

9.8 The poem as Coleridge's 'touch'

To end this chapter and this analysis of the poem, I return briefly to my discussion in Section 6.4, where I explained Coleridge's notion of *single* and *double touch* as part of the poet's wider interest in the nightmare. For Coleridge, a nightmare manifests itself through a complex series of physiological and psychological phenomena, interrelated and combining to disrupt bodily and mental functioning in the most terrifying of experiences. The emphasis on the physical, on being 'touched', stands out in all of the poet's accounts of his nightmares. Explicit in their detailing of an increasingly powerless self, they represent closely the experience of 'This living hand, now warm and capable':

> a claw-like talon-mailed Hand grasped hold of me, interposed between the curtains, I haved just before with my foot felt something seeming to move against it (for in my foot it commenced) – I detected it, I say, by my excessive Terror, and dreadful Trembling of my whole body, Trunk & Limbs - & but my piercing out-cries – Good Heaven! (reasoned I) were this real, I never should or could be, in such agony of Terror.
>
>   (Coleridge 1973: e.4046)

It is only possible of course to speculate that Keats may have been influenced by Coleridge's ideas on the nightmare but since the older poet spoke of them to

Keats during a meeting and these were later relayed in a letter (see Section 3.5), we might assume that they resonated with Keats at least to some degree. Moreover, in navigating the worlds of Keats' final poem, we experience the movement across and between world edges as the felt physicality of the reading of this poem. Its ability to touch, to reach out and to terrify is, as I have suggested, most keenly felt at the transition points between worlds and amplified in conceptualising the entire composite nightmare experience. The hand's potential to *touch* through its agency and to haunt the reader through its demonstrable power is the defining characteristic of the poem. For as Milnes suggests:

> the power of this poem lies in the deictic gestures ... but it is above all their ostension. 'See here it is –'that ensures that readers look to the reality.
>
> (Milnes 2010: 102)

9.9 Review

In this final analytical chapter, I have provided an innovative reading of 'This living hand, now warm and capable' that builds on my work on the nightmare world in previous chapters and aims to further demonstrate the potential of text world theory as a critical tool. Since, in line with existing critical opinion, I am less concerned with meaning or attempting to explain the effect of nightmares in terms of their thematic function, my argument here has centred on the way the poem can be understood as one that is not so much read as experienced. Consequently, I have argued that this experience of reading can be explained through the poem's embedded world structure and in particular through the reader's movement between and across different world edges and layers. In addition, I suggested that the entire reading can be reconfigured and read as a framing nightmare experience, which I termed a composite nightmare world. I explained that this nightmare world in turn will necessarily variously engage readers as is typical of poems addressed in the second person and suggested that these different positions or degrees of self-implication can be understood as text world models of detachment, involvement and empathy. This chapter has therefore followed previous ones in applying text world theory while exemplifying in a more radical way how the concept of the nightmare world might be useful in undertaking literary criticism.

Conclusion

10.1 Overview

This book began from the premise that the current text world theory model had yet to be developed to account in a systematic way for both the complex phenomenon of the dream and its associated states and the notion of desire. Consequently, a cognitive poetic analysis of the distinctive nature and use of dreams, desires and nightmares in Keats' poetry was not possible using the existing version of text world theory. This book has therefore sought to develop text world theory to allow for such discussion and analysis to take place. The need to address this operational aspect remains significant and pressing for text world theory as a discipline, since it will consequently allow more sustained work in both Keats studies and poetry dealing with dreams in general. This book has therefore provided a timely set of modifications to Werth's model to account for particular kinds of conceptualisation, building on the significant work in reconfiguring modality within the text world theory model by Gavins (2005a, 2007a).

In developing text world theory to account for specific mentation states, I have argued that it is important to maintain the model's multi-disciplinary approach, both to further draw on those areas that text world theory has historically found useful and to tread new interdisciplinary ground. For the former, I have drawn on those models such as contextual frame theory and deictic shift theory and to a wide range of work in cognitive linguistics; for the latter, I made use of innovative connections from and across the fields of dream theory and sleep medicine to provide a contextual backdrop for my discussion of mentation states and nightmares and consequently my models of the dream and nightmare worlds. In Chapter 4, I provided a review of work in modality and the important key notions of attitude and factuality, gradience and modal force. Here, I made use of work from more general pragmatic positions in conjunction with established models in cognitive linguistics. Furthermore, I proposed a revised continuum of boulomaic forms that utilises Hartmann's (1998) wake-dreaming continuum as a basis for differentiating between different mentation states. These theoretical backgrounds are important in the light of Werth's insistence on the model as a cognitive discourse grammar and the particular attention he affords to the 'human viewpoint' nature of the model, which stresses the importance of human experience and the need to model and replicate human emotions, beliefs and mental processes in the widest sense.

In emphasising the need for a re-evaluation of certain aspects of text world theory, I have proposed a number of additions and modifications to the model. The central modification presented here is focused on how text world theory treats the notion of a dream and its associated mental states. In Chapter 4, I distinguished between boulomaic desire worlds and two kinds of dream worlds: a type A boulomaic dream world and a type B dream world that may be viewed as displaying either peripheral boulomaic properties or those more in line with epistemic forms. Furthermore, placing each of the three kinds of world along a continuum helps to distinguish them on the basis of volition, their reality status and their modal force. I suggested that desire worlds that are prototypically characterised as focused waking thought have stronger degrees of volition and are more likely to represent states of reality. In addition, I accounted for the stronger modal force associated with prototypical boulomaic constructions by drawing attention to how their linguistic realisations have deontic image-schematic forms and are in Langacker's (2008) cognitive grammar terms ground-effecting. Desire worlds and stronger type A dream worlds will therefore necessarily have higher degrees of modal force and be less prone to decomposing. Consequently, I suggested that they will hold a relative functional significance and will be viewed and treated by a reader as such in the act of reading. The modifications I suggested within the boulomaic domain offer a more developed way of accounting for the range of mentation states and have yet to be fully accounted for in existing text world theory models.

The revised notion of desire and dream worlds allows for the identification of a further extreme kind of type B world, the nightmare world, which I have argued has iconic properties and seeks to simulate or emulate a real nightmare experience either through a recount of a nightmare or through its representation in a literary context. As I argued in Chapter 6, work in text world theory has tended to pay less attention to accounting for or explaining the feel or texture within worlds that hold similar global conceptual structures. Consequently, I showed that developing and expanding the notion of different kinds of dream world allows for the explanation of the stylistic texture of a nightmare space. Once again, in Chapter 6, I drew widely from dream theory, sleep medicine and cognitive psychology as a way of broadening text world theory's range of influences. In establishing this unique conceptual space, I proposed three key identifiers. First, I suggested that the automaticity of a nightmare experience means that it has both an establishing and a waking trigger; the experiencer of the nightmare will awaken as a result of the experience and be 'worldswitched' back to the parent space. I demonstrated through my analyses that the world-switch can be seen as having a significant impact on the way in which the revisited parent space is understood, since a form of dynamic world-updating known in text world theory as incrementation will have taken place. I argued that this intended impact mirrors the phenomenon known in sleep medicine as nightmare distress, which accounts for the degree of emotional impact following a nightmare. In the case of literary nightmares, I suggested that it should therefore be possible to measure the residual strength of a nightmare episode by measuring its ripple effect on both characters and readers throughout the remainder of the literary episode.

Secondly, nightmare worlds make extensive use of negation following Givón (1993), in one of its three forms of syntactic, morphological and inherent negation. As I demonstrated in Chapter 6, the patterning of particular examples of each of these forms can produce interesting and significant stylistic effects in their own right. So, I argued that a focus on negation within the text world model also offers the opportunity to review the way in which the model accounts for distinctive examples of negation within a nightmare world. To this end, I highlighted how negation is understood as a process of conceptual contrast in addition to Werth's own discussion of negation as an incrementing force.

Thirdly and finally, I proposed that the striking intensity of nightmare experiences, which has been measured in sleep medicine by using the notion of the central or contextualising image (Hartmann 2008), can be seen in a similar intensity in the nightmare world. Here, I argued that this can be measured stylistically by looking for clusters of salient and attractive lexical items by using the attention-resonance model suggested by Stockwell (2009).

This book represents a timely work on the poetry of John Keats since it represents the first full-length analysis of a canonical English poet using text world theory. However, it also aims to demonstrate how a cognitive poetic approach can supplement existing more conventional approaches to literary criticism. In my four analytical chapters, I have used my development of Werth's model, in conjunction with existing readings, to provide cognitive poetic analyses of four of Keats' poems, all of which I have argued rely on the use of desire and dream structures to generate particular literary effects. The four analytical chapters therefore represent an exemplification of my suggested adaptations to the text world theory model but equally stand as literary appreciations of the poems in their own right, both discretely and as a uniform set of comments on Keats' use of desires, dreams and nightmares. So, in Chapter 5, I showed how much of *The Eve of St Agnes* can be understood as the texture of desire and dream worlds. In Chapter 7 on *Isabella; or the Pot of Basil*, I placed Keats' presentation of Isabella's nightmare experience as the functional heart of the poem. In Chapter 8 on 'La belle dame sans merci', I explored the text world concepts of accessibility and reader tracking in a reading that explores the constraints inherent in experiencing the poem. And, in my final chapter, I provided the most comprehensive reading to my knowledge of Keats' final fragment 'This living hand, now warm and capable'.

10.2 Further implications

This study has offered a re-evaluation of how text world theory deals with desire, dreams and associated states and explores such phenomena in four of Keats' poems. As such, it has attempted to break new ground in text world theory, linguistic-oriented studies of Keats and the analysis of nineteenth-century poetry in cognitive poetics in general. Some further implications arising from this study are presented below.

First, although I have focused solely on poetry and on one particular poet, there is clearly scope for my revisions to text world theory to be applied to a wider range of texts that make use of the variation of the mentation states with which I work. Equally, I believe that there is scope for text world theory to be used across disciplines, for example, in sleep medicine, to account for the specific texture of dream and nightmare recounts by patients, particularly where these are integrated into larger narrative structures and yet represent important episodes in their own right.[1]

As I noted in my introduction to the study, this book has predominantly dealt with the general kinds of constraints that a reader might face in negotiating and tracking the various text worlds in the poems I have analysed. However, in my engagement with and discussion of critical opinion on Keats, I have drawn attention to the kinds of discourse world knowledge that have been used in conjunction with specific textual detail to create rich text worlds and consequent ideas about themes and meaning. So secondly, although beyond the parameters of this book, there is scope and potential for text world theory and my suggested modifications to it to undertake this type of analytical exercise. Again, I would suggest that there is as much potential for this type of work to take place within non-literary contexts as literary ones. It would be interesting, for example, to explore the notions of nightmare distress and degrees of implication and involvement by considering discourse world knowledge in more detail among groups of readers as part of an empirical study.

Finally, it is clear that text world theory will undoubtedly evolve as researchers seek to expand and revise the model and explore new discourse events in innovative ways, mindful of Werth's claim for the model as the ultimate descriptive linguistic framework. It is therefore hoped that this book forms part of a broad and cross-disciplinary movement in cognitive poetics that, where necessary, seeks to both maintain and further renovate Werth's original ideas.

Notes

Chapter 1

1 A distinction between ordinariness and alterity, with degrees of distance between the two, allows for a model which draws attention to key differences as well as similarities. In this way, I am able to highlight both the shared properties and peculiarities of states along this continuum, for example, in what I term 'type A and type B dream worlds' (see Chapter 4).

2 This can be seen in a growing number of historical and political readings of Keats that emerged towards the latter end of the twentieth century. See Sandy (2006) for an overview.

3 Since text world theory presents itself as a discourse grammar and places a key importance on the types of knowledge and beliefs that inform the motivations of discourse participants in the construction of meaning, it should be to account for the readings of different literary critics, working at different times and within different theoretical (and often specialist) parameters (i.e. a *discourse world*). Furthermore, it can draw attention to the different types of world knowledge used by these critics to enrich text-driven world structures (see Gavins (2012) for recent exemplification of this). Subsequently, I use a number of critical readings to either inform my own work or draw attention to how certain world structures have been interpreted in different, conflicting yet possible ways. I also maintain important premise of work in cognitive poetics: that it should be as concerned with hermeneutics (interpretation) as much as poetics (a model of the mind). Consequently, although this chapter and subsequent analytical ones offer new ways of thinking about the conceptualisation of desire and dream states in the poem and make some further suggestions to text world theory model, they are very much underpinned by a strong sense of *interpretation*, whether that be to supply a fresh reading, revise an existing opinion or simply to draw attention to how readerly prominence given to one kind of world structure can explain a reading position. Needless to say, I consider my analytical chapters as exercises in literary criticism.

4 See Martindale and Dailey (1995).

Chapter 2

1 Gavins (2007) is the best comprehensive account of Werth's model, as well as her
   own revisions to it.

2 See Evans and Green (2006) and Geeraerts (2006) for useful summaries.

3 See also Lakoff (1987: 582–5) for a summary of criticism of generative semantics
   and key principles of an alternative cognitive approach.

4 These key areas in cognitive linguistics are given focus in most introductory
   readers and text books (e.g. see Ungerer and Schmidt 1996; Croft and Cruse 2004;
   Evans and Green 2006 and the chapters in Geeraerts 2006).

5 Fillmore's (1977: 106ff) COMMERCIAL EVENT frame provides a good example
   of the way in which a frame represents a particular structure within which a
   related set of lexical items is understood. Here, *buy, pay, charge, cost, money* and
   payment are all responsible for activating a conceptualisation of the frame event
   (they act in a similar way to Langacker's concept of an *access node* (1987: 163))
   and are understood in relation to the participant roles that we might expect
   to find in this particular situation: BUYER, SELLER, GOODS and MONEY.
   Fillmore draws attention to the valence of verbs that form part of the frame, such
   as *buy* and *pay*, in so far as they rely on different configurations of participants
   and place an emphasis on the different relationships between those participants
   within a particular syntactic pattern. The verb *buy* provides a structure within
   the frame for the relationship between a buyer (subject) and the goods (object),
   while a different structure is profiled by the verb phrase *sold*, which provides
   structure between buyer, goods and seller. Alternatively, the verb choice *charged*
   provides an example of the internal structure between all four participant roles.
   In each case, the perspective within the frame is altered to draw attention towards
   a different participant.

6 Bühler distinguishes between *demonstratio ad oculos*, where addresser and
   addressee share the same perceptual space and can use deictic language to
   refer to entities physically present within that shared space; and *deixis am
   phantasma*, where the addresser and addressee do not have access to shared
   physical entities or are in different situational contexts (an additional third
   type is *anaphora*). Since *deixis am phantasma* occurs through the accounts of
   absent narrators or refers to entities imagined rather than present, its primary
   distinguishing feature resides in the role of deictic projection as readerly
   immersion into deictic centres acting as anchoring points for future outward
   projection. The deictic centre then becomes a viewpoint or vantage point from
   which a reader or listener conceptualises events. *Deixis at phantasma* therefore
   shares a similar operational structure to that of Werth's *split discourse world* (see
   Section 2.3.1).

7 McIntyre (2006: 105–6) points out that edgework was originally used by Young (1987) to describe the textual indicators of deictic boundaries rather than the process of moving between them. Despite McIntyre's concern that this double reference and consequent double focus are problematic, in this book I use the term *edgework* when exploring both world edges and the movement between them, since I view the processing and tracking of world boundaries themselves as governed to some extent by the constituent parts of those edges and worlds. So, in Chapter 5 on *The Eve of St Agnes*, I explore the movement between desire and dream worlds as a textural phenomenon dependent on the defining characteristics of those worlds themselves. And in Chapter 9, I suggest that the edgework required by a reader to negotiate a series of embedded worlds in 'This living hand, now warm and capable' is both concerned with movement across and a felt sense of the edges of distinct worlds.

8 In his model, Werth defines the frame not as an actual situation but rather a 'distillation of repeated experiences' (1999: 111) that are shaped through human conceptualisation into a structured representation of knowledge and are open to reshaping through subsequent discourse events.

9 This is a situation which is the case in the vast majority of written literary discourse.

10 The principle of text-drivenness is therefore able to account for the use of contextual information and knowledge in a rigorous and systematic way. It stands as the key innovation that distinguishes text world theory from the other approaches to schematised knowledge.

11 In possible words theory (Ryan 1991), the notion of *accessibility* is used to measure the perceived distance between an unrealised world and the actual world. This is different from text world theory's treatment of the term.

12 Werth (1999: 214) has referred to this as being similar to *hearsay* in the context of a court case. Here, a judge and jury can only evaluate the truthfulness and reliability of what they hear from a co-present witness rather than what we have heard through report. The latter is generally inadmissible as evidence.

13 Werth's ideas on incrementation are similar to those on tracking and updating in Emmott's contextual frame theory (see Section 2.2.1).

14 See Givón (1979: 133–8) and further discussion in Chapter 6.

Chapter 3

1 See Pagel et al. (2001: 197–8) for a good overview of these.

2 See Kahan (2001) for a summary.

3 A recent and detailed study of consciousness can be found in Metzinger (2009). Metzinger argues that consciousness is the 'appearance of a world', which is 'graded . . . and comes in many different shades' (18–19).

4 A cognitive emphasis is also present in Hartmann's claim that through visual
   cross-domain mapping, dreams provide *explanatory metaphors* for a dreamer's
   state of mind (1998: 4). Domhoff's neurocognitive model also suggests that dreams
   make use of the same kinds of conceptual metaphors and metonymies as waking
   thought (2001a: 26), and Lakoff (1993, 2001) provides a detailed overview of how
   conceptual metaphors structure both the dream process and the interpretation
   of that particular dream. Lakoff replaces Freud's *symbolism*, *displacement*,
   condensation and *regression* with the cognitive linguistic models of *conceptual
   metaphor*, *conceptual metonymy*, *conceptual blending* and *irony* to account for how
   unconscious concerns become consciously realised (Lakoff 2001: 2).

5 This belief can be seen in the work of the philosopher David Hartley (1749), a
   firm advocate of psychological associationism, who suggested that dreaming was
   simply a result of physical problems and the mind's creating of its own images
   based on the residue of previous experiences from the day's waking state.

6 Indeed, the poem could be seen as representing an early template for text world
   theory.

7 This is a sentiment echoed by Coleridge who proposes that the dream and drama
   are analogous entities, going so far as to describe characters in his dreams as
   'dramatis personae' (Coleridge 1990: e.5360), differentiating between them and
   their real-life versions in a kind of forerunner of the concept of an *enactor*.

8 See, for example, *Letters* II, 113, n.164; II, 181, n. 197; II, 186, n.199 and II, 329, n.290.

9 Gavins' intention here is to revise Werth's treatment of the modal system within
   text world theory into a better and more usable model rather than to explore every
   possible type of world-switching trigger.

Chapter 4

1 For example, Bybee and Pagliuca (1985: 63–4) use the term 'agent-oriented' to
   stress the role of the agent in effecting propositional force as opposed to a focus on
   a judgement on the truth value of a proposition itself.

2 These principles are similar to those of *prototype theory* (Rosch 1975, 1978, 1988).

3 The ground in this sense is different from that identified as part of a figure/ground
   relationship, which refers to a background against which an attentional figure has
   perceptual prominence. See, for example, Ungerer and Schmid (1996: 156–60) and
   Chapter 6.

4 In Langacker's *Cognitive Grammar*, the traditional grammatical category
   noun represents a kind of 'thing', while a *verb* represents a type of 'process'. See
   Langacker (2008: 103–12).

5 In this case, of course, real may or may not be real in *real world* terms; it is the
   conception that is important.

6 For example, 'must' as in 'You must cover your eyes or they'll be burned' is understood as the COMPULSION schema, while 'may' as in 'We may be able to cure his illness' is based on REMOVAL OF CONSTRAINT.

7 Clearly, there are some subtle differences here, arising as a consequence of the different kind of force-dynamic suggested by the deontic form. It also suggests a difference between 'can' used deontically rather than as a dynamic modal expression and 'will', which exists as a stronger, more emphatic representation of the agonist's tendency, ability and desire. Talmy discusses these differences in a schematic way by suggesting that for deontic forms, with some exceptions,

> a notable semantic characteristic of the modals in their basic usage is that they mostly refer to an agonist that is sentient and to an interaction that is psychological, rather than physical.
>
> (Talmy 1988: 79)

8 See, for example, Werth's own illustration of a job advertisement for the King of France (1999: 230–1).

9 (A) I hope I win the race, (B) I wish I was rich, (C) I want that car
In the above examples, the desire world-building predicates 'hope', 'wish' and 'want' set up stipulative contexts in which sets of conditions are required (respectively winning a race, being rich and having/owning a car) to actualise the processes. In the first example, the conceptual arrangement evident in the explicit desire contains a different temporal deictic centre (some time in the unspecified future) but spatially refers to the same location as the matrix world. Furthermore, the enactors specified in the space, which we could call a *desire world*, remain close to those in the matrix world; the imagined distance between *counterparts* (Fauconnier 1997: 42–3; Werth 1999: 294; Stockwell 2002: 94) is relatively close. This is mirrored in examples (B) and (C) where counterparts of the speaker *I* are conceptualised as part of desire worlds formed by the world-building predicates 'wish' and 'want', and in the final example, accompanied by a counterpart of the desired vehicle. In both examples, counterparts of the locations in which the utterances are spoken are also assumed, in the absence of any further information (compare, for example, the utterance 'When I was in Madrid, I wanted that car').

10 In fact, this distinction has proved difficult across linguistics as a whole. So for example, although the notions of desire and dream are represented in Halliday and Matthiessen's four sub-types of sensing (2004: 208) as examples of *desiderative* and *cognitive higher sub-types*, the authors do point out that

> the system of TYPE OF SENSING construes experience as indeterminate: the four different types of sensing shade into one another.
>
> (Halliday and Matthiessen 2004: 210)

Chapter 5

1 The poem's history of revision is complex, with Stillinger suggesting that there
   were three main versions that Keats 'had some direct hand in: the draft, the
   revised manuscript text, and the first printing' (1999: 25). The most contentious
   changes made by Keats involved making the sexual union between Porphyro
   and Madeline more explicit, a move which both embarrassed and angered Keats'
   lawyer, adviser and editor Richard Woodhouse who despite admitting that 'the
   interest on the reader's imagination is greatly heightened', thought that it would
   make the poem 'unfit for ladies, & indeed scarcely to be mentioned to them'
   (*Letters* II, 163, n.192). Leader (1996: 303) suggests that these revisions were made
   in response to Keats' desire to appear 'manly' in reaction to the very self-conscious
   anxieties that had haunted him since the publication of *Endymion*. In any case,
   these were later removed by Woodhouse before the published 1820 text (Stillinger
   1999: 28).

2 This commercial concern, evident in Keats' letter to his brother and sister where
   he speaks of his jealousy towards Byron's success in selling '4000 coppies' (*Letters*
   II, 62, n.159) of the final canto of *Childe Harolde*, manifests itself in his remark
   about 'making by some means a little to help on' and in doing so hoping to
   'trounce' Byron (*Letters* II, 84, n.159).

3 See Wolfson (1990) for examples of these accusations aimed at Keats, and a
   subsequent history of Keats and female readers.

4 Indeed, it could be said that the process of world-building is similar to the
   cinematic notion of mise-en-scène (Bordwell and Thomson (2003)).

5 Although Porphyro and Madeline have no history as such that is relayed to us
   in the poem, we assume that they must know each other and have come into
   contact before.

6 Stockwell (2009) uses a similar notion to explain the degrees of identification that
   readers may undertake in Kipling's poem 'If'. In exploring how the primary-level
   'you' of the matrix text-world is affected and updated through accessing secondary-
   level enactors in more remotely switched worlds, Stockwell suggests that

   > it might even be a principle of text world theory dynamics if I suggest
   > that attributes assigned to world-switched counterparts of a text world
   > entity are always passed back up and out to the text world entity in order
   > to enrich this higher level enactor.
   >
   > (Stockwell 2009: 149)

   Although Stockwell focuses on enactors of the reader rather than enactors of
   characters within the fictional text, it would seem viable to extend this rule out
   to all text world entities as a specific type of text-world incrementation. In effect

then, we can say that modalised and other world-switches have a 'feeding back' quality that allows their conceptualisations to cross back over the edges to enrich and update the matrix world and in terms of characterisation, provide a way for explaining how readers track and understand more fully formed composites of enactors.

7 The poem has long been read as one concerned with the different kinds of power inherent in the poetic imagination.

Chapter 6

1 I have emphasised this important aspect in Chapter 3. See also Kramer (1982), Fiss (1986) and Domhoff (1993, 2001a) for comprehensive and convincing arguments.

2 For example, Jones (1931) sees nightmares as extreme versions of dreaming that are little more than repressed erotic dreams and Freud (1973a) attempts to account for the phenomenon by differentiating between two further dream sub-types, anxiety and punishment, which nonetheless remain part of a more general categorisation of the dream as wish-fulfilment. Freud explains the anxious dream as the consequence of a repressed wish holding more force than the censorship mechanism that is usually in place in normal dreams. This results both in the anxiety manifest in the dream content and in the understanding of the dream as failed dream functioning, since the fact that the dreamer does not wake up means that sleep is not protected. In a believable thesis but one devoid of any clinical or empirical evidence, Freud proposes that the displeasure caused by traumatic dreams can be explained by seeing the dreamer fighting against his own wishes in a counterpart relationship: as two 'separate people who are linked by some strong element in common' (Freud 1973a: 253). By splitting the dreaming-self, Freud suggests that the lack of pleasure experienced can simply be explained in the fact that the anxiety dream is a fight against a wish that remains not 'an acceptable one but a repudiated one' (1973a: 254). In a similar way, Freud's second type of dream, the punishment dream, is viewed as a contrary fulfilment of a kind: in this case, the wish is brought about due to the self-censoring and critical super-ego part of the mind (1973a: 257; 1973b: 91).

There is, however, one particular kind of bad dream that Freud admits is incompatible with a view of dreaming as wish-fulfilment. His brief discussion of traumatic dreams, defined by Domhoff (1993: 295) as those that replay emotionally negative states of affairs in a continual repetition of a traumatic event 'in all its emotional detail and horror', leads him to conclude that they can again only be explained in the absence of any other justified explanation as examples of failed dream functioning (Freud 1973b: 58). Freud's failure to develop work on such phenomena in any further detail leads him to view these as simply exceptions to his general theory, merely an example of 'trivial interferences with the functions of dreams' (1973b: 59).

3   However, some researchers have avoided this distinction and have defined the nightmare simply as any unpleasant emotional dream (e.g. Belicki 1992a; Wood and Bootzin 1990; Wood et al. 1992; McNamara 2008).

4   See also Kuiken and Sikora (1993) and Hartmann (1999). For an overview of nightmares and the intensity of negative emotions, see Zadra et al. (2006).

5   See also Hobson (2005: 80–2).

6   In my revised model for desire-dream worlds, this supports placing the nightmare as an extreme example of a type B dream world, exhibiting a prototypical lack of volition.

7   Others have also found that this leads to the sharing of content with others (Vann and Alperstein 2000), and the use of nightmares for creative purposes (Hartmann 1984; States 1997; Pagel 2008).

8   McNamara also suggests that nightmares tend to be less metaphorical than ordinary dreams, although this characteristic is often disputed (see Hartmann 1984, 1996, 1998; Hartmann et al. 2001; Oudiette et al. 2009).

9   Other writers of the period make extensive reference to supernatural and demonic presence. Macnish (1834: 122) refers to 'unearthly shrieks and gibberish of hags, witches and fiends' as components of the nightmare, while Clodd (1891: 171) ascribes the phenomenon to a 'vast army of nocturnal demons' that invades a sleeper's dreams. Drawing together the nightmare and the supernatural, Jones (1931) traces how nightmare experiences have influenced and accounted for the longevity of superstitious belief in werewolves, vampires and witches.

10 Although the work has occasionally been read as a fantasy of revenge directed at a woman who had rejected him (see Myrone 2001: 70), it also presents an idea of the nightmare consistent with that suggested by theorists of his time. The presence of the horse in Fuseli's painting can also be read as the presence of some additional external spirit, although it is possible that there is an additional play on the word *mare* (female horse): see Jones (1931: 245) for an explanation on the assimilation of the words *mara* and *mare*.

11 Coleridge preferred this spelling to *nightmare*: see Coleridge (1906: 210).

12 There are some late letters to Fanny Brawne that are littered with references to the nightmare-type phenomena described by Coleridge. These generally arise from extreme physical and emotional distress in melodramatic descriptions of love-sick states. See, for example, *Letters* II, 123, n.172; II, 224, n.204.

13 In fact, Jordan argues that in many if not most instances, negative statements can be more informative than positive ones (1998: 707) and that ultimately, assigning

different informational levels to positive and negative statements in language use is inappropriate since they serve different functions (1998: 709).

14　Since literary discourse is designed to 'effect a change in the schemata' (Cook 1994: 191) of readers, it follows that literary texts will tend to fit into the category of schema-refreshing discourse, although as Cook points out, 'This is not to say, however, that all literature is schema refreshing or that all schema-refreshing discourse is literature' (1994: 192). Equally, the quality of schema-refreshment is not understood to be universal but rather to be seen as reader-dependent (1994: 192).

15　However, by reversing the figure/ground relationship to make the non-event more salient, the negative construction becomes a felicitous one, against the background of the positive conception:

> I waited and waited there. Finally, when John **didn't** come, I left.
>
> Givón (1993: 193)

16　Lakoff (2004: 3) views the understanding of all negative constructions as reliant on this type of conceptual contrast, stressing that 'when we negate a frame, we evoke the frame'.

17　See also Clark and Clark 1977: 452–8).

18　See my discussion of boulomaic desire and dream worlds in Chapters 4 and 5 for an example of this.

19　Thus, Stockwell's *maintenance* can be viewed as operating in a similar way to the kinds of anti-shifting devices explicit in deictic shift theory (Zubin and Hewitt 1995: 144ff.).

20　See Allan (2009: 627).

Chapter 7

1　Bennett (1994: 82) suggests that initially the motivation for Keats to write *Isabella* was to make money and to develop a more substantial following of readers since translations of Boccaccio had proved to be very popular among the general reading public (see also Wright 1957). Heinzelman (1988: 165) notes that Keats may have been influenced by William Hazlitt's *Essay on the Principles of Human Action*, which condemned the strong motivational force of the human attribute of self-interest and its effects. Following Hazlitt's remark in his lecture 'On Dryden and Pope' that 'some of the serious tales in Boccaccio . . . if executed with taste and spirit, could not fail to succeed' (Hazlitt 1930: 82), Keats inevitably saw the collaboration as an opportunity to secure the kind of readership that *Endymion* had failed to provide. The fact that the collaboration did not ultimately take place is more down to Keats' own dissatisfaction with, and insecurities about, the poem than any problem working with Reynolds. Indeed, according to Heinzelman (1988: 171), Reynolds was unable to initially complete his planned poems due to illness.

2   This was a view not shared by Woodhouse who believed that the poem would 'please more [than] *the Eve of St Agnes* (*Letters* II, 162, n.192).

3   Since these modal constructions refer to ability, they would normally be considered as examples of *dynamic modality* (Palmer 2001 and see Section 4.1.4).

4   This point is emphasised by Everest (1995: 120).

5   This image of Isabella is incremented into an updated view of her character in the poem. Indeed, the premonition of death foregrounds the arrival of, and focus on, Lorenzo's ghost in subsequent stanzas, and of course Isabella, at the end of the poem.

6   Indeed, Keats affords a significant amount of space (seven stanzas) to detailing the contents of this vision, which like the preceding nightmare world is participant-accessible.

7   Following her vision, Isabella resolves to disinter Lorenzo's body, remove the head and plant it, as a way of regenerating, albeit in a perverse manner, the brief intimacy she and Lorenzo shared in the opening sections of the poem. Ironically of course, the enactor of Lorenzo acting as the ghost in the nightmare world is afforded a considerably more vocal presence than that in the opening sections of the poem, and this greater sense of intimacy is matched following the nightmare by the physical proximity Isabella shares with Lorenzo's body in stanzas XLVII and LI.

8   It is this kind of sentimentality in the celebration of the literary over the economic that may have caused Keats to suggest that the poem was too 'smokeable' and prone to the kind of criticism levelled at *Endymion*.

9   Indeed, it is tempting to view a similarity between rooms in this sense and text worlds, both of which have defined boundaries.

Chapter 8

1   The two versions of the poem have attracted varying degrees of critical comparison, with the earlier one generally regarded as being both the textually superior and authoritative text (see Stillinger 1974). However, McGann (1993) argues for the supremacy of the 1820 *Indicator* version since it represents the only version that Keats chose to publish in his lifetime. Kelley (1987) distinguishes between the two not on any literary merit but on their respective different contexts of reception. She reads the first – but now established version – as being originally for a private, family audience while the second with its changes reflecting a more conscious sensitivity to the *Indicator's* likely readership and revisions that were intended to secure a more sympathetic reception from critics than both his earlier poetry and the earlier version of the poem would allow.

2 This is a common reading of the poem and can be seen, for example, in Wasserman (1953), Perkins (1959), D'Avanso (1967) and Motion (1997).

3 I use the term *initial speaker* as a way of referring to this particular enactor to draw attention to the poem's emphasis on speech and representation. Traditionally, critical readings of the poem tend to use the term *narrator*.

4 See Wise (1976: 21) for a discussion of the difference between the terms 'man-at-arms' and 'knight-at-arms' in the context of the organisation of a medieval cavalry.

5 However and ironically, we do of course have to accept its contents to some degree for any reading to take place at all. As Gavins (2010: 405) explains, although enactor-created and consequently enactor-accessible worlds cannot be verified for truth by discourse participants, these worlds are frequently accepted by readers as existing at the same ontological level as participant-created worlds.

6 Sandy (2000) argues that Keats rejects the 'Wordsworthian consolation' of nature, evident, for example, in 'Resolution and Independence' and instead presents inherently negative landscapes in both waking and dreaming modes that serve to highlight the failure of the imagination to transcend reality.

7 For a detailed example of this reading, see Bloom (1961).

8 Spatially then, the new world is consistent with that of the first focalised world of the initial speaker and probably understood as consistent with that of the empty or inferred text world.

9 Keats' own remarks on the poem can also be read in the light of this particular scepticism. He explains the choice of la belle dame's 'four kisses' in the same letter-journal to his brother and his brother's wife that contained the original version of the poem, by stressing the need to 'temper the Imagination as the Critics say with Judgment' (*Letters* II, 97, n. 159), reversing words originally spoken by Hazlitt.

10 In his reading that sees the poem as the merging of a medieval poetic concern with melancholy and early nineteenth-century ideas on the nightmare state, Kiessling (1983: 9) suggests that the knight, like Keats' poetic psyche, remains forever stranded between the worlds of haunting vision and cold reality following his dream. Such a reading clearly acknowledges the influence of Coleridge on Keats' thinking.

Chapter 9

1 For example, see Bate (1963: 626) who suggests that the poem represents 'the last serious lines he was ever to write', and composed as a thematic and stylistic antidote to stanza LI of *The Cap and Bells*, was probably intended for some future dramatic work. Alternatively, Motion (1997: 476) proposes that the lines were intended to form part of another failed composition, the dramatic work *King Stephen*.

2 Unsurprisingly, given the content of these letters, the poem has often been read as one of an imagined revenge on a lover (Fanny Brawne), However, this reading has been challenged, see, for example, Hopkins (1989) and Waters (2001, 2003).

3 Yet again, the poem's indeterminate nature means that both readings are possible and choosing one over the other does little to affect the poem's text world macro-structure beyond that of assigning a body-as-enactor as a world-builder in the focalised space.

4 In Gavins' (2005a) reconfiguration of modal worlds, she integrates these ideas by accounting for hypothetical structures as *hypothetical epistemic modal worlds*.

5 In fact, the lexical choice 'haunt' with attention concentrated on the psychological impact of the hand's possible actions means that it is possible to view this world as a fleeting nightmare world, represented through a central image of fear, and imagined briefly.

6 Indeed, the world-switch itself provides the primary means of *tracing* that Werth suggests is necessary since the trace is a simple one between entities within the same text world. Furthermore, Werth suggests the following about anaphora where there are a number of possible references.

> Where there is a potential ambiguity of chaining...we assign a probability to each possible reference, based on our frame knowledge of the specific situation and our general knowledge of the situation-type.
>
> (Werth 1999: 293)

7 Since I am arguing that the entire poem attempts to emulate a nightmare experience for the reader, this latter and more supernatural reading is of course plausible.

8 A text world account of this phenomenon can therefore explain Waters' (2003:15) suggestion that poems explicitly referring to the second person seem to entrap the reader by 'begging identification'.

Chapter 10

1 I also believe there is considerable scope for exploring other additions to the text world theory model that I have suggested, for example, my notions of the *establishing world*, the *world zoom* and the operational structure of my ideas on *composite enactors* in Chapter 5.

Bibliography

Allan, K. (2009) 'The connotations of colour terms: colour-based X-phemisms', *Journal of Pragmatics* 41(3), 626–37.

Allen, G. O. (1960) 'Kisses four: La belle dame as Phoebe', *The News Bulletin of the Rocky Mountain Modern Language Association* 13(3), 3–4.

Al-Mansoob, H. (2005) *The Text Worlds of Raymond Carver: A Cognitive Poetic Analysis*, Unpublished PhD thesis, University of Nottingham.

Antrobus, J. (1993) 'Dreaming: could we do without it?', in A. Moffitt, M. Kramer and R. Hoffman (eds), *The Function of Dreams*, Albany, NY: State University of New York Press, pp. 549–58.

Arseneau, M. (1997) 'Madeline, mermaids, and medusas in *The Eve of St Agnes*', *Papers on Language and Literature* 33, 227–43.

Bachelard, G. (1969) *The Poetics of Reverie: Childhood, Language and the Cosmos* (translated from the French by Daniel Russell), Boston, MA: Beacon Press.

Bahti, T. (1986) 'Ambiguity and indeterminacy: the juncture', *Comparative Literature* 38(3), 209–23.

Barrett, D. (ed.), (1996) *Trauma and Dreams*, Cambridge, MA: Harvard University Press.

Bate, W. J. (1963) *John Keats*, Cambridge, MA: Harvard University Press.

Baxter, A. (1733) *An Enquiry into the Nature of the Human Soul; Wherein the Immateriality of the Soul is Evinced from the Principles of Reason and Philosophy*, London.

Belicki, K. (1992a) 'Nightmare frequency versus nightmare distress: relations to psychopathology and cognitive style', *Journal of Abnormal Psychology* 101, 592–7.

— (1992b) 'The relationship of nightmare frequency to nightmare suffering with implications for treatment and research', *Dreaming* 2, 143–8.

Belicki, K. and Cuddy, M. (1996) 'Identifying sexual trauma histories from patterns of sleep', in D. Barrett (ed.), *Trauma and Dreams*, Cambridge, MA: Harvard University Press, pp. 46–55.

Bennett, A. (1994) *Keats, Narrative and Audience: The Posthumous Life of Writing*, Cambridge: Cambridge University Press.

Bentley, P. (2003) 'Caviare from the count: Blackwood's and John Keats's "La belle dame sans merci"', *Romanticism* 9, 55–67.

Berkowitz, L. (2000) *Cause and Consequences of Feelings*, West Nyack, NY: Cambridge University Press.

Bex, T. (1995) 'Keats and the disappearing self: aspects of deixis in odes', in K. Green (ed.), *New Essays on Deixis: Discourse, Narrative, Literature*, Amsterdam: Rodopi, pp. 161–78.

Blagrove, M. and Akehurst, L. (2000) 'Personality and dream recall frequency: further negative findings', *Dreaming* 10(3), 139–48.

Blagrove, M. and Haywood, S. (2006) 'Evaluating the awakening criterion in the definition of nightmares: how certain are people in judging whether a nightmare woke them up?', *Journal of Sleep Research* 15, 117–24.

Blagrove, M., Farmer, L. and Williams, E. (2004) 'The relationship of nightmare frequency and nightmare distress to well-being', *Journal of Sleep Research* 13, 129–36.

Blake, W. (2004) *The Complete Poems*, A. Ostriker (ed.), Harmondsworth: Penguin.

Bloom, H. (1961) *The Visionary Company: A Reading of English Romantic Poetry*, Garden City, NY: Doubleday.

— (1970)'The internalization of quest-romance', in H. Bloom (ed.), *Romanticism and Consciousness: Essays in Criticism*, New York: W. W. Norton, pp. 3–24.

Bond, J. (1753) *An Essay on the Incubus, or Nightmare*, London: Wilson and Durham.

Bordwell, D. and Thomson, K. (2003) *Film Art* (4th edn), London: McGraw-Hill.

Bosinelli, M. (1995) 'Mind and consciousness during sleep', *Behavioural Brain Research* 69, 195–201.

Brooks, C. (1947) *The Well Wrought Urn: Studies in the Structure of Poetry*, New York: Harcourt Brace.

Bruhn, M. (2005) 'Place deixis and the schematics of imagined space: Milton to Keats', *Poetics Today* 26(3), 387–432.

Bühler, K. (1982) 'The deictic field of language and deictic worlds', in R. Jarvella and W. Klein (eds), *Speech, Place and Action: Studies in Deixis and Related Topics* (translated from *Sprachtheorie*, 1934), Chichester: John Wiley, pp. 9–30.

Bulkeley, K. (ed.) (2001) *Dreams: A Reader on the Religious, Cultural and Psychological Dimensions of Dreaming*, New York: Palgrave.

Burke, E. (1958) *A Philosophical Enquiry into the Origin of Our Ideas of the Sublime and Beautiful*, J. Boulton (ed.), London: Routledge and Kegan Paul.

Burke, K. (1943) 'Symbolic action in a poem by Keats', *Accent* 4, 30–42.

Bush, D. (1966) *John Keats: His Life and Writings*, New York: Macmillan.

Bybee, J. and Pagliuca, W. (1985) 'Cross-linguistic comparison and the development of grammatical meaning', in J. Fisiak (ed.), *Historical Semantics, Historical Word Formation*, Berlin: Morton de Gruyter, pp. 59–84.

Bybee, J., Perkins, R. and Pagliuca, W. (1994) *The Evolution of Grammar: Tense, Aspect and Modality in the Languages of the World*, Chicago, IL: Chicago University Press.

Byron, G. G. (1905) *The Poetical Works of Lord Byron*, E. H. Coleridge (ed.), London: John Murray.

Carstensen, K. (2007) 'Spatio-temporal ontologies and attention', *Spatial Cognition and Computation* 7(1), 1–19.

Cartwright, R. (1991) 'Dreams that work: the relation of dream incorporation to adaptation to stressful events', *Dreaming* 1, 3–10.

Chung, S. and Timberlake, A. (1985) 'Tense, aspect and mood', in T. Shopen (ed.), *Language Typology and Syntactic Description*, Volume III, Cambridge: Cambridge University Press, pp. 202–58.

Clark, H. H. and Clark, E. V. (1977) *Psychology and Language: An Introduction to Psycholinguistics*, New York: Harcourt Brace.

Clodd, E. (1891) *Myths and Dreams*, London: Chatto and Windus.

Coates, J. (1983) *The Semantics of the Modal Auxiliaries*, London and Canberra: Croom Helm.

Coates, J. and Leech, G. (1980) 'The meanings of modals in modern British and American English', *York Papers in Linguistics* 8, 23–4.

Coleridge, S. T. (1906) *Biographia Literaria*, G. Watson (ed.), London: J. M. Dent.

— (1962) *The Notebooks of Samuel Taylor Coleridge, Volume 2*, K. Coburn (ed.), London: Routledge and Kegan Paul.

— (1973) *The Notebooks of Samuel Taylor Coleridge, Volume 3*, K. Coburn (ed.), London: Routledge and Kegan Paul.

— (1987) *Lectures 1808-1819: On Literature, Volume 2*, R. A. Foakes (ed.), London: Routledge and Kegan Paul.

— (1990) *TheNotebooks of Samuel Taylor Coleridge, Volume 4*, K. Coburn (ed.), London: Routledge and Kegan Paul.

Collins, P. (1974) 'The analysis of the English modal auxiliaries as main verbs', *Kivung* 7, 151–66.

Cook, G. (1994) *Discourse and Literature*, Oxford: Oxford University Press.

Corcoran, B. (2009) 'Keats's death: towards a posthumous poetics', *Studies in Romanticism* 48(2), 321–50.

Cowen, D. and Levin, R. (1995) 'The use of the Hartmann boundary questionnaire with an adolescent population', *Dreaming* 5, 105–14.

Cox, J. (ed.), (2009) *Keats's Poetry and Prose*, New York: W. W. Norton & Company.

Crews, F. and Bulkeley, K. (2001) 'Dialogue with a skeptic', in K. Bulkeley (ed.), *Dreams: A Reader on the Religious, Cultural and Psychological Dimensions of Dreaming*, New York: Palgrave, pp. 361–77.

Croft, W. and Cruse, D. A. (2004) *Cognitive Linguistics*, Cambridge: Cambridge University Press.

Cruickshank, T. and Lahey, E. (2010) 'Building the stages of drama: towards a text world theory account of dramatic play texts', *Journal of Literary Semantics* 39, 67–91.

Culler, J. (1977) 'Apostrophe', *Diacritics* 7(4), 59–69.

D'Avanso, M. (1967) *Keats's Metaphors for the Poetic Imagination*, Durham, NC: Duke University Press.

Damasio, A. (1994) *Descartes' Error: Emotion, Reason and the Human Brain*, New York: Grosset/Putnam.

— (2001) 'Fundamental feelings', *Nature* 413, 781.

— (2004) *Looking for Spinoza: Joy, Sorrow and the Feeling Brain*, London: Vintage.

Darwin, E. (1789) *The Botanic Garden*, London: J. Johnson.

— (1796) *Zoonomia; or The Laws of Organic Life*, London: J. Johnson.

De Quincey, T. (1993) *Confessions of an English Opium-Eater*, Ware: Wordsworth Classics.

de Selincourt, E. (ed.), (1926) *The Poems of John Keats*, London: Methuen.

Delacour, J. (1995) 'An introduction to the biology of consciousness', *Neuropsychologia* 33(9), 1061–74.

Domhoff, G. W. (1993) 'The repetition of dreams and dream elements: a possible clue to the function of dreams', in A. Moffitt, M. Kramer and R. Hoffman (eds), *The Function of Dreams*, Albany, NY: State University of New York Press, pp. 293–320.

— (1999) 'Drawing theoretical implications from descriptive empirical findings on dream content', *Dreaming* 9(2/3), 201–10.

— (2001a) 'A new neurocognitive theory of dreams', *Dreaming* 11(1), 13–33.

— (2001b) 'Using content analysis to study dreams: applications and implications for the humanities', in K. Bulkeley (ed.), *Dreams: A Reader on the Religious, Cultural and Psychological Dimensions of Dreaming*, New York: Palgrave, pp. 307–20.

— (2010) 'Dream thought is continuous with waking thought based on preoccupations, concerns and interests', *Sleep Medicine Clinics* 5, 203–15.

Easthope, A. (1989) *Poetry and Phantasy*, Cambridge: Cambridge University Press.

Ekman, P. (1992) 'An argument for basic emotions', *Cognition and Emotion* 6, 169–200.

Emmott, C. (1994) 'Frames of reference: contextual monitoring and narrative discourse', in M. Coulthard (ed.), *Advances in Written Text Analysis*, London: Routledge, pp. 157–66.

— (1997) *Narrative Comprehension: A Discourse Perspective*, Oxford: Oxford University Press.

— (2003) 'Constructing social space: socio-cognitive factors in the interpretation of character relations', in D. Herman (ed.), *Narrative Theory and the Cognitive Sciences*, Stanford, CA: CSLI, pp. 283–309.

Enscoe, G. (1967) *Eros and the Romantics: Sexual Love as a Theme in Coleridge, Shelley and Keats*, The Hague: Mouton.

Evans, V. (2009) 'Cognitive Linguistics', in L. Cummings (ed.), *The Pragmatics Encyclopaedia*, London: Routledge, pp. 46–9.

Evans, V. and Green, M. (2006) *Cognitive Linguistics*, Edinburgh: Edinburgh University Press.

Everest, K. (1995) '*Isabella* in the market place: Keats and feminism', in N. Roe (ed.), *Keats and History*, Cambridge: Cambridge University Press, pp. 107–26.

Fauconnier, G. (1994) *Mental Spaces: Aspects of Meaning Construction in Natural Language*, Cambridge: Cambridge University Press.

— (1997) *Mappings in Thought and Language*, Cambridge: Cambridge University Press.

Fauconnier, G. and Turner, M. (2002) *The Way We Think: Conceptual Blending and the Mind's Hidden Complexities*, New York: Basic Books.

Fillmore, C. (1968) 'The case for case', in E. Bach and R. T. Harms (eds), *Universals in Linguistic Theory*, New York: Holt, Rinehart and Winston, pp. 1–88.

— (1977) 'Scenes-and-frames semantics', in A. Zampolli (ed.), *Linguistic Structures Processing*, Amsterdam: North Holland, pp. 55–82.

— (1982a) 'Towards a descriptive framework for spatial deixis', in R. Jarvella and W. Klein (eds), *Speech, Place and Action: Studies in Deixis and Related Topics*, Chichester: John Wiley, pp. 31–59.

— (1982b) 'Frame Semantics', in The Linguistic Society of Korea (ed.), *Linguistics in the Morning Calm*, Seoul: Hanshin Publishing Co., pp. 111–37.

— (1985) 'Frames and the Semantics of understanding', *Quaderni de Semantica* 6(2), 222–54.

Finney, C. L. (1964) *The Evolution of Keats's Poetry*, New York: Russell and Russell.

Fish, S. (1980) *Is There a Text in This Class? The Authority of Interpretive Communities*, Cambridge MA: Harvard University Press.

Fisher, C., Byrne, J., Edwards, A. and Kahn, E. (1970) 'A psychophysiological study of nightmares', *Journal of the American Psychoanalytic Association* 18, 747–82.

Fiss, H. (1986) 'An empirical foundation for a self psychology of dreaming', *Journal of Mind and Behavior* 7, 161–91.

Fludernik, M. (1995) 'Pronouns of address and 'odd' third person forms: the mechanics of involvement in fiction', in K. Green (ed.), *New Essays in Deixis: Discourse, Narrative, Literature*, Amsterdam: Rodopi, pp. 99–129.

Fogle, R. H. (1945) 'A Reading of Keats *The Eve of St Agnes*', *College English* 6, 325–8.

Ford, J. (1998) *Coleridge on Dreaming: Romanticism and the Medical Imagination*, Cambridge: Cambridge University Press.

Fosse, R. Stickgold, R. and Hobson, J. A. (2001) 'The mind in REM sleep: reports of emotional experience', *Sleep* 24, 947–55.

Foulkes, D. (1979) 'Home and laboratory dreams: four empirical studies and a conceptual re-evaluation', *Sleep* 2, 233–51.

— (1985) *Dreaming: A Cognitive-Psychological Analysis*, Hillside, NJ: Lawrence Erlbaum.

— (1990) 'Dreams and consciousness', *European Journal of Cognitive Psychology* 3(1), 39–55.

Foulkes, D., Sullivan, B., Kerr, N. and Brown, L. (1988) 'Appropriateness of dream feelings to dreamed situations', *Cognition and Emotion* 2, 29–39.

Fowler, R. (1986) *Linguistic Criticism*, Oxford: Oxford University Press.

Frayling, C. (2006) 'We live in Gothic times', in M. Myrone (ed.), *The Gothic Reader: A Critical Anthology*, London: Tate Publishing, pp. 12–20.

Freud, S. (1973a) *Introductory Lectures on Psychoanalysis*, (ed.) A. Dickson (translated from the German by James Strachey), Harmondsworth: Pelican.

— (1973b) *New Introductory Lectures on Psychoanalysis*, (ed.) J. Strachey (translated from the German by James Strachey), Harmondsworth: Pelican.

— (1976) *The Interpretation of Dreams*, (ed.) A. Richards (translated from the German by James Strachey), Harmondsworth: Penguin.

— (1985a) 'Creative writers and day-dreaming', in A. Dickson (ed.), *Art and Literature* (translated from the German by James Strachey), Harmondsworth: Penguin, pp. 129–41.

— (1985b) 'The uncanny', in *Art and Literature* (translated from the German by James Strachey), Harmondsworth: Penguin, pp. 335–76.

Galbraith, M. (1995) 'Deictic shift theory and the poetics of involvement in narrative', in J. F. Duchan, G. A. Bruder and L. E. Hewitt (eds), *Deixis in Narrative: A Cognitive Science Perspective*, Hillsdale, NJ: Lawrence Erlbaum, pp 19–60.

Garfield, P. (1996) 'Dreams in bereavement', in D. Barrett (ed.), *Trauma and Dreams*, Cambridge, MA: Harvard University Press, pp. 186–211.

Gavins, J. (2000) 'Absurd tricks with bicycle frames in the text world of *The Third Policeman*', *Nottingham Linguistic Circular* 15, 17–33.

— (2001) *Text World Theory: A Critical Exposition and Development in Relation to Absurd Prose Fiction*, Unpublished PhD thesis, Sheffield Hallam University.

— (2003) 'Too much blague? An exploration of the text worlds of Donald Barthelme's *Snow White*', in J. Gavins and G. Steen (eds), *Cognitive Poetics in Practice*, London: Routledge, pp. 129–44.

— (2005a) '(Re)thinking modality: a text world perspective', *Journal of Literary Semantics* 34(2): 79–93.

— (2005b) 'Text world theory in literary practice', in B. Petterson, M. Polvinen and H. Velvo (eds), *Cognition and Literary Interpretation in Practice*, Helsinki: University of Helsinki Press, pp. 89–104.

— (2007a) *Text World Theory: An Introduction*, Edinburgh: Edinburgh University Press.

— (2007b) 'And everyone and I stopped breathing': familiarity and ambiguity in the text-world of "The day lady died"', in M. Lambrou and P. Stockwell (eds), *Contemporary Stylistics*, London: Continuum, pp. 133–43.

— (2010) "Appeased by the certitude': the quiet disintegration of the paranoid mind in *The Mustache*', in D. McIntyre and B. Busse (eds), *Language and Style*, Basingstoke: Palgrave Macmillan, pp. 402–18.

— (2012) 'Leda and the stylisticians', *Language and Literature* 12(4): 345–62.

Geeraerts, D. (ed.), (2006) *Cognitive Linguistics: Basic Readings*, Berlin: Walter de Gruyter.

Genette, G. (1980) *Narrative Discourse*, New York: Cornell University Press.

Gerring, R. (1993) *Experiencing Narrative Worlds: On the Psychological Activities of Reading*, New Haven, CT: Yale University Press.

Giovanelli, M. (2010) 'A text world theory approach to the teaching of poetry', *English in Education* 44(3), 214–31.

Gittings, R. (1954) *John Keats: The Living Year*, Cambridge, MA: Harvard University Press.

— (1968) *John Keats*, Harmondsworth: Penguin.

Givón, T. (1979) *On Understanding Grammar*, New York: Academic Press.

— (1984) *Syntax: A Functional-Typological Introduction Volume I*, Amsterdam: John Benjamins.

— (1989) *Mind, Code and Context: Essays in Pragmatics*, Hillsdale, NJ: Lawrence Erlbaum.

— (1993) *English Grammar: A Function-Based Introduction: Volume 1*, Amsterdam: John Benjamins.

— (2005) *Context as Other Minds: The Pragmatics of Sociality, Cognition and Communication*, Philadelphia, PA: John Benjamins.

Goellnicht, D. C. (1984) *The Poet-Physician: Keats and Medical Science*, Pittsburgh, PA: University of Pittsburgh Press.

Greenberg, R. and Pearlman, C. (1993) 'An integrated approach to dream theory: contributions from sleep research and clinical practice', in A. Moffitt, M. Kramer and R. Hoffman (eds), *The Function of Dreams*, Albany, NY: State University of New York Press, pp. 363–80.

Grice, H. P. (1975) 'Logic and conversation', in P. Cole and J. L. Morgan (eds), *Syntax and Semantics, Volume 3: Speech Acts*, New York: Academic Press.

Griffiths, P. (1997) *What Emotions Really Are*, Chicago: University of Chicago Press.

Hall, C. (1973) 'A cognitive theory of dreams', in S. G. M. Lee and A. R. Mayes (eds), *Dreams and Dreaming*, Harmondsworth: Penguin, pp. 361–70.

Hall, G. (2009) 'Texts, readers – and real readers', *Language and Literature* 18(3), 331–7.

Hall, J. (1991) 'Romance to ode: love's dream and the conflicted imagination', in W. H. Evert and J. W. Rhodes (eds), *Approaches to Teaching Keats's Poetry*, New York: Modern Language Association of America, pp. 126–30.

Halliday, G. (1987) 'Direct psychological therapies for nightmares: a review', *Clinical Psychology Review* 7, 501–23.

Halliday, M. and Matthiessen, C. (2004) *An Introduction to Functional Grammar* (3rd edition), London: Edward Arnold.

Hartley, D. (1749) *Observations on Man, His Frame, Duty and Expectations*, London: Samuel Richardson.

Hartmann, E. (1984) *Nightmares: The Psychology and Biology of Terrifying Dreams*, New York: Basic Books.

— (1991) *Boundaries in the Mind: A New Psychology of Personality*, New York: Basic Books.

— (1996) 'We do not dream of the three r's: a study and implications', *Sleep Research* 25, 136.

— (1998) *Dreams and Nightmares*, New York: Perseus Books.

— (1999) 'The nightmare is the most useful dream', *Sleep and Hypnosis* 1, 199–203.

— (2007) 'The Nature and functions of dreaming', in D. Barrett and P. McNamara (eds), *The NewScience of Dreaming, Volume III*, Westport: Praeger Publishing, pp. 171–92.

— (2008) 'The central image (CI) makes 'big' dreams big: the central image as the emotional heart of the dream', *Dreaming* 18(1), 44–57.

Hartmann, E. and Brezler, T. (2008) 'A systematic change in dreams after 9/11/01', *Sleep* 31(2), 213–18.

Hartmann, E. and Kunzendorf, R. (2005) 'The central image (CI) in recent dreams, dreams that stand out, and earliest dreams: relationship to boundaries', *Imagination, Cognition and Personality* 25, 383–92.

— (2006) 'Boundaries and dreams', *Imagination, Cognition and Personality* 26(1–2), 101–15.

Hartmann, E., Kunzendorf, R., Rosen, R. and Gazells, G. N. (2001) 'Contextualizing images in dreams and daydreams', *Dreaming* 11(2), 97–104.

Hartmann, E., Zborowski, M., McNamara, P., Rosen, R. and Gazells, G. N. (1999) 'Contextualizing images in dreams: relationship to the emotional state of the dreamer', *Sleep* 22(2), 131.

Hartmann, E., Zborowski, M. and Kunzendorf, R. (2001) 'The emotion pictured by a dream: an examination of emotions contextualized in dreams', *Sleep and Hypnosis* 3, 33–43.

Hazlitt, W. (1930) *Complete Works of William Hazlitt, Volume 5: Lectures on the English Poets/A View of the English Stage*, P. P. Howe (ed.), London: J. M. Dent.

— (1931) *Complete Works of William Hazlitt, Volume 12: The Plain Speaker/Opinions on Books/Men and Things*, P. P. Howe (ed.), London: J. M. Dent.

Heinzelman, K. (1988) 'Self-interest and the politics of composition in Keats's *Isabella*', *English Literary History* 55, 159–93.

— (1988) 'Layers and operators in functional grammar', *Journal of Linguistics* 25, 127–57.

Hermansen, M. (2001) 'Dreams and dreaming in Islam', in K. Bulkeley (ed.), *Dreams: A Reader on the Religious, Cultural and Psychological Dimensions of Dreaming*, New York: Palgrave, pp. 73–91.

Hidalgo Downing, L. (2000a) *Negation, Text Worlds and Discourse: The Pragmatics of Fiction*, Stanford, CA: Ablex.

— (2000b) 'Negation in discourse: a text world approach to Joseph Heller's *Catch-22*', *Language and Literature* 9(4), 215–40.

— (2000c) 'Negation World creation in advertising discourse', *Revista Alicantina de Estudios Ingleses* 13, 67–88.

— (2002) 'Creating things that are not: the role of negation in the poetry of Wislawa Szymborska', *Journal of Literary Semantics* 30(2), 113–32.

— (2003) 'Negation as a stylistic feature in Joseph Heller's *Catch-22*: a corpus study', *Style* 37(3), 218–341.

Hobson, J. A. and McCarley, R. W. (1977) 'The brain as dream state generator: an activation-synthesis hypothesis of the dream process', *The American Journal of Psychiatry* 134, 1335–48.

Hobson, J. A. (1988) *The Dreaming Brain*, New York: Basic Books.

— (2005) *Dreaming: A Very Short Introduction*, Oxford: Oxford University Press.

Hobson, J. A., Pace-Schott, E. F. and Stickgold, R. (2000) 'Dreaming and the brain: toward a cognitive neuroscience of conscious states', *Behavioral and Brain Sciences* 23, 793–842.

Hodge, R. and Kress, G. (1988) *Social Semiotics*, Cambridge: Polity Press.

Holland, N. (1993) 'Foreword', in C. Rupprecht (ed.), *The Dream and The Text: Essays on Literature and Language*, New York: SUNY, pp. ix–xx.

Holmes, R. (1974) *Shelley: The Pursuit*, Harmondsworth: Penguin.

Homans, M. (1990) 'Keats reading women, women reading Keats', *Studies in Romanticism* 29, 341–70.

Hopkins, B. (1989) 'Keats and the uncanny: "This living hand"', *The Kenyon Review* 11(4), 28–40.

Hopkins, L. (2005) *Screening the Gothic*, Austin, TX: University of Texas Press.

Horder, L. (2007) *'I'm angry because I understand, not because I don't': A Text World Theory Approach to Making Sense of the Unfamiliar in Sarah Kane's 4.48 Psychosis*, Unpublished MA dissertation, University of Nottingham.

Hunt, H. (1991) 'Dreams as literature/science of dreams: an essay', *Dreaming* 1(3), 235–42.

Hwang, S. (1992) 'The functions of negation in narration', in S. Hwang and W. R. Merrifield (eds), *Language in Context: Essays for Robert E. Longacre*, Dallas, TX: Summer Institute of Linguistics and The University of Texas at Arlington Publications in Linguistics, pp. 321–37.

Jedrej, M. and Shaw, R. (1992) *Dreaming, Religion and Society in Africa*, Leiden: E. J. Brill.

Johnson, M. (1987) *The Body in the Mind: The Bodily Basis of Meaning, Imagination and Reason*, Chicago, IL: Chicago University Press.

Jones, E. (1931) *On the Nightmare*, London: The Hogarth Press.

Jones, J. (1969) *John Keats's Dream of Truth*, London: Chatto & Windus.

Jordan, M. P. (1998) 'The power of negation in English: text, context and relevance', *Journal of Pragmatics* 29, 705–52.

Kahan, T. L. (2001) 'Consciousness in dreaming: a metacognitive approach', in K. Bulkeley (ed.), *Dreams: A Reader on the Religious, Cultural and Psychological Dimensions of Dreaming*, New York: Palgrave, pp. 333–60.

Kelley, T. (1987) 'Poetics and the politics of reception: Keats's "La belle dame sans merci"', *English Literary History* 54, 333–62.

Kemp, A., Rawlings, E. I. and Green, B. L. (1991) 'Post-traumatic stress disorder (PTSD) in battered women: a shelter sample', *Journal of Traumatic Stress* 4(1), 137–48.

Kiessling, N. (1983) 'An anatomy of melancholy and the nightmare', in M. Lazar (ed.), *The Anxious Subject: Nightmares and Daymares in Literature and Film*, Malibu, CA: Undena Publications, pp. 1–11.

King, J. and Sheehan, J. R. (1996) 'The use of dreams with incest survivors', in D. Barrett (ed.), *Trauma and Dreams*, Cambridge, MA: Harvard University Press, pp. 56–67.

Kozmová, M. and Wolman, R. N. (2006) 'Self-awareness in dreaming', *Dreaming* 16(3), 196–214.

Kramer, M. (1982) 'The psychology of the dream: art or science?', *Psychiatric Journal of the University of Ottawa* 7(2), 87–100.

— (1991) 'The nightmare: a failure in dream function', *Dreaming* 1(4), 277–84.

Kramer, M., Schoen, L. and Kinney, L. (1987) 'Nightmares in Vietnam war veterans', *Journal of the American Academy of Psychoanalysis* 15, 67–81.

Kruger, S. F. (1992) *Dreaming in the Middle Ages*, Cambridge: Cambridge University Press.

Kuiken, D. and Sikora, S. (1993) 'The impact of dreams on waking thoughts and feelings', in A. Moffitt, M. Kramer and R. Hoffman (eds), *The Function of Dreams*, Albany, NY: State University of New York Press, pp. 419–76.

Kuiken, D., Miall, D. S and Sikora, S. (2004) 'Forms of self-implication in literary reading', *Poetics Today* 25(2), 171–204.

Kunzendorf, R., Hartmann, E., Thomas, L. and Berensen, L. (2000) 'Emotionally directing visual sensations: generating images that contextualize emotion and become "symbolic" ', *Imagination, Cognition and Personality* 19(3), 269–78.

Lagory, M. (1995) 'Wormy circumstance: symbolism in Keats's *Isabella*', *Romanticism* 34, 321–42.

Lahey, E. (2003) 'Seeing the forest for the trees in Al Purdy's "Trees at the Arctic Circle" ', *Belgian Journal of Language and Literatures* 1, 73–83.

— (2004) 'All the world's a sub-world: direct speech and sub-world creation in 'After' by Norman Craig', *Nottingham Linguistic Circular* 18, 21–8.

— (2005) *Text World Landscapes and the English-Canadian National Identity in the Poetry of Al Purdy, Alden Nowlan and Milton Acorn*, Unpublished Ph.D. thesis, University of Nottingham.

— (2006) '(Re)thinking world-building: locating the text-worlds of Canadian lyric poetry', *Journal of Literary Semantics* 35, 145–64.

Lakoff, G. (1987) *Women, Fire and Dangerous Things: What Categories Reveal About The Mind*, Chicago, IL: Chicago University Press.

— (1990) 'The invariance hypothesis: is abstract reason based on image schemas?', *Cognitive Linguistics* 1, 39–74.

— (1993) 'How metaphor structures dreams: the theory of conceptual metaphor applied to dream analysis', *Dreaming* 5(2), 77–98.

— (2001) 'How unconscious metaphorical thought shapes dreams', *PsyArt*, http://www.psyartjournal.com/article/show/lakoff-metaphor_and_psychoanalysis_how_metaphor (last accessed 29 December 2012).

—. (2004) *Don't Think of an Elephant! Know Your Values and Frame the Debate*, White River Junction, VT: Chelsea Green Publishing Company.

Lakoff, G. and Johnson, M. (1980) *Metaphors We Live By*, Chicago, IL: Chicago University Press.

Lakoff, G. and Turner, M. (1989) More *Than Cool Reason: A Field Guide to Poetic Metaphor*, Chicago, IL: University of Chicago Press.

Lamb, C. (1987) *Elia and The Last Essays of Elia*, J. Bate (ed.), Oxford: Oxford University Press.

Langacker, R. (1987) *Foundations of Cognitive Grammar, Vol I: Theoretical Prerequisites*, Stanford, CA: Stanford University Press.

— (1991) *Foundations of Cognitive Grammar, Vol II: Descriptive Application*, Stanford, CA: Stanford University Press.

— (2008) *Cognitive Grammar: A Basic Introduction*, New York: Oxford University Press.

Lansky, M. R. and Bley, C. R. (1995) *Posttraumatic Nightmares: Psychodynamic Explorations*, Hillsdale, NJ: Analytic Press.

Lau, B. (1991) *Keats's Reading of the Romantic Poets*, Ann Arbor, MI, University of Michigan Press.

Lavie, P. and Kaminer, H. (1996) 'Sleep, dreaming and coping style in holocaust survivors', in D. Barrett (ed.), *Trauma and Dreams*, Cambridge, MA: Harvard University Press, pp. 114–24.

Lawler, J. (2010) 'Negation and negative polarity', in P. C. Hogan (ed.), *The Cambridge Encyclopaedia of the Language Sciences*, Cambridge: Cambridge University Press, pp. 554–5.

Lazar, M. (ed.) (1983) *The Anxious Subject: Nightmares and Daymares in Literature and Film*, Malibu, CA: Undena Publications.

Leader, Z. (1996) *Revision and Romantic Authorship*, Oxford: Oxford University Press.

LeDoux, J. (2000) 'The amygdala and emotion: a view through fear', in J. P Aggleton (ed.), *The Amygdala*, Oxford: Oxford University Press.

— (1996) *TheEmotional Brain: The Mysterious Underpinnings of Emotional Life*, New York: Simon and Schuster.

Leech, G. (1983) *Principles of Pragmatics*, London: Longman.

Leech, G. and Coates, J. (1980) 'Semantic indeterminacy and the modals', in S. Greenbaum, G. Leech and J. Svartvik (eds), *Studies in English Linguistics*, London: Longman.

Leech, G. and Short, M. (2007) *Style In Fiction: A Linguistic Introduction to English Fictional Prose* (2nd edition), Harlow: Pearson Education.

Levin, R., Gilmartin, L. and. Lamontanaro, L. (1998) 'Cognitive style and perception: the relationship of boundary thinness to visual-spatial processing in dreaming and waking thought' *Imagination, Cognition and Personality* 18, 25–41.

Levinson, M. (1988) *Keats's Life of Allegory: The Origins of a Style*, Oxford: Blackwell.

Lindop, G. (2004) 'Romantic poetry and the idea of the dream', *The Keats-Shelley Review* 18, 20–37.

Lipking, L. (1981) *The Life of the Poet: Beginning and Ending Poetic Careers*, Chicago, IL: University of Chicago Press.

Lyons, J. (1977a) *Semantics: Volume 1*, Cambridge: Cambridge University Press.

— (1977b) *Semantics: Volume 2*, Cambridge: Cambridge University Press.

Macario, M. M. A. (1978) *du Sommeil, des Reves et du Somnambulisme Dans L'etat de Sante et de Maladie*, Nendeln, Liechtenstein: Krans Reprint.

Macnish, R. (1834) *The Philosophy of Sleep*, Glasgow: McPhun.

Mahowald, M. W., Woods, S. R. and Schenck, C. H. (1998) 'Sleeping dreams, waking hallucinations and the central nervous system', *Dreaming* 8(2), 89–102.

Martindale, C. and Dailey, A. (1995) 'I. A. Richards revisited: do people agree in their interpretations of literature?', *Poetics* 23, 299–314.

Maquet, P., Péters, J.-M., Aerts, J., Delfiore, G., Degueldre, C., Luxen, A. and Franck, G. (1996) 'Functional neuroanatomy of rapid-eye-movement sleep and dreaming', *Nature* 383, 163–6.

McGann, J. (1993) 'Keats and the historical method in literary criticism', in K. Kroeber and G. W. Ruoff (eds), *Romantic Poetry: Recent Revisionary Criticism*, New Brunswick, NJ: Rutgers University Press, pp. 439–64.

McIntyre, D. (2006) *Point of View in Plays: A Cognitive Stylistic Approach to Viewpoint in Drama and Other Text Types*, Amsterdam: John Benjamins.

McNamara, P. (2008) *Nightmares: The Science and Solution of Those Frightening Visions During Sleep*, Westport, CT: Praeger.

Mellor, A. K. (2001) 'Keats and the complexities of gender', in S. Wolfson (ed.), *The Cambridge Companion to Keats*, Cambridge: Cambridge University Press, pp. 214–29.

Metzinger, T. (2009) *The Ego Tunnel: The Science of the Mind and the Myth of the Self*, New York: Basic Books.

Miall, D. and Kuiken, D. (1994) 'Foregrounding, defamiliarisation and affect: response to literary stories', *Poetics* 22, 389–407.

— (1997) 'Coleridge and dreams: an introduction', *Dreaming* 7(1), 1–11.

Milnes, R. M. (ed.) (1848) *Life, Letters and Literary Remains of John Keats*, London: Edward Moxon.

Milnes, T. (2010) *The Truth About Romanticism: Pragmatism and Idealism in Keats, Shelley, Coleridge*, Cambridge: Cambridge University Press.

Miró, E. and Martinez, M. P. (2005) 'Affective and personality characteristics in function of nightmare prevalence, nightmare distress, and interference during nightmares', *Dreaming* 15, 89–105.

Mithun, M. (1999) *The Languages of Native North America*, Cambridge: Cambridge University Press.

Motion, A. (1997) *Keats*, London: Routledge.

Muller, K. (1996) 'Jasmine: dreams in the psychotherapy of a rape survivor', in D. Barrett (ed.), *Trauma and Dreams*, Cambridge, MA: Harvard University Press, pp. 148–58.

Murry, J. M. (1925) *Keats and Shakespeare: A Study of Keats's Poetic Life from 1816 to 1820*, London: Oxford University Press.

Myrone, M. (2001) *Henry Fuseli*, London: Tate Publishing.

Nader, K. (1996) 'Children's traumatic dreams', in D. Barrett (ed.), *Trauma and Dreams*, Cambridge, MA: Harvard University Press, pp. 9–24.

Nader, K. and Pynoos, R. (1991) 'Play and draw techniques as tools for interviewing traumatized children', in C. E Schaefer, K. Gitlin and A. Sandgrund (eds), *Play Diagnosis and Assessment*, New York: John Wiley and Sons, pp. 375–89.

Nahajec, L. (2009) 'Negation and the creation of implicit meaning in poetry', *Language and Literature* 18(2), 109–27.

Narrog, H. (2005) 'Modality, mood, and change of modal meanings: a new perspective', *Cognitive Linguistics* 16(4), 677–731.

Nelmes, J. (ed.), (2003) *An Introduction to Film Studies* (3rd edition), London: Routledge.

Nielsen, T. and Levin, R. (2007) 'Nightmares: a new neurocognitive model', *Sleep Medicine Reviews* 11, 295–310.

Nir, Y. and Tonini, G. (2009) 'Dreaming and the brain: from phenomenology to neurophysiology', *Trends in Cognitive Science* 14(2), 88–100.

Nørgaard, N. (2007) 'Disordered collarettes and uncovered tables: negative polarity as a stylistic device in Joyce's "Two Gallants" ', *Journal of Literary Semantics* 36(1), 35–52.

Nuyts, J. (2001) *Epistemic Modality, Language and Conceptualization*, Amsterdam: John Benjamins.

— (2005) 'The modal confusion: on terminology and the concepts behind it', in A. Klinge and H. H. Müller (eds), *Modality: Studies in Form and Function*, London: Equinox, pp. 5–38.

— (2006) 'Modality: overview and linguistic issues', in W. Frawley (ed.), *The Expression of Modality*, Berlin: Walter de Gruyter, pp. 1–25.

O'Connell, A. (2006) *A Place of Vision: Romantic Dream Poetry and the Creative Imagination*, Unpublished PhD thesis, University of Durham.

Oatley, K. and Jenkins, J. M. (1996) *Understanding Emotions*, Oxford: Blackwell.

Oudiette, D., Leu, S., Pottier, M., Buzare, M-A., Brion, A. and Arnulf, I. (2009) 'Dreamlike mentations during sleepwalking and sleep terrors in adults', *Sleep* 32(12) 1621–8.

Packer, S. (2002) *Dreams in Myth, Medicine and Movies*, Westport, CT: Greenwood.

Pagano, A. (1994) 'Negatives in written text', in M. Coulthard (ed.), *Advances in Written Text Analysis*, London: Routledge, pp. 250–65.

Pagel, J. (2008) *The Limits of Dream: A Scientific Exploration of the Mind/Brain Interface*, Oxford: Elsevier.

Pagel, J. F., Blagrove, M., Levin, R., States, B., Stickgold, B. and White, S. (2001) 'Definitions of dream: a paradigm for comparing field descriptive specific studies of dream', *Dreaming* 11(4), 195–202.

Palmer, F. (1976) *Semantics*, Cambridge: Cambridge University Press.

— (1979) *Modality and the English Modals*, London: Longman.

— (1986) *Mood and Modality*, Cambridge: Cambridge University Press.

— (2001) *Mood and Modality* (2nd edition), Cambridge: Cambridge University Press.

Papafragou, A. (2000) *Modality: Issues in the Semantics-Pragmatics Interface*, Oxford: Elsevier.

Pavel, T. G. (1986) *Fictional Worlds*, Cambridge, MA: Harvard University Press.

Perkins, D. (1959) *The Quest for Permanence: The Symbolism of Wordsworth, Shelley and Keats*, Cambridge, MA: Harvard University Press.

Perkins, M. (1983) *Modal Expressions in English*, London: Frances Pinter.

Porter, L. M. (1993) 'Real dreams, literary dreams and the fantastic in literature', in C. Rupprecht (ed.), *The Dream and The Text: Essays on Literature and Language*, New York: SUNY, pp. 32–47.

Premack, D. and Woodruff, G. (1978) 'Does the chimpanzee have a theory of mind?', *Behavioral and Brain Sciences* 1, 515–26.

Pynoos, R. and Nader, K. (1989) 'Children's memory and proximity to violence', *Journal of the American Academy of Child and Adolescent Psychiatry* 28(2), 236–41.

Radden, G. and Dirven, R. (2007) *Cognitive English Grammar*, Amsterdam: John Benjamins.

Rescher, N. (1968) *Topics in Philosophical Logic*, Dordrecht: Reidel.

Revonsuo, A. (2000) 'The reinterpretation of dreams: an evolutionary hypothesis of the function of dreaming', *Behavioral and Brain Sciences* 23, 877–901.

Richardson, A. (2001) 'Keats and Romantic Science', in S. Wolfson (ed.), *The Cambridge Companion to Keats*, Cambridge: Cambridge University Press, pp. 230–45.

Ricks, C. (1974) *Keats and Embarrassment*, Oxford: Clarendon Press.

Roberts, G. L., Lawrence, J. M., Williams, G. M. and Raphael, B. (1998) 'The impact of domestic violence on women's mental health', *Australian and New Zealand Journal of Public Health* 22(7), 796–801.

Rosch, E. (1975) 'Cognitive representations of semantic categories', *Journal of Experimental Psychology: General* 104, 192–233.

— (1978) 'Principles of categorization', in E. Rosch and B. B. Lloyd (eds), *Cognition and Categorization*, Hillside, NJ: Lawrence Erlbaum, pp.27–48.

— (1988) 'Coherences and categorization: a historical view', in F. S. Kessel (ed.), *The Development of Language and Language Researchers: Essays inHonor of Roger Brown*, Hillsdale NJ: Lawrence Erlbaum, pp. 373–92.

Rosenfeld, N. (2000) '"Eve's dream will do here": Miltonic dreaming in Keats's *The Eve of St Agnes*', *Keats-Shelley Journal* 49, 47–59.

Rowe, A. and Wells, P. (2003) 'Film form and narrative', in J. Nelmes (ed.), *An Introduction to Film Studies* (3rd edition), London: Routledge, pp. 53–90.

Rumelhart, D. (1975) 'Notes on a schema for stories', in D. G. Brobow and A. M. Collins (eds), *Representation and Understanding: Studies in Cognitive Science*, New York: Academic Press, pp. 211–36.

— (1980) 'Schemata: the building blocks of cognition', in R. Spiro, B. Bruce and W. Brewer (eds), *Theoretical Issues in Reading Comprehension*, Hillsdale, NJ: Lawrence Erlbaum, pp. 33–58.

— (1984) 'Understanding understanding', in J. Flood (ed.), *Understanding Reading Comprehension: Cognition, Language, and the Structure of Prose*, Newark, New York: International Reading Association, pp. 1–20.

Rupprecht, C. (ed.) (1993) *The Dream and The Text: Essays on Literature and Language*, New York: SUNY.

Ryan, M. (1991) *Possible Worlds, Artificial Intelligence and Narrative Theory*, Bloomington and Indianapolis, IN: Indiana University Press.

Sandy, M. (2000) 'Dream lovers and tragic romance: negative fictions in Keats's *Lamia, The Eve of St. Agnes* and *Isabella*', *Romanticism on the Net* 20, 1–12, http://id.erudit. org/iderudit/005955ar (last accessed 29 December 2012).

— (2006) 'Twentieth and twenty-first-century Keats criticism', *Literature Compass* 3/6, 1320–33.

Schank, R. C. (1982) *Dynamic Memory*, New York: Cambridge University Press.

Schank, R. C. and Abelson, R. P. (1977) *Scripts, Plans, Goals and Understanding: An Inquiry into Human Knowledge Structures*, Hillsdale, NJ: Lawrence Erlbaum.

Schwartz, L. M. (1973) *Keats Reviewed by His Contemporaries: A Collection of Notices for the Years 1816–1821*, Metuchen, NJ: The Scarecrow Press.

Schwartz, S. (2000) 'A historical loop of one hundred years: similarities between 19th century and contemporary dream research', *Dreaming* 10(1), 55–66.

Segal, E. M. (1995a) 'Narrative comprehension and the role of deictic shift theory', in J. F. Duchan, G. A. Bruder and L. E. Hewitt (eds), *Deixis in Narrative: A Cognitive Science Perspective*, Hillsdale, NJ: Lawrence Erlbaum, pp. 3–17.

— (1995b) 'A cognitive-phenomenological theory of fictional narrative', in J. F. Duchan, G. A. Bruder and L. E. Hewitt (eds), *Deixis in Narrative: A Cognitive Science Perspective*, Hillsdale, NJ: Lawrence Erlbaum, pp. 61–78.

Semino, E. (1995) 'Deixis and the dynamics of poetic voice', in K. Green (ed.), *New Essays in Deixis: Discourse, Narrative, Literature*, Amsterdam: Rodopi, pp.145–60.

Sharrock, R. (1961) 'Keats and the young lovers', *Review of English Literature* 2(1), 76–86.

Shelley, M. (1998) *Frankenstein or The Modern Prometheus*, Cambridge: Cambridge University Press.

Shelley, P. B. (1909) *Literary and Philosophical Criticism*, J. Shawcross, (ed.), London: Henry Frowde.

— (1977) *Shelley's Poetry and Prose* (eds), D. Reiman. and S. Powers, New York: W. W. Norton.

Shulman, D. (1999) *Dream Cultures: Explorations in the Comparative History of Dreaming*, Cary, NC: Oxford University Press.

Simpson, P. (1993) *Language, Ideology and Point of View*, London: Routledge.

— (2004) *Stylistics: A Resource Book for Students*, London: Routledge.

Smith, L. Z. (1974) 'The material sublime: Keats and *Isabella*', *Romanticism* 13, 299–311.

Sperry, S. (1973) *Keats the Poet*, Princeton, NJ: Princeton University Press.

Squier, L. and Domhoff, G. W. (1998) 'The presentation of dreaming and dreams in introductory Psychology textbooks: a critical examination with suggestions for textbook authors and course instructors', *Dreaming* 8(3), 149–68.

States, B. (1997) *Seeing in the Dark: Reflections on Dreams and Dreaming*, New Haven, CT: Yale University Press.

— (2003) 'Dreams, art and virtual worldmaking', *Dreaming* 13(1), 3–12.

Stillinger, J. (1971) *The Hoodwinking of Madeline and Other Essays on Keats's Poems*, Urbana, IL: University of Chicago Press.

— (1974) *The Texts of Keats's Poems*, Cambridge, MA: Harvard University Press.

— (1999) *Reading The Eve of St Agnes: The Multiples of Complex Literary Transaction*, Oxford: Oxford University Press.

— (2009) *Romantic Complexity: Keats, Coleridge and Wordsworth*, Chicago, IL: University of Chicago Press.

Stockwell, P. (2000) *The Poetics of Science Fiction*, London: Longman.

— (2002) *Cognitive Poetics: An Introduction*, London: Routledge.

— (2005) 'On cognitive poetics and stylistics', in B. Petterson, M. Polvinen and H. Velvo (eds), *Cognition and Literary Interpretation in Practice*, Helsinki: University of Helsinki Press, pp. 267–81.

— (2009) *Texture: A Cognitive Aesthetics of Reading*, Edinburgh: Edinburgh University Press.

— (2011) 'Authenticity and creativity in reading lamentation', in J. Swann, R. Pope and R. Carter (eds), *Creativity in Language*, Basingstoke: Palgrave, pp. 203–16.

Strachan, J. (ed.), (2003) *A Routledge Literary Sourcebook on the Poems of John Keats*, London: Routledge.

Styles, E. (2006) *The Psychology of Attention*, London: Psychology Press.

Su, P. S (1994) *Lexical Ambiguity in Poetry*, Harlow: Longman.

Swann, K. (1988) 'Harassing the muse', in A. K. Mellor (ed.), *Romanticism and Feminism*, Bloomington, IN: Indiana University Press, pp. 81–92.

Sweetser, E. (1990) *From Etymology to Pragmatics: Metaphorical and Cultural Aspects of Semantic Structure*, Cambridge: Cambridge University Press.

Szpakowska, K. (2001) 'Through the looking glass: dreams in ancient Egypt', in K. Bulkeley (ed.), *Dreams: A Reader on the Religious, Cultural and Psychological Dimensions of Dreaming*, New York: Palgrave, pp. 29–44.

Talmy, L. (1988) 'Force dynamics in language and cognition', *Cognitive Science* 12, 49–100.

Tassi, P. and Muzet, A. (2001) 'Defining the states of consciousness', *Neuroscience and Biobehavioral Reviews* 25, 175–91.

Thayer, M. (1945) 'Keats and Coleridge: "La belle dame sans merci"', *Modern Language Notes* 60(4), 270–2.

Thompson, M. P., Kaslow, N., Kingree, R., Thompson, N. and Meadows, L. (1999) 'Partner abuse and posttraumatic stress disorder as risk factors for suicide attempt in a sample of low income, inner city women', *Journal of Traumatic Stress* 12(1), 59–72.

Tomasello, M. (1992) 'The social bases of language acquisition', *Social Development* 1, 67–87.

— (2003) *Constructing a Language: A Usage-Based Theory of Language Acquisition*, Cambridge, MA: Harvard University Press.

— (2006) *First Verbs: A Case Study of Early Grammatical Development*, Cambridge: Cambridge University Press.

Tooby, J. and Cosmides, L. (2001) 'Does beauty build adapted minds? Towards an evolutionary theory of aesthetics, fiction and the arts', *Substance* 94/95, 6–27.

Tsur, R. (2003) *Onthe Shore of Nothingness: A Study in Cognitive Poetics*, Exeter: Imprint Academic.

— (2008) *Toward a Theory of Cognitive Poetics* (2nd edition), Eastbourne: Sussex Academic Press.

Turley, R. M. (2004) *Keats's Boyish Imagination*, London: Routledge.

Ungerer, F. and Schmid, H. J. (1996) *An Introduction to Cognitive Linguistics*, Harlow: Longman.

Van de Kolk, B., Blitz, R., Burr, W., Sherry, S. and Hartmann, E. (1984) 'Nightmares and trauma: a comparison of veterans', *American Journal of Psychiatry* 141, 187–90.

Vann, B. and Alperstein, N. (2000) 'Dream sharing as social interaction', *Dreaming* 10(2), 111–20.

von Wright, E. H. (1951) *An Essay in Modal Logic*, Amsterdam: North Holland.

Waldoff, L. (1977) 'Porphyro's imagination and Keats's Romanticism', *Journal of English and Germanic Philology* 76, 177–94.

— (1985) *Keats and the Silent Work of Imagination*, Urbana and Chicago, IL; University of Illinois Press.

Ward, A. (1963) *John Keats: The Making of a Poet*, New York: Viking.

Wason, P. C. (1961) 'Response to affirmative and negative binary statements', *British Journal of Psychology* 52, 133–42.

— (1965) 'The contexts of plausible denial', *Journal of Verbal Learning and Verbal Behavior* 4, 7–11.

Wasserman, E. R. (1953) *The Finer Tone: Keats' Major Poems*, Baltimore, MD: The John Hopkins Press.

Waters, W. (2000) 'Poetic address and intimate reading: the offered hand', *Literary Imagination* 2(2), 188–220.

— (2003) *Poetry's Touch: on Lyric Address*, Ithaca, NY: Cornell University Press.

Watkins, D. (1989) *Keats's Poetry and the Politics of the Imagination*, Rutherford, NJ: Fairleigh Dickinson University Press.

Werth, P. N. (1981) 'Tense, modality and possible worlds', *Rapport des Activities de L'Institut de Phonetique* 16, Brussels: Universite Libre de Bruxelles, pp. 17–30.

— (1994) 'Extended metaphor: a text world account', *Language and Literature* 3(2), 79–103.

— (1995a) 'How to build a world (in a lot less than six days and using only what's in your head)', in K. Green (ed.), *New Essays on Deixis: Discourse, Narrative, Literature*, Amsterdam: Rodopi, pp. 49–80.

— (1995b) '"World enough and time": deictic space and the interpretation of prose', in P. Verdonk and J-J. Weber (eds), *Twentieth Century Fiction: From Text to Context*, London: Routledge, pp. 181–205.

— (1997) 'Conditionality as cognitive distance', in A. Athanasiasdou and R. Dirven (eds), *On Conditionals Again*, Amsterdam: John Benjamins, pp. 243–71.

— (1999) *Text Worlds: Representing Conceptual Space in Discourse*, London: Longman.

White-Lewis, J. (1993) 'In defense of nightmares: clinical and literary cases', in
   C. Rupprecht (ed.), *The Dream and The Text: Essays on Literature and Language*,
   New York: SUNY, pp. 48–72.

— (2001) 'Reflecting on a dream in Jungian analytic practice', in K. Bulkeley (ed.),
   *Dreams: A Reader on the Religious, Cultural and Psychological Dimensions of
   Dreaming*, New York: Palgrave, pp. 189–93.

Wierzbicka, A. (1985) *Lexicography and Conceptual Analysis*, Ann Arbor, MI: Karoma.

Willet, T. (1988) 'A cross-linguistic survey of the grammaticalization of evidentiality',
   Studies in Language 12, 51–97.

Wilmer, H. A. (1982) 'Vietnam and madness: dreams of schizophrenic veterans', *Journal
   of the American Academy of Psychoanalysis* 10, 47–65.

Wilson, D. B. (1993) *The Romantic Dream: Wordsworth and the Poetics of the
   Unconscious*, Lincoln, NE: University of Nebraska Press.

— (1997) '"Surprised by sleep": Coleridgean dejection and self-analysis', *Dreaming* 7(1)
   67–81.

Wise, T. (1976) *Medieval Warfare*, London: Osprey.

Wolfson, S. (1990) 'Feminising Keats', in H. de Almeira (ed.), *Critical Essays on John Keats*,
   Boston, MA: G. K. Hall, pp. 317–56.

— (2001) 'Late lyrics', in S. Wolfson (ed.), *The Cambridge Companion to Keats*,
   Cambridge: Cambridge University Press, pp. 102–19.

Wood, J. M. and Bootzin, R. R. (1990) 'The prevalence of nightmares and their
   independence from anxiety', *Journal of Abnormal Psychology* 99, 64–8.

Wood, J. M., Bootzin, R. R., Rosenhan, D., Nolen-Hoeksma, S. and Jourden, F. (1992)
   'Effects of the 1989 San Francisco earthquake on frequency and content of nightmares',
   Journal of Abnormal Psychology 101, 219–24.

Wordsworth, W. (1936) *Poetical Works*, Oxford: Oxford University Press.

Wright, H. G. (1957) *Boccaccio in England from Chaucer to Tennyson*, London: Athlone.

Young, K. G. (1987) *Taleworlds and Storyrealms: The Phenomenology of Narrative*,
   Hingham, MA: Kluwer.

Young, S. (2001) 'Buddhist dream experience', in K. Bulkeley (ed.), *Dreams: A Reader
   on the Religious, Cultural and Psychological Dimensions of Dreaming*, New York:
   Palgrave, pp. 9–28.

Zadeh, L. (1965) 'Fuzzy sets', *Information and Control* 8, 338–53.

— (1970) 'Fuzzy languages and their relation to human and machine intelligence',
   Proceedings of the International Conference on Man and Computer, Bordeaux,
   130–65.

— (1971) 'Quantitative fuzzy semantics', *Information Sciences* 3, 159–76.

— (1972) 'A fuzzy-set-theoretic interpretation of linguistic hedges', *Journal of
   Cybernetics* 2(3), 4–34.

Zadra, A. and Donderi, D. C. (2000) 'Nightmares and bad dreams: their prevalence and
   relationship to well-being', *Journal of Abnormal Psychology* 109(2), 273–81.

Zadra, A., Assaad, J. M., Nielsen, T. A. and Donderi, D. C. (1995) 'Trait anxiety and its relation to nightmares, bad dreams and dream content', *Sleep Research* 24, 150.

Zadra, A., Pilon, M. and Donderi, D. C. (2006) 'Variety and intensity of emotions in nightmares and bad dreams', *The Journal of Nervous and Mental Disease* 194(4), 249–54.

Zubin, D. A. and Hewitt, L. E. (1995) 'Deictic shift theory and the poetics of involvement in narrative', in J. F. Duchan, G. A. Bruder and L. E. Hewitt (eds), *Deixis in Narrative: A Cognitive Science Perspective*, Hillsdale, NJ: Lawrence Erlbaum, pp. 129–55.

Index

Lightning Source UK Ltd.
Milton Keynes UK
UKOW02f1120200215

246602UK00001B/62/P